To Kate

Thank you for your guidance.

Louis A. Borsh

A BROOKLYN BOY'S

STORIES

TRUE SHORT STORIES AS TOLD
BY THE AUTHOR WHO GREW UP
IN THE EAST NEW YORK SECTION
OF BROOKLYN.

TALES FROM THE 1940s THRU THE 70s

Written by

LOUIS S. BOREK

Copyright © 2013 by Louis S. Borek Enterprises Inc.
All rights reserved.

ISBN:-10: 1484884752
ISBN-13: 978-1484884751
LCCN: 2013910228

No part of this publication may be reproduced, or stored in a retrieval system or transmitted
In any form or by any means, electronic, mechanical, photocopying, recording or otherwise used without the express written permission of the author, except by reviewers who may quote brief excerpts in connection with a review.

The first printing is by CreateSpace. DATE June 2013

Printed in the USA

Dedication

To: My wonderful parents.

Frank and Lucille

Without their early guidance, patience and street smarts, God only knows where I could have wound up.

And

Francyn, my beautiful wife, who spent many hours reading my memoirs, assisted in reviewing and acquired an authentic awareness of where I came from.

Introduction

Throughout years of socializing with both men and women, each time I told a story it had everyone's undivided attention. Afterwards they asked questions, which lead to another story. When my brother Billy was present, he contributed facts and the stories became more exciting. Many people suggested that I write a book.

I grew up in the East New York section of Brooklyn. It seemed to me, that most people who lived in that area had the same life style and whatever I had to write may seem like old hat to them.

Recently, I met a fellow at the gym, located here in the Panhandle of Florida. The new person I befriended is John Motlow. We spoke a few times while working out, and then one evening we went for a beer at Beef O Brady's, a local pub. John, being a literate person seemed very interested in a couple of stories I told him. He suggested like many other people, that I write a book. I asked him "Who would be interested?" John explained that most people do not have a clue of what it was like living where you came from including me and would find it interesting. He said many people from that old neighborhood would love to reminisce with the stories, including your friends and the members of your own family. He suggested I begin by typing a few old memories just so he may read them. Therefore, I did. He said, "Your memory is exceptional and you have a lot to offer," then asked me to write a short story. After giving it some thought, I began typing. As I progressed, more and more memories became reality. The writing seemed to work similar to talking with people, one story leads to another as a result, I continued writing. I will tell you stories from my childhood up until I moved from N.Y. Including many Street games, we played at no expense to our parents, the hustling to earn a buck, and the battles to keep it. Some are funny, some are sad. You will have to take the good with the bad just as I did.

The forthcoming stories are all true. When telling a story that took place many years ago, one must rely on memory. Stories can preserve memories, just like a photo, and just like a photo, they can be touched up. There is always going to be a little embellishment when you tell a story. How can you not embellish? Maybe you substitute a phrase from how it actually happened just to induce humor or emphasize a fact. These are all stories that I vividly remember. To add to the humor and to make each story a little more interesting, I have added small icons prior to each story to give you a lead on what is coming up next. My writing technique is in the manner in which the people actually speak in East New York. For that reason, you will also find an additional page consisting of Brooklyn slangs. You can look at it to help you understand just what the odd words mean. I hope you will enjoy reading these stories as much as I did writing them.

I Am from Brooklyn.

    I come from a borough called Brooklyn. Specifically, I reside in the section of East New York.
We call a Hoagie or a Sub a Hero.
Shopping carts, we call wagons.
Roads, we call streets. Going on the Avenue is a night out.
Everyone knew someone or somehow related to them.
Our parents sat on a stoop all night while we played handball, box-ball, hide and seek, hopscotch, tag or ring-o-leeveeo.
Our moms called us from the window or pop whistled signaling us to come in and eat.
We had block parties that lasted until morning.
Neighbors spent lots of time having parties in the alleyway cooking over charcoal.
We ate the best Italian bread, pastries and cookies. Available to us was Italian ices...not water ice, Mr. Softie, egg creams, pretzel sticks and candy dots on paper from the candy store.
We hung out in the park, not the playground.
We took gypsy taxi cabs, not the checkered yellow cabs.
We rode the train, not the railroad.
These were the best of times. Too bad, it all had to end.
Please read on.

BROOKLYN SLANG

SLANG WORD	ENGLISH
Adda	Out of
Anutta	another
Alotta	A lot of
Autta	Ought to
Bacala	Cod fish salad (Italian)
Botz	crazy (Italian)
Callfaya	I will call for you
C'mere	Come here
Dares	There is
Dat	that
Dem	them
Den	than
Ding	thing
Dink	think
Doin	doing
Fugeddaboutit	Forget about it
Gatootz	squash (Italian)
Getaddahere	Get out of here
Ginny stinkers	Small Italian cigars
Gonna	Going to
Hadda	Had to
Howya doin?	How are you doing?
How'dja?	How did you?
I aint	I'm not
I daught dat	I thought that
I'm doin good	I am doing good
Jeweatjet?	Did you eat yet?
Kiddin	kidding

Let's gedadda here --------------- Let's get out of here
Na--------------------------------- no
Spall deen ------------------------A pink rubber ball
Stoop ---------------------------- Entrance stairway
Utter ---------------------------- other
Wha ----------------------------- what
Watta ---------------------------- What do?
Warrin --------------------------- wearing
Whack --------------------------- A smack or to kill
Wit ------------------------------ with
Wooda --------------------------- Would have
Yeah ----------------------------yes
Ya--------------------------------- you
Ya kiddin me? --------------------- Are you kidding me?
Youse guys ------------------------ You guys
Yo--------------------------------- hey

EAST NEW YORK BROOKLYN

East New York is a residential neighborhood located in the eastern section of the borough of Brooklyn. Its boundaries starting from the north and moving clockwise are Cypress Hills to the north. To the East is the borough of Queens, Jamaica Bay to the south and the railway tracks next to Van Sinderen Ave. to the west. Linden Boulevard and Atlantic Ave are the primary thoroughfares through East New York. The 75th Police Precinct patrols the area.

The population consisted of mostly working class Italians, Jewish and Irish residents. The area closest to where we lived is (City Line.) It is the borderline between Brooklyn and Queens.

During the period of the stories which you are about to read, many nice people subsided in this area. However, times changed and so did the types of people. Many of the youths turned out to be successful and productive citizens. Others turned out to be criminals, thugs, racketeers and Mafiosi.

THE FAMILY

Our house 1011 Glenmore Ave.

As far as I could remember, I always lived on Glenmore Ave. in the East New York section of Brooklyn. My parents were also born in Brooklyn. Their parents were immigrants from Europe. Dad's parents both came to Brooklyn from Poland. Mom's parents were from Italy. It was common for the children of immigrants to date and marry outside their origin of decent.

Mom had four sisters and one brother. On pop's side there was four boys and one girl. All of mom's siblings married Italians, making it one big family which all of them spoke Italian. Dad, who they called the Pollock, fit right in with the clan. Dad knew a few words in Italian, mostly curse words, which was fine with all of his brother in-laws. They all got along well with him because he was a regular guy with a great sense of humor.

All of the people on dad's side could speak Polish. Dad's siblings did not reproduce like the Italians. There is only one cousin from the polish side and a gang of cousins on the Italian side.

Whenever someone asks me, what is your decent? I answer, "I am half Italian and half Polish. They once made me an offer that I could not understand." The people who get it always laugh at my answer.

Military Guys: Pop and all of his brothers were in the military. They all served their country in World War II in the U.S. Army. Dad's youngest brother Adam participated in the Normandy invasion in France. Uncle Willie went to Burma India. Uncle Charlie was in the Army Air Corps. Dad went to join the Army but Mom proceeded to the draft board and claimed hardship. She told them that she had a new baby and needed him at home. She said that pop never forgave her for doing that. He then joined the National Guard. He could not stand by at home while all his brothers were at war. Pop did the best he could under the circumstances. I am proud of all of them.

Our House: We always had some kind of a freshly baked cake, pie, cookies, cupcakes or donuts. Mom always encouraged us to invite our friends to the house in the afternoon to have something to eat and a glass of milk. Therefore, we did bring home many of our friends. She knew all of them extremely well. It was usual occurrences to have friends eat supper with us too. She cooked extra just in case someone decided to dine with us.

Mom often put up a large pot of Italian tomato sauce, or as some called it, (Gravy.) She would send me to the

Italian bakery a couple of block from our house to get a loaf or two of Italian bread. By the time, I returned home, the ends of the bread were gone. Most of the Italian kids ate the heels of the bread on the way home from the bakery.

Our apartment was small, however, mom always made everyone feel comfortable.
She taught my brother and me never to leave the house eating something unless we had enough to share with whoever was outside playing with us at the time. If we had a cookie in our hand, she asked.

"How many kids are out there?"

"There are three kids Ma."

"Then bring out four cookies, don't ever eat in front of someone without offering."

Brother Billy: I was born on July 7, 1940. Billy came along on December 31 1944 at 9:00 P.M. He was a New Year's Eve baby. People always asked Mom, why did you not wait another three hours? He could have been the first baby of the year. Mom would reply. "Because now! We can claim him as a dependent on our income tax for 1944."

It had snowed the day before mom came home from the hospital. I recall running out in the snow to get a look at him. When she brought him into the house, I was so excited that I had a baby brother. She then removed the blanket then placed him in his crib. "Ma what are you doing? Put him on the floor so I could play with him." Everyone started to laugh. She explained that he was too small right now, but give him some time and he will be ready to play with you. Therefore, I settled for just reaching into the crib and touching him. It is hard to remember how many times a day I did that while looking to see if he had grown any bigger. Our parents never had any more children.

Mother: Our home is spotless. Everything was neat and clean. All things were in their own place. In the summer, we played on shinny parquet wood floors. Mom always kept them polished; she never used water on them in fear of ruining the wood. Winter months were different. Our parents brought up from our bin in the cellar a carpet, which they had rolled up in a special storage bag. It always smelled of camphor when it was unwrapped. They put mothballs in the bag to prevent any moths or bugs from doing damage to the carpet. It did not take too long for the smell to disappear. Then everything was back to normal.

Mother washed all of our clothes by hand with a washboard in the kitchen sink, and then hung them out on a clothesline to dry, folded then placed in a neat order. Tee shirts and underwear folded and placed in a drawer along with socks. Trousers ironed with a crease; shirts were starched and hanged in the closet. There was a gizmo hanging on the closet door with a dial on it. When you turned the dial, it would suggest the proper color co-ordination for shirts, ties and trousers. She made sure that all our shoes shined too. The three men in her life never had an excuse to look sloppy.

Pop got up very early each morning for work. By the time we got up to go to school, he was gone. If he came home after we were finished eating, there would always be a plate of food set aside for him. Sometimes, he would return home when Billy and I were already asleep, but I could always feel him kissing me, and then tucking me in.

At suppertime, mom made a point of having all of us sitting down at the same time to eat. There was no sitting in another room watching TV or talking on the phone. Suppertime was very special at our house. This was the time when she told us stories and asked us questions about how our day went. All this began when we were at a very young age. She asked questions about any of the new kids that had come for milk and cake, then occasionally mentioned someone specifically, asked what his last name is and where did he live. We went along with her and tried to answer all of her questions the best we could. When she found out enough about someone in question, she would tell us that she was not too fond of him, suggesting that we do not become too friendly because the kid was destined for trouble. She was correct one hundred percent of the time.

Momma grew up in the same neighborhood and knew many people. She occasionally alerted us to watch out for some of the kids. This was especially true after finding out their last name, and where they lived. She told us that his uncle or his father is in the Mafia, that we should be friends with these kids but *NEVER* go into business with them and *NEVER* get involved with their sisters. Someday it will be beneficial to you, if you keep them as friends.

While never dumping too much on us at one time, we were always aware of what was going on around us. She taught us just how the wise guys operated. She then told us that we should *NEVER* become one of them. *NEVER* take favors from them. *NEVER* borrow anything from them. However, she suggested once again that we always stay friends with them. You will attend weddings, drink at the same bars and go to the same parties with them. They will introduce you to more of their friends and family. That is a good thing. Get to know all of them. However, always remember these things you were just told. Because once they own you, you can never get away. When mom spoke to us, she had a very special way of capturing our undivided attention. We always listened attentively. Upon asking her how she knew so much about all of these people. She answered, "Because I went to school and lived in the same neighborhood with them."

Mom had a lot of common sense and was very streetwise. Although she only went as far as a sixth grade in school, she was a wealth of knowledge, and a step ahead of her time.

The Butcher: Momma always shopped for fresh food. We rarely ate canned food. When she went shopping, she took her two sons with her. We would go into the butcher shop where there was always sawdust on the floor. We would play with it, kicking it at each other and skidding on it, pretending to be baseball players sliding into a base. Mom would yell at us, but the butcher handed each of us a slice of baloney or a frankfurter. He told us to calm down and eat the meat. He was a smart man. However, so were we? Each time we entered the butcher shop we would start milling around until we got the frankfurter.

The Haberdasher: While living with Jewish people, mamma learned their traits, beliefs and habits. At Easter time, Billy and I got a new outfit to wear. Mom took us shopping in the Brownsville section of Brooklyn. She woke us up extra early so that we would be the first ones in the store to try on suits. Mother told us to be quiet in the store, just try on the suit and let me do all the talking. She greeted the man with a nice good morning how are you sort of thing, then told him to fit us in a suit, mentioning to the sales clerk. "Show him a Shark Skin," This was supposed to be a tougher type of material. The name sounded tough anyway. After trying on a few suits, she told us to pick out the one we liked best. The man then began to mark it up with a chalk the tailors used for alterations. If the jacket were a little too big, the man let us face mom while he pulled on the back of it telling her.

"See it fits him well."

He would do this to avoid doing more alterations to the suit. I would yell,

"Ma he's trying to trick you, watch him."

The man with the Yamaka (A small religious skullcap) on his head pleaded his innocents.

By the time, we were finished, or rather say by the time mamma was finished with him, she paid only half the price he was asking and got all free alterations. Mom knew that according to Jewish belief, if a merchant lost his first sale he was doomed for a terrible day at the store. Mamma always told us *"THE EARLY BIRD GETS THE WORM."*

Father: Dad was a hardworking man. He provided for his family, we were a happy household. He loved to make people laugh. He did not love anything more than that, besides his family.

He always had a sense of humor, even as a child. In church, a nun asked the children. "What must we do to save our souls?" Pop raised his hand. When called on to answer the question, he told the nun. "We must walk on our heels."

In my first grade class, the teacher gave us an assignment to go home and ask our parents of our descent. My father told me that he is Polish, your mother is Italian and that makes you an Indian. The next morning the teacher made each student stand and explain to the class of their ancestry. When I stood up and told the class just what my dad told me, everyone including the teacher laughed. Other teachers came in to hear me recite my little riddle over a few more times. When I went home and told pop, he began to laugh too. "Hey dad, tell me the truth where did I come from?" "Well son, the truth is I won you in a crap game."

Baseball was his favorite sport. He played the game a lot when he was young. His position was a catcher. He was also a Brooklyn Dodger fan. Whenever he had time off work, he spent it teaching me how to play the game.

Pop met many people while making deliveries for the United Parcel Service. (UPS) He surprised us with many different things. One day he made a delivery to the home of Jackie Robinson. (Brooklyn Dodger 2nd baseman) Jackie was not at home at that time; however, dad asked his wife Rachael if she could give him a photograph of her husband. She gave him a picture but apologized that he was not here to sign it. Therefore, Pop asked her to sign it and she did. He then brought it home. It is still amongst my other baseball stuff.

Back in the old days, The UPS delivered furniture for the large stores. Dad drove one of those big trucks. He delivered heavy stuff up flights of steps into customer's apartments. On occasion, his route brought him into our neighborhood. Each time one of the big brown trucks came down the street, I looked for the number 16266. That was the number on his truck. It is funny how some things always stick with me. When I spotted it, I became excited while running alongside the curb while the truck moved slowly. Occasionally he allowed me to hop on the running board to take a short ride. Whenever dad was in the area, he always came up to the house with his helper to eat lunch. He cooked eggs with potatoes and peppers then told us what a good cook he is. He said he cooked in the army for many men. At an older age it became clear to me, Pop was probably always on KP (Kitchen Patrol.)

Both our parents smoked cigarettes. Dad tried to quit but found it very hard to do. He later stopped smoking cigarettes and started smoking cigars. The cigars were worse than cigarettes. Everything stunk of smoke. We grew up in this environment like many other kids, while becoming accustomed to the smell. However, that did not mean we liked it.

One day at a very young age, Dad began talking about his smoking habit. He said to watch while he took out a nice clean white handkerchief, taking a drag on his cigarette, and then blowing it thru the handkerchief.

"Look at the brown mark in the handkerchief."

"What the heck is dat?"

"Nicotine;" he said, then explained to me,

"If this is what the handkerchief looks like from only one puff, imagine what my lungs look like? I smoke two packs a day."

He then took a pink spall deen and said.

"This is the color of your lungs because ya have never smoked. Try naming something dat ya dink the color of my lungs look like."

"The United Parcel truck ya drive every day."

"Yes! That is exactly right, nicotine is addicting, once ya start smoking, it is almost impossible to quit. As hard as I try, I cannot stop."

"Sit there and dink about it."

He left the room for a moment, giving it time to sink in. When he returned, he laid a new pack of cigarettes on the table.

"From this day on ya have my permission to begin smoking if ya wish to start."

Without hesitating, I pushed the pack of butts back at him and told him

"No Thanks!"

"Good" he said, "besides all ya do is watch your money go up in smoke right before your eyes. Only a fool would start smoking."

Pop was wise to do what he did that day because I have never smoked a cigarette in my life.

Dad and I were riding down Glenmore Ave. one afternoon in his 1948 Dodge when we saw smoke coming from out of a building. There were several fire trucks on the scene. He parked the car and we started to walk towards the fire. As we got closer, we saw a broom factory burning. The black smoke was gushing out from the front entrance while several firefighters were on the roof chopping away with hatchets and long pointed poles to let the smoke out of the building. I knew some of the firefighters from our firehouse. I recognized the tools we played with when the firefighters left the firehouse.

All of a sudden, there was a big explosion; the large glass storefront windows blew out of the building and two firefighters went flying out along with the glass into the street. "Holy Mackerel Dad did you see dat?" "Yes, Stay put do not move." He began running towards the fire. Dad picked up one of the firefighters and carried him behind a fire truck. Just then, there was another explosion and the flames went shooting out of the roof. The hoses were blasting water on the fire from the Johnny pumps like crazy. What a friggin blaze.

It took a very long time to put the fire out that day. We heard from the firefighters that the explosions came from fifty-five gallon drums filled with some sort of liquid like shellac. It was very exciting to see all my pals from the firehouse in action, but I was most impressed and proud of the way my dad jumped into action. He picked up the fallen firefighter, placed him on his shoulder and brought him to safety.

"Ya gotta love the guy."

Comic Books: Dad knew we liked to read comic books. He would never hesitate to ask people along his route if they had comic books that they have already read and did not want anymore. He stored them in his locker at work. When he saved up a nice pile, he tied them up with string and brought them home. In the morning, we'd be surprised to find a new stash. Mom stored them behind a chair it the living room. Our friends knew where she kept them. They arrived at our house extra early on their way to school just to get the latest scoop on Superman, Batman and Archie. After school, they returned at our house again for milk, cake and another look at the newly arrived comic books.

The Catskill Mountains: Daddy worked hard but played just as hard. He always took his two-week vacation time around the middle of summer during the last week of July and the first week of August. I do not know where he found this place up in the Catskill Mountains called Villa Paragone. It was a vacation area owned by an Italian family by the name of Paragone. It had a lot of cabins and other buildings with rooms similar to a hotel. There was a main dining room where all the guests ate three meals a day. They had a swimming pool with a diving board. The first time we went to the Villa, we all had a great time. There was a lot to do besides; it was quite a contrast from the hot city streets back in Brooklyn. Pop took us to nearby places like the Catskill game farm where we saw many different animals besides the cats and dogs that roamed in the streets and alleyways back home. He also took us to the Howe Caverns. These caves were unlike the holes and tunnels we dug out in the lots. You had to take an elevator to find the underlying cause of the cave. This place was neat. We went sightseeing to many unique places. He bought us stickers to place on the side windows indicating everywhere we had visited. "Man was we the *RITZ?*" We even visited the place where Rip Van Winkle slept for about a hundred years. "As legend goes."

One day we went to Albany N.Y. Wow! This was the capital of the state. While driving thru the city my kid brother had to take a dump. Pop told him to hold it until he finds a place with a toilet. However, Billy kept telling him.

"I can't hold it." I said,

"Hey Dad, dare's a fire house he could go dare."

"Yeah, dats a great place for me to go dump."

Dad pulled over, Billy jumped out of the car and made a dash for the firehouse. He knew that the firefighters would let him use the toilet because he used the one behind our house all the time.

When he came out smiling dad told him to get back into the car. He then stopped and bought him an Albany sticker for the window and told him, "If anyone ever asks you if you have been to Albany; tell them yes I took a dump in the fire house." We still mention that occasionally.

Pop made friends with many people. He teamed up with a couple of guys who loved to have fun and were good at telling jokes along with other antics to make people laugh. He kept in touch with these people throughout the year, always planning for their next vacation. It was usual to see him bringing home lots of crap such as wigs, costumes and musical instruments. Mom would ask, "what the hell are you gonna do with all that stuff?" Dad told her, "wait till vacation time, you will see."

The following summer rolled around and pop was set to head for the mountains with a car full of stuff. Upon our arrival his friends were already there waiting for him with their stuff. It did not take long before they went into action. They had planned different skits to perform on a little stage, which was located in the large dining room.

After the evening meal, they asked the guests to hang around for some entertainment. These gents came out dressed in different costumes along with musical instruments and began telling jokes with musical sounds in the background. Everyone was laughing and had a good time. When it was over, the folks gave them a standing ovation. These gents continued doing funny things impulsively around the swimming pool or just about anywhere on the grounds of the villa. They played revelry in the morning with a bugle and sometimes tap in the evening while bringing down the American flag. The people loved them. One night dad said that I was going to be in the next show. He put some boot black over my face, taught me some lines to say. "Now pretend to be a little Al Jolson." The crowd went crazy.

The following year we all met at a place, a few blocks away from the villa. Dad had us play a musical instrument while wearing wigs as we marched along the country road, to the villa. There were loads of people waiting at the front of the villa to greet us. Everyone was yelling and screaming, you would have thought someone very important had arrived.

The Paragons told us that every room was booked in advance early in the season for the same two weeks we were coming up there. The Paragons were also from Brooklyn and naturally; dad had them over our house for dinner after the season was over. "You gotta love the guy he was a good time Charlie."

Cousin Joann: Next door to our house lived mom's oldest sister Viola. She and her husband Tony had two daughters: Celia, and Joann who is twelve years younger. Celia was pretty, smart and had a lot of class. Joann, on the other hand, was also pretty but a spoiled brat, which she learned to accept with ease. Uncle Tony worked as a cab driver; Aunt Viola owned and operated a sewing shop called (Francine Frock.) She employed several operators who fabricated garments in bulk. My aunt was a very busy woman. She worked a full week and then some. Therefore, someone had to look after Joann. This someone was our mother. We cannot blame Joann for being the way she was. The way I see it, my aunt could not give her all the attention that she deserved, for that reason, she tried to make it up to her by giving her whatever she asked for: aka guilt. This caused her to become a little monster. Joann was with us every day after school and sometimes on Saturday. She ate supper with us every evening and was like a sister to us. Our mom was different from her sister Viola. She did not give to us everything we asked for. When she told us NO to something that is just what she meant; NO! Our cousin caused us much grief. Both Billy and I caught many whippings from mom because of her pranks. She'd tell mom we hit her, which we did not do. We would then receive a smack and a lecture to go along with it about how boys do not hit girls.

Joann made evil faces at us at the dinner table, stuck her tongue out when mother was not looking and kick us under the table along with a bunch of other crap just to provoke an incident so that mom would holler at us.

I was fixing a bicycle on the cellar steps with many parts spread out neatly so that I could remember how to put it back together. Along came Joann with a bucket of water and dumped it over my head scattering all the parts down the cellar steps. I became furious. While chasing her into the house, she was screaming at the top of her lungs "Aunt Lucy (My mother's name.) Boobie (My nickname.) just hit me" and she began to cry. Bam! Without asking any questions, I got a smack.

On Saturday afternoons, we would go to the local movie theater named the Earl, located on Liberty Ave. on City Line. Cousins Anthony, his sister Elaine, Joann, Billy and I met up with other cousins who lived over the city line in Queens. These cousins were mom's sister Millie's kids. They are Agnes, Joyce, Rosalie and Kathy. Poor old Uncle Frank never had a son.

The theater showed two full-length movies, ten cartoons and a continuing serial of some sort each week like, (Superman or Robin Hood.) Aunt Viola, who was a wonderful and kind woman, would give Joann money to get into the movie. It cost something like fourteen cents, and another dollar to buy candy for herself and all of her cousins. "Yeah sure, when hell freezes over." While Joann stuffed her face with candy, all of the other cousins looked on with envy. She told us her mother gave her plenty of money to buy candy and if we were nice to her and did whatever she told us to do; she might buy us some candy too. Well, that went over like a ton of bricks. Now you know the antics of Cousin Joann. In spite of that, all of us still love her.

One year, the Barnum and Bailey three-ring circus came to Madison Square Garden in Manhattan. My aunt Viola took Joann along with Billy and me. I still remember that day with all the animals, clowns and acrobats. It was something we had never seen before and it excited us. I recall these beautifully dressed girls in feathered costumes flying through the air on ropes. The star of that act was Minnie Ho- Ho; she had on a purple colored costume, and she flew through the air with the greatest of ease. I could hear the guys back in Brooklyn, "Minnie Who? She sounds like a flying whore."

There was a person in the show with a leather whip. He had a woman companion who held a cigarette in her mouth while he cracked the whip and knocked the thing right out of her mouth without hitting her. Thinking, gee we could do that. Therefore, before we went home I asked my aunt if she would buy me one of the whips that they sold at the souvenir shop. She bought me the whip however, she never knew that I intended to have her daughter Joann hold a candy cigarette in her mouth while performing the trick.

When we got home, I practiced with the whip until I was good at it. I told Joann that I had an idea how we could make money. How? She asked. I told her that we could charge a nickel to watch an act that they did at the circus. It is not much but the kids would pay. We practiced with the candy cigarette before we did it in front of anyone. Joann finally felt confident that she would not get hurt. We did it a few times but never collected too much money but the whole idea was fun.

Grandfather Louie: There was talk in the family about mom's father Louis; He died just before I was born. I guess the traditional thing to do was name someone after him. That is how I got the name Louis.

Occasionally, I heard my aunts talking about him. They mentioned the time their house blew up down near the Old Mill. (*The Old Mill* is a section in East N.Y.) My grandfather ran a still in the basement and made alcohol. I believe that is why my grandmother knew all about running a booze business. They never said much about it. If they knew we kids were listening, they would begin speaking in Italian so that we could not understand them. When they spoke Italian, we knew that they were saying something that we should not know about, because the only other times they spoke Italian, was when they spoke with grandma.

Although we never heard much about what happened the day the house blew up, some of the old timers from down the Old Mill knew about it. As I became older and associated with different people, I found out a little more about what happened. Soon as any of the old timers found out that, we were from the Fuccillo family. (This was my mother's maiden name.) We heard them say "Oh yeah that was the fella Louie that made alcohol in the basement." Who knows, they may have been some of his customers? I never questioned my mother about it too much. I already knew that this was something that she was not very proud to be associated with and I never wanted to put her in an embarrassing situation. I was just glad to hear that no one was in the house at the time.

The Neighborhood

Glenmore Ave: I remember a schoolteacher telling us "It's a shrinking world." Meaning that as time went by traveling became easier and people moved further away from their place of birth. This was not true with our family. Everyone settled close to each other. Glenmore Ave. seemed to be the hub. There were four brick buildings, each of which housed four families. Most of our family on mom's side lived in an apartment in one of the buildings or close by.

Between the buildings is a space of about twenty feet. It is an alley, no grass just concrete. This is where everyone congregated. The kids played all sorts of games. The summers were always a lot of fun. We all ate dinners outside together.

Not all families were Italian, many Jewish people too. Whenever everyone gathered, there was a variety of food as a result; we learned to eat many different things. I remember always hearing music from someone's radio sitting on a windowsill or my uncle Danny played music with a mandolin. There were always ethnic jokes as well as singing and dancing. No one ever felt offended by the jokes. Everyone lived close together as one big happy family. The buildings were so close together that a telephone was not necessary, neighbors spoke to each other through the windows. The women hung clothes on a clothesline attached to a couple of wooden poles in the back yard. They also ran a line between buildings and passed a sample of whatever was on their menu that night.

The Old Mill was a section not far from where we lived. Mostly Italian families lived there. It seemed to generate many Wise Guys. This is a slang expression used, meaning Gangsters or Hoodlums. Another term often used is Goodfellas.

There was another section known as *"The Hole."* This was an area south of the Sunrise highway that dropped off in elevation. I guess that is why they called it The Hole. It was another section of mostly Italian families, it also breed Wise Guys. We lived in a higher elevated section that everyone knew as *"The City."* for that reason we are City people.

Just about, everyone went to public school. I started in the Kindergarten at P.S 159, which went up to the sixth grade. From there I went to P.S. 214. Both schools were within walking distance. High school (Franklin K. Lane H.S.) was a little further away so we took a bus, which cost us a nickel. On pleasant afternoons, it was a nice walk home.

Everything was very convenient. My parents did not always own a car therefore; we walked or took public transportation. The subway was one block away on Euclid Ave. This was the last stop on the IND line. I remember when the line officially opened in 1948. There was a celebration and the mayor of N.Y. City (Mayor O' Dwyer) was there to make a speech. When they opened up this new station, things started to change in the neighborhood. Loads of people came from Long Island to board the train that took them into Manhattan. Every empty lot became a parking lot for their cars. New bus lines added even more congestion. An elevated train also ran down Euclid Ave., which was a half a block from our house.

Across the street from us was a brickyard. It stretched a half block along Euclid Ave. Flatbed trucks were loaded there with bricks, to make deliveries. The place had a large sign that read (William Gerier Brick Co.,) some phone numbers and a list of different kinds of brick.

Bingo Cards & Craps: My mother belonged to a Bingo club, which consisted of twelve members; it included a few of her sisters and close friends. They met at a different home every Friday night to play Bingo and socialize. While the women enjoyed their time together, the men gathered at another house to play cards. Remembering the card games at our house, almost all of the men smoked. It was either cigarettes or cigars. The worst smelling cigars were the old Ginny Stinkers. It was a smaller cigar with a funny shaped roll and they stunk like hell.

The men drank beer or whiskey and cussed at each other or at the crummy hand that the dealer dealt to them. The cussing was not bad. They showed respect for any of the kids that were present. Billy and I played with toys on the floor. The apartments were quite small so we were always within hearing distance of what was going on during the card games.

Recollecting, the men speaking about what they could have had, or should have done. They talked about properties that were cheap at one time but now the asking price was outrageous. "I could-a bought it then but now it's too expensive." Alternatively, "Dat business is doin great today I should-a bought it for a song a few years ago."

We were too young to comprehend much of this business talk. However, the whining form these old men always made an impression. As we got older, while talking to Billy, trying to educe, that when we got older we should try different ideas. Venture into whatever we thought could pan out for us. Let us not sound like the old men at the card games! Explaining to him, "If we tried things and were not successful we could always try something else. It would be better in the end to try and to fail, than not to have tried at all and become two whining old folks."

The back yards were very small. There was a cover over a cellar door and about a ten by twenty foot area of dirt. The property owner, who was Jewish, was not much into planting anything so we had many weeds in the back of the house. On Sunday mornings, some of the men gathered to shoot craps against the side of the cellar door. Once again the smell of smoke filled the air while the men who lost a few bucks at the card game tried to win it back playing dice.

Figs: Behind the adjacent building where our grandmother lived was quite different. Our step grandfather Angelo, who they all called "The old Geezer," planted tomatoes and other vegetables. He also had a fig tree. The old Geezer was so proud of this tree. He wrapped it up with tarpaper every winter to protect it from the frost. In the summer, the figs sprouted out in abundance. Billy and I kept a sharp eye on those figs. We knew just when they were ripe enough to eat. Now, we had to be careful not to eat too many at one time because my grandfather also had a sharp eye and this Fig tree was his pride and joy.

Wine: Our grandfather also made wine. Each season, he bought a truckload of grapes. He had a press and a bunch of wine barrels, which he kept in the back yard. The old man made a ton of wine. We could not imagine how he and grandmother could drink so much wine. He was a real stingy man, rarely offering a drink to anyone. This being a reason he earned the name Old Geezer. Thinking back, grandma probably sold some of it and gave him the money. We did not put it past her to sell wine; after all, she used to sell alcohol too. When entering her cellar, there were groups of bottles of all different flavors of liquors on a shelf. She mixed them with alcohol and then sold them.

Grandma was a cool old woman, doing her own thing with the alcohol. She always went somewhere with two big green canvas shopping bags at her side. Granny was a strong woman and had no problem carrying these bags while traveling on a trolley car that ran a block from our house, the elevator train that was also a block away, or a bus that was close by. Granny was real slick. She knew that if the law approached her all she had to do was drop the bags against the ground to break the bottles and the evidence was gone in a heartbeat. As slick as the woman was, she was not as professional as she may have thought. The law kept an eye on her.

Grandma followed through with her normal routine until one day as we kids were playing in the backyard, mom's sister Irene climbed through a bedroom window with a couple of gallons of raw alcohol in her hands. She ran to the garden and smashed the glass bottles as we all stood there watching the white liquid as it soaked into the black garden soil. Not long after, detectives entered the apartment searching for grandma's stash of booze. If not for the quick thinking of Aunt Irene, the old lady would have been carted off in a pie wagon for the illegal possession of raw alcohol.

Grandma was a lonely woman after Grandpa Louie died. She had her family around her however, that certainly could not fill her craving for a man. The old Geezer most likely filled that need for her.

Many Italian Americans often speak about how they spent numerous hours at the home of their grandparents. There are many stories of the Sunday dinners at Nonna's

(Grandma in Italian) house and all of the fabulous things that she cooked and baked. We lived just next door to our grandparents and we have no such stories to tell. I cannot recall ever eating a dinner at grandma's house. Maybe it was because of the stingy old Geezer. We will never know.

Fire Station: On the same block just behind our house was Fire House Engine Co 236. The front of the firehouse faced Liberty Ave. A trolley car ran along this street. Every time an alarm signal went off the engines would start and the sirens blasted to let everyone know that they were coming out of the building.

We were always pals with the firefighters. They kept a metal cup attached to a water spigot so that we could always get a drink. These fellas did not have much to do during the day while waiting for a signal from a fire alarm, so they had plenty of time to spend with us kids. We always treated them with respect as we did with all our elders. Mother taught this to us at an early age. They took a liking to us therefore, allowing us to sit on the fire trucks, ring the bell and hang off the back to make believe we were firefighters.

Whenever we heard the sound of the signal, we knew that they were going to a fire. We waited until they were far enough away before entering the firehouse. That is when each of us went upstairs to the living quarters put on a pair of boots and a hat then jump onto the brass pole to slide down through a hole in the floor and land on the concrete below. We did this a couple of times but were very cautious because many times, it was a false alarm and the firefighters would return almost immediately.

When it was obvious that they were at a real fire, it was time for us to eat. These fellas always had plenty of food in the refrigerator. There were always lots of cold cuts, bread and drinks. Therefore, we chowed down and then made our exit before they returned to the firehouse. Once again, down the brass pole.

During the hot summers, it was noisy in the neighborhood. Air conditioners were not too popular in those days unless you had a window unit. Our folks put one in years later but most of the time we had window screens to keep the bugs out and let fresh air in.

The streets were always full of people. You could always see mother pushing a baby carriage, people walking, or just sitting on the stoop. There was never a shortage of kids. The Italian families on the next block had seven eight or nine kids each. Around the corner on Doscher Street there were plenty of other kids of every decent. It was never a problem finding someone to play with or just hang out.

Events: I was the first-born on the Polish side of the family. Therefore, it was only natural-like in most families to give that child a lot of attention. My Uncles and especially dad pushed me to indulge in athletic activities. As a young child, my uncle bought me a work out set consisting of springs, those handgrip squeeze things and boxing gloves. What was I going to do with all this stuff? I was too young to use them. Pop held onto everything until I got older. He stashed it all away in a small bin in the basement.

I caught a baseball with my father when he was off work on Sundays and Mondays. It was a ritual. Pop was a catcher therefore, he knew all about the position. He began teaching me how to catch. It started at a very young age with him rolling oranges to me. Later, we stood on opposite sides of Glenmore Ave. as he pitched to me. We did this for years, as I developed very sharp reflexes.

Pop began to teach me how to box, I always followed his instructions on how to stand, move around, dance throw left jabs and right crosses. He put on a pair of gloves and we spared together.

When he felt I was good enough to handle the gloves, he called on my Cousin Anthony, who lived across the street from us. We put the gloves on, pop called out "Bong. Round one, come out shake hands and start boxing." Anthony is five years older than I am, and at that age, it makes a big difference. The punches landed, Bam! Slam! He always gave me a shellacking. When it was over pop would say, "You did well today, that's my boy." Besides Anthony, other kids in the neighborhood were all willing to take a shot at me. Pop never picked a small kid for me to box with. He did not want me pounding on a small dude. That would not have looked too good in front of the neighbors.

We called these little matches in the alleyway, "smokers." On Sundays, a couple of the fathers gathered with their kids to teach them how to box. Well, it did not take long before they were betting on the matches. This was always a thing in Brooklyn. If it was not a card game, it was shooting craps or they went to Aqueduct racetrack, which was not too far away. The men lite up their cigars or butts filling the air with smoke as we kids spared with each other in the alley.

The New Kid: A new family moved into an apartment across the street from us. Somehow, related to our uncle Frank who lived in Queens just past the city line. One Sunday this new neighbor named Sam came over to our alleyway to check out the action. He was with his son Richie. Not long after they arrived, dad asked Sam, would you like our sons to box? Sam told dad that his son Richie was much bigger, besides he was about four or five years older than your son. Dad told him it was OK and that he should not worry about it. When Sam finally agreed to have his son box, pop asked him if he would like to place a bet on the outcome of the match. Sam could not resist such an offer. Therefore, they placed a wager.

Richie put on a pair of boxing gloves. It looked like it was the first time he had ever seen boxing gloves much less wear them. I looked at dad and said, "Gee another big guy?" "Do not worry he said, just do what I tell you to do. Rush into him from the start. Do not give him a chance to think of what he has to do. Just hit him with left jabs and feel him out. Then whack him with the old one two. Now go get him." Well, it did not take but a few seconds. After following pop's instructions Richie ripped the gloves off, threw them on the floor and started to cry. Sam got pissed off he kicked his son in the ass and chased him home. It was obvious that the man was embarrassed.

Sam turned out to be a nice person. He drove a good-sized truck, which he used to deliver bananas. After work, he parked his truck in front of the house. It did not take long before I climbed inside the rear of the truck looking for anything good that may be lying in there. The truck always had lots of shredded newspaper lying on the floor. I began sifting thru the paper and found a few nice bananas. "Wow": So, from that day on I kept an eye out for the banana truck. Meanwhile, Richie became a good friend.

The Nuns: When becoming a little older but still attending elementary school I went down near The Old Mill area. This is where our Catholic church (Saint Fortunata) is located. As you can tell by its name, mostly Italians frequented it. On Friday nights, they had open house for sports minded kids. Many people from The Old Mill and The Hole went there. I found one activity very exciting. It was the boxing matches. They matched the boys according to size. I could now box with some kid without getting my ass kicked.
These matches were enjoyable, because after all the lessons from dad along with the experiences of boxing with all the bigger boys, it was to my advantage to box with someone the same size as me.

Wednesday afternoons was religious instruction day for everyone. The kids from each faith would gather outside P.S. 159 and along with monitors, usually a teacher or a volunteer parent marched us to our church.

While sitting in the church, or the church basement, the priests and nuns taught us prayers and preached to us about different kinds of sins. A Venial sin was like a minor offence similar to a misdemeanor. A Mortal sin was a real bad one, similar to a felony.

After listening attentively to their stories' it was time to ask questions. For instance, the sister would tell us that it was a Venial sin to gamble. After trying to reason with what she said, and thinking of all the old fellas who gambled every week, they raised good respectful children and provided for their families. What was wrong with gambling? Besides, they all enjoyed themselves. Therefore, I raised a hand and asked. "What is so bad about gambling? Do you not, set up booths every year at the church feast? Many of them are games of chance. You have different kinds of big wheels with numbers or dice on them, there are crap tables and people all bet with cash." The nuns could not handle questions like that. They said to be quiet and stop acting like a Jew. Well, the conversation got a good laugh from everyone. After the religious class was over, the nuns dismissed all the students and we went home. We City Kids were not the only ones attending these classes. The kids from The Old Mill and The Hole were there too. We all mixed and made many new friends.

Dancing: On special nights, the church held a dance. They provided Rock and Roll music along with the nuns to supervise. This was always a good time. Many good-looking Italian girls attended and this was a great way to meet them. If a couple danced too close, one of the nuns told them to back off. Mother Helen was like the head honcho of all the nuns, who are termed Sisters. Everyone feared the big dog of the yard. Anyone that stepped out on line got a whack from her.

When you put a bunch of new kids together from different neighborhoods, some of them will try to stand out from the rest. Someone will mouth off just to look smart or tough, just like at the school. We settled all differences after three o clock with a fistfight in the schoolyard, some street corner or an empty lot. After the church classes ended, there was usually a fight. It was always be between a City Kid and someone from another neighborhood.

My mom was not the type of women who babied her children. Surely, pop broke her of that right from the start. When coming home on Wednesday afternoons with cuts and bruises, filthy and ripped clothes. She would just give a harsh looking stare and say something like "I guess you went to church today? Throw those clothes in the hamper and get yourself cleaned up, supper will be ready soon."

Pat's Old Man: While still in elementary school, during a church class one Wednesday afternoon, a big kid sat behind me. His name was Patrick. He kept hitting the back of my head. After telling him to stop, he continued. All of his pals from the

Old Mill giggled every time he smacked me. This was a time when a fellow must make a stand. Either he continues to make a clown of me, or it stops right now. If it did not stop now, it would happen repeatedly every Wednesday. I turned around and told him that we will settle this at the end of class. The class ended and everyone left the church. We walked across the street; I then grabbed him in front of his friends, pushing him up against a brick wall right there on the corner of Linden Blvd. and Crescent Street. He threw a punch that is when I began to pound his face in with both hands. Wow! A crowd gathered to watch this spectacle. It turned out that Patty was not as tough as he pretended to be.

The guy was bleeding form his face when someone yelled out "Here comes Mr. Mafia you better run." Asking, "Who is Mr. Mafia"? (This was his real name) Someone said he was Patrick's father. Do not let him get you. While running down Crescent Street, this big man was right on my tail. I ran down into an empty lot and through some weeds, but he was catching up to me and yelling threats and curse words. This gent was really pissed off. I tried running through another lot but he was faster than I was. I made a turn and headed for the church figuring it was my best shot to escape this mad man.

Saint Fortunata had a real big stairway at the front entrance of the church. If I could make it up those steps and through the door, I would be home safe. The big lug was too fast for me. He caught me at the top of the steps and began to pound me. I could not believe that I was taking such a beating from this big ape right there in front of the church entrance. This is where everyone came each Sunday to pray. I was glad it was Wednesday afternoon. When it was over, I went home. I never mentioned anything to mom. It was just another day.

I will tell more about Mr. Mafia later.

You Must Work Hard: Time went on and my little brother began to grow bigger. I pinched his cheek every day and give him kisses. I loved the little fellow. My brother liked to play with his toys. He could play for hours making believe cowboys or soldiers were in battle. He devised little sounds to emphasize what was going on at the time. He made the sound of a bugle then yelled, "Charge em men," while moving the little soldiers toward each other again yelling commands. He was very contented being at home playing with his toys.

My dad and I continued to play catch with the baseball. I was about five years old when he began pitching the ball to me very fast. One day I complained that the ball hurt my hand. For that reason, he got me a little sponge to put in my catchers' mitt. "There how's that?" he said, "Now don't complain anymore." I learned very fast not to shy away from the baseball. He instructed me to never be afraid of the ball, always be in control. Pop became angry when I flinched away from the ball causing me to miss catching it.

After building up a good sweat, he rewarded me at the candy store across the street from our house with a cold soda. My favorite was cherry. We sat at the counter sipping our drinks while talking about baseball. He told me that when I got older I could play ball on neighborhood teams. Then when I reached high school, I could play for the school team. After that comes college. That is where the Baseball Scouts look for the good players. If you are good, enough they will offer you a contract to play professional baseball. However, to get that far, you will have to work very hard at becoming a good player. Pop had it all figured out? I loved hanging out with him.

During the time, we caught the baseball, different people passed. They stopped to watch those fastballs come burning in at me. The mail carrier once told my father that he was throwing the ball too fast to me. He also said that I was too small to be catching such a fast baseball. Dad told him that he had everything under control.

"You do not see him shying away from the ball do ya."

"If he were my kid I would never do dat."

"Well he aint your kid so mind your own business and just go deliver the mail."

The mail carrier shook his head and left us.

The Farms:

Alongside our house on Euclid Ave., starting from Glenmore Ave to Liberty Ave., there was a real shabby looking fence. It was made of all worthless pieces of wood. We called it "The Ginny Fence." As you walked along the fence every so often, there was a gate. Inside each gate of this large lot, was a partition fence, constructed with more worthless wood. I have no idea who owned this land, but many different people grew vegetables there.

We called them "The Farms." Most people would have considered them big gardens. However, what did we know? We were City Kids and never saw a real farm except in the movies.

Euclid Ave. is a dirt road. Above it, the elevator train traveling down Pitkin Ave. made a turn on Euclid Ave. went for two blocks passing the brickyard and the farms and turned on Liberty Ave. It past City Line then traveled on down into Queens.

My brother was growing older and began to hang out with me. I pinched his cheek and asked if he wanted to go check out the farms. Billy never refused to go with me. Climbing the fence was never a problem for us. Once we got inside, it was like a feast. We could eat anything that was ripe, and we did. We made it easier for ourselves to get from one farm to another by making small holes in the Ginny Fences so we could crawl thru instead of climbing over. When we left, we were sure to close the holes so that no one would know we were there.

Some of these farms have a well to provide water for the plants. These people worked very hard at farming this land, we were always careful not to step on any plants or eat too much. Besides, we never wanted the farmers to catch us.

A couple of the farms had a shack with gardening tools and fertilizers. We never touched any of their stuff. The farmers grew heads of lettuce, peppers, tomatoes, eggplants, basil, oregano, carrots, parsley and Gagootz. (That is squash in Italian.) You name it and they grew it.

Directly across the street from our house is where my cousins Anthony and Elaine live. Elaine, (nicknamed Clowny) is one year older than I am. She is a real Tom Boy. She is always game for anything and never had a problem climbing fences or keeping up with the boys. Whenever we went to the farms, she came along to eat her share of fruit and vegetables.

As my brother got older and learned the ropes, he began taking his friends into the farms for a treat. He warned them; never break anything or touch their tools. Now, all of us City Kids had our own farm and we never had to work it.

Peaches: Located at the rear of one of these farms was a short fence that separated the back yard of a household from the farms. The yard has two humongous peach trees. In the summertime, they bared the best peaches I have ever tasted. The owner was a man named Jimmy, a tall skinny dude nicknamed Slim. He had two hunting dogs, named Zeke, Judy and hunted rabbit with my uncle Frank in the wintertime. Slim was always very nice to us. We could never sneak into his yard without the dogs howling. Therefore, Slim knew that we climbed into his trees, sat there and ate a few peaches however, he did not object. We never took advantage of the opportunity and besides, he and his family could never eat so many peaches.

Grapes: One sunny afternoon Billy told me to come with him to one of the farms. He said, "I know where there are some real good grapes." So, down Euclid Ave. we went, walking under the El towards the farm. "OK." he said "This is it; lets climb over the fence." A Ginny fence is not easy to scale. The thing shakes big-time. There is a good chance of a serious injury. We climbed over, walked in about twenty feet, then looked up. Staring us in the face was, *The Man!* This was sort of a slang word used by all the kids. "It meant the owner." I yelled, "Run, he's coming after us!" We both hit the fence together, climbed up over and down the other side like two monkeys. The man reached the fence and just easily pushed the gate opened. "Otz, we coulda did dat." As we ran down the dirt road along a broken sidewalk made of stone, the man wound up and threw a big tomato at us, hitting Billy square in the back of his head (Squish) seeds and crushed tomato dripped all over him. I was hysterical laughing as we ran away. It was not a clean getaway, but a getaway. We will eat the grapes another day.

OTZ is another slang word used by the Italian kids. The real word in Italian is "Gotz," it is a curse word and if my mother ever heard us say it, we would get a crack across the mouth with the back of her hand. Therefore, we all said *OTZ* and sort of got away with it.

Matiuch: One of the people who planted stuff at the farms was an old woman named Mary. Her nickname was Matiuch; I guess it meant something in Italian. She always had a big brown dog to accompany her. This dog looked vicious. Whenever she came to the farms, we made sure not to be in there. As she passed our house, the dog started barking while trying to get at us. She would pull on the leash and yell at the dog, but he kept on barking and growling as if he knew that we had made a visit to get some of Mary's tomatoes.

Always making sure, we were nice to her. "Good morning Matiuch, Good afternoon Matiuch," but under our breaths we would be saying, "Screw you Mary, we just ate some of your tomatoes." As time went by, the people stopped gardening. Weeds began to grow. This was all right with us because now we had a big empty lot to play in without a fence. Mother always shopped for fresh vegetables and fruits so we never missed the farm food, it was just a little something extra to pick on.

Street Games

Skates: There were different seasons and each one dominated a variety of games played by everyone. In the fall season, street skating was always a big thing. The skates had a clamp on the front; it fastened to the shoe with a skate key. Every kid had a key in his or her pocket besides a lot of other crap, including a piece of chalk to mark lines in the streets.

There were not many cars in those days so we always played in the streets, that were made of what we called tar. Actually, it was macadam, which was super smooth and easy on the skate wheels.

One of the competitive games we played was Street Hockey. Goals were set in two locations of the street. The boundaries marked with chalk. Hockey sticks were available at the corner candy store and not expensive; the puck was made of wood. When the sticks broke, we later used them as swords to duel. When skates became old we took them apart, nailed half a skate with two wheels to each end a 2x4 piece of lumber about five feet long. A wooden fruit box from a grocery store nailed on top of it; two handles nailed on top of the box in order to hold on to it and steer. Bingo! You had a homemade scooter. We painted them with any color paint we could find. To jazz them up a little, we popped a couple of reflectors off a truck then nailed them to the box. By adding another piece of wood at the bottom of the box, formed a compartment. This was a great place to stash some lunch, a slingshot, or whatever else you needed for the day.

Marbles: We played marble games as long as it was not too cold and the ground was not too hard. Everyone carried a few "Mibs." (Is a Slang word for marbles) in their pocket. You never knew when you might run into a marble game. There were several games played like, Shimmy, Pottsy, Hit the carbola; (Carbola is a big marble). Sometimes a kid would have a shoebox with various size holes cut in it. The holes were numbered. If you rolled a marble into a hole, the number was your pay off in Mibs. If you missed, you lost the marble.

There were two brothers, Albee and Joey. Joey was an odd-looking kid. He rather looked like half a dwarf. His nickname was Peewee. This little dude would have made a great character in the movies. You could always find them wherever there was a marble game in progress. Peewee was a little cheater. He kicked his shooter to get a better position. When no one was looking, he used a steel ball bearing instead of a regular marble to knock more Mibs from the pot, and occasionally stole your marble. The fellas let him get away with all his petty crap because he was so small. No one wanted to hurt him. Whenever he won, Peewee danced around shaking his ass, throwing his hands in the air singing "One two three ou gottza, one two three ou gottza", just to piss everyone off.

One afternoon after playing marbles with Peewee, I began walking home; mamma was sitting on the stoop talking with some of the neighbors. Upon my arrival, with both my hands in the air as I mimicked Pee Wee. I sang "one two three ou gottza." Whack! I just caught a crack across the mouth from mom. She had just been embarrassed in front of all the Italian women with this Italian curse word from my mouth. The next time I saw Peewee I gave him a good hop in the hole and told him that was for nothing.

Stickball: This was always a warm weather game. We played in the street, against a concrete wall, or in the schoolyard on the softball court. It was better to play in the schoolyard for a couple of reasons. Playing in the street most always ended up breaking someone's window. Between stickball, stoopball, baseball or football there was always that risk. Each time a window was broken, mom taught us to confess to the owner and have a new windowpane replaced which I had to pay for. Replacing windows became expensive. There was a Glazier on Pitkin Ave. named Jack. We all knew him as (Jack the Glazier.) Thinking, if speaking with him, maybe we could make a deal. Suppose that I were to do some work around his shop, run some errands, and then maybe, he would fix all of the busted windows at a lower cost. This worked out well. The Glazier was now a pal and agreed to repair them at a low rate.

The other reason for playing in the schoolyard was a beneficial one. P.S. 159 was a five-story building. The school auditorium was only three stories high and it had a flat tar roof. At least a couple of balls went on the roof during a game. There was no way to go on the roof thru the school building because the custodian locked all of the doors at a certain time of the day. There were only two other ways. One was to shimmy up a skinny steel pipe, or climb the large flight of steps leading to a vestibule entrance to the auditorium. Together, my friend Roy and I waited around after the games were finished and most of the players left the schoolyard. After walking to the top of the stairway, we climbed onto the vestibule roof. Then one of us stood with his back against the corner of the brick wall. The other person got a boost until he was able to grab onto the parapet coping and then pull himself onto the auditorium roof.

BINGO! We hit pay dirt, cashing in on the entire cluster of the pink Spalding's. We also found softballs, handballs, and if lucky, a football. It was a hell of a risk because if one of us ever fell from that height, he would be minced meat on the concrete below. For that reason, no one else ever tried it except for us two morons. Nevertheless, we had balls.

After school was out, the custodian locked the gates at the entrances to the yard. When everyone was gone the (Jocks), "a term used that identified an athletic type kid," climbed over the fence to play ball. This went on for a long time until some smart fellow cut a hole in the chain-linked fence. Now everyone was able to get into the schoolyard. "I wonder why someone did not think of doing that sooner."

Basketball: Nowadays, while driving down any street, one can find a basketball stand along with a backstop in many yards, and rarely see any kids playing basketball.

Around the corner from our house on Doscher Street, there was a streetlight in the middle of the block, which attached to a tall wooden pole. At the end of the block there was a grocery store called Bohack. Momma always shopped there so the men who ran the store knew us well. These men always supplied us with a new vegetable bushel any time we needed one. We made a backboard out of old wood, and then nailed a bushel to it that represented the basket. Bada-Bing! There was a homemade basketball court, and we are able to play night games too. We played for many hours under the light and replaced many worn out bushels.

Most of the games we played during the day at the schoolyard. There were always many people and you had to challenge the winners in order to play on the court. The schoolyard had only one basketball court. It had a metal backboard and a steel rim with a steel chain for a net. A little bit stronger than the bushel court.

During the cold winter nights, we went to one of the other schools in the neighborhood. The gymnasium was available for kids to play sports. Basketball and Dodge ball were the most popular games. At these other schools, we met many kids from different neighborhoods. There was never a shortage of people to play with. Dodge ball was a rough game. You had to hit someone with the ball to knock him out of the game. It usually ended up with a fistfight.

Football: We played Football in the street, an empty lot or the schoolyard. The game was always two-hand touch instead of tackling. No one had any sort of equipment to protect us. Ever since the farms were gone, the lot was a great place to play. One sunny afternoon while playing a game, my brother Billy tripped over a shoebox wrapped in newspaper. Once on his feet again he picked up the box. Someone yelled out

"What's in it?"

"I don't know,"

"Well, open the damn ding."

Everyone gathered around while Billy tore open the box. It was something wrapped with more newspaper. Suddenly the thing rolled out of the newspaper into his hands. It was a dead baby. The baby looked like it was just born. Someone had stabbed it in its side then dumped it in the lot. Wow! "What should we do?" Someone suggested we call the Firemen, they will know what to do with it. Before you could say Jackie Robinson, police were on the scene asking us questions. The news reporters came next, again asking questions and taking notes.

"Who found the baby?"

"I did" say Billy.

"What's your name"?

Suddenly, I stepped up and told Billy not to give anyone his name. Just tell them what happened. The story hit the Daily news the next day but the article read "some kid," they never mentioned my brother's name. We learned at a young age never to talk about what went on in the neighborhood. Keep your eyes and ears opened and your mouth shut.

Football in the schoolyard was always a rough game. When we played a game of football, nothing else would be going on. Everyone in the yard played football. There were these two brothers, Marty and Patty, a few years older than most of us. We classified them as the 'big guys'.

The brothers choose to see who would pick first. Odds or Evens were the most frequent way to choose. It went like this: One person would pick odds; naturally, the other person had evens. On a count of, one-two-three shoot. Both guys threw out either one or two fingers at the same time. The total fingers added up to an odd or an even amount. That is what determined who won to choose first. After picking sides, the two brothers appointed themselves as Quarterbacks while the rest of us played the other positions. They also appointed the receivers. Naturally, the best catchers and runners were the receivers. The rest of the people played the line. At the beginning, this was a lot of fun but after we all became banged up it got old very fast. The people that had the most fun were the two brothers. The rest of us went home with cuts and bruises from the cold concrete playground.

We played Football games in the street too. The sewer tops became the goals just as they had become the bases in stickball. When playing football in the street there was always the risk of breaking someone's window on the kick off. This did not happen too often however, whenever it did happen, it was Jack the Glazier to the rescue.

Punch ball: This is a great game. All the equipment you needed to play is a Spalding. It is a high bouncing pink rubber ball. Most of the kids pronounced it Spall Deen. It is just like baseball, with the same rules. A bat is not used; instead, we threw the ball up in the air about a foot then punched it with our fist. Every one played similar positions as in baseball. After hitting the ball, you ran the bases.

All of these games were great to play except for one set back, the sewers. These friggin things ate up more balls than Carter had Liver pills. Everyone kept an eye in the sewer to see how many balls were floating in the dirty water. When there were no more balls left to play with, this was the time to do the nasty job of lifting off the sewer top, being very careful not to let the steel top fall into the sewer. Once the top was off, two people held one person by his legs lowering him head first into the sewer to retrieve all the balls. We then replaced the sewer cover and the games continued. No one ever gave thought to what would happen if he fell into the sewer.

On a hot summer afternoon, it was ball-retrieving day. At the street corner, there was a sewer with two tops adjacent to one another. Some of the big guys from the next block were attempting to lift off one of the sewer tops. They used a stick to lift it up enough to grab it. "I will never forget this day as long as I live." After lifting the top, I stuck my hand under to grab it. The top weighed about fifty pounds. It slipped off the stick and fell back onto the sewers rim with my finger caught in between. Screaming, there on my knees with a finger pinned, the big guys tried to lift it again but it only squashed the finger more. "Damn it, get me loose." It seemed like it was stuck there for hours until they got it off my finger. The finger looked like a pancake. It was a wonder that it did not break. Now, how do I explain this to mom? Thinking back today, it would have made good sense to place a piece of wood or cardboard in front of the sewers hole to stop the balls from dropping into the water. "Damn! Those big guys, you'd think they would have known better."

Stoop Baseball: Again, the only thing needed to play this game is a Spall Deen and a stoop. The rules of this game are similar to baseball. It takes two people to play. The person, who is up at bat, throws the ball against the stoop. His opponent in the field tries to catch it on a fly for out one. If the ball bounces one time, it is a single, twice a double, and so on. After three outs, the batter then takes the field and the fielder is now the batter. The game consists of nine innings. Stoop Baseball is a fast game. It is mental. There are no scorecards, pencils nor paper. There is always someone waiting to challenge the winner. A new person would show up and call, "Next." Next, is a common word we used in all street games, it simply means that he is in line to play the winner.

The front doors to all of the brick buildings on Glenmore Ave. had small windowpanes. When playing Stoop Baseball sometimes the ball bounced off the stoop, went the wrong way and broke a glass. It is ruled a foul ball. This did not happen very often but when it did, it was another job for Jack the Glazier.

Stoopball: Another simple game is "Stoopball." It is completely different from the above-mentioned game. Standing on the sidewalk, a person threw the Spall Deen at the stoop. If caught on one bounce, it was five points, a fly, was ten points. If the ball hit the point where the tread and riser of the step meet, the ball returned at a high speed. Catching this ball is worth fifty points. The first person to reach one thousand is the winner. If it bounced more than once, you were out. It was mental. There was not a kid in the neighborhood that could not continuously pitch the ball at a fast pace while adding the numbers in his head accurately. Today, you can go to almost any store to buy something and if the cash register does not tell the clerk how much the total of the purchase, and the amount of change to give back, he or she is in trouble.

As we played Stoopball across the street from our house, next to the candy store. I was fidgeting around with a steel grating covering a cellar window. The neighborhood kids always checked out the gratings, looking to see if there was anything worth fishing out.

To this day, I still cannot figure out how I managed to get a foot caught between the steel bars. Everyone tried to get it loose but could not do it. The woman that owned the candy store came out to help. Her name was Beatty. Beatty, being the oldest one there at the time, supervised. "Twist it to the left," she said; "now try twisting it to the right, pull up on your leg." Nothing worked and the pain was getting worse. Finally, Beatty said, "Gee, I don't know what else to do." I asked her if she would please call the Firemen; they will know what to do. It did not take long when my pals arrive. They looked at the situation, walked over to the fire truck, and pulled out a long bar that they used to break things at a fire. BINGO! It took them less than a minute to get my foot free. "Ya gotta love those Firemen." Anxiety began to build. What would happen if Mom found out about it? Then it would be real trouble trying to explain how the foot got in there in the first place.

The Fire Alarm: Cousin Elaine could always get me into trouble at the snap of a finger. While playing in front of the candy store late one afternoon, she said to look at the hole located on the side of the fire alarm box, attached to a wood pole. I asked her why the hole was there. She knew that if she got my curiosity going, I would do whatever she suggested. She said if you take the old mop stick, which we were playing with at the time, and use it to pull down that handle, a bullet would shoot out of the hole. After looking at the hole for a while, curiosity began to build. I pulled down hard on the handle, *CLANK-CLANG* the fire alarm went off. Elaine ran like hell. I waited only a moment to see the flying bullet that never came. Elaine yelled Run! As we ran up the stoop and into her house, we heard the fire trucks outside and hid under a bed. We were alarmed. "No pun intended."

The Firemen chalked it off as a false alarm and returned to the firehouse. Aunt Mary, (Elaine's mother) could not get me out from under the bed. After refusing to come out, she went across the street to summon our downstairs neighbor Bernie. He worked as a security guard. Bernie came up to escort me home. He told me not to be scared because he had a gun and he will not allow anyone to stop us from going home. I was in trouble again. It was impossible to explain this one to my mother. "I just had to take my licks." The hole in the fire alarm box was a key hole to open the box. How naïve I was at about six years old.

Baseball: When not catching ball with Dad, I was somewhere in the neighborhood playing either Hardball (Baseball) or Softball (Larger ball.) We played Softball either in the street or in the schoolyard. When we played in the street, we would be soon calling on Jack the Glazier to do a window repair. The schoolyard was always good because it was fenced-in. It had a flat, smooth concrete floor, painted bases, and no windows to break. Sometimes, balls went on the assembly roof.

However, Roy and I will shortly be the new owners of the balls.

Euclid Park: Located approximately seven blocks from our house was Euclid Park. This park had many good things to play on. Including, swings, sliding ponds, seesaws, monkey bars, drinking fountains, a small wading pool and rest rooms. It also had a place to store equipment and a Parkies quarters. The man in charge of the park was called a' Parkie' by all the kids. Nevertheless, the best thing about the park was the baseball field. It was gigantic with beautiful green grass. On one corner of the field is a gorgeous baseball diamond, manicured by the Parkies. Euclid Field was second best only to Ebbets Field where the Brooklyn Dodgers played.

Only league games or special bookings played on this field. There was a chained link fence around it. It also has a backstop behind home plate made of chained link. Behind the backstop is a large seating area made of concrete that went up to about four levels. The Parkies kept anyone from going on the baseball diamond besides permitted teams.

Two Parkies worked at Euclid Park for a long time. One named Carmine, I do not remember the other man's name but he was a big fat person. These men wore a uniform while at work. The color was Army green so you can always spot the Parkies.

The Backstop:  Everyone played ball on another field at the other end of the park. I always longed to play on the big Euclid diamond someday, frequently dreaming about it.

One afternoon after playing ball on the grass area of the park with my friend Roy, we decided to walk over to the big diamond and check it out. Roy suggested that we climb up on top of the chain-linked backstop. It seemed like a good idea at the time, so up we went. All of a sudden, we could hear a whistle blowing from left field. It was the fat Parkie; he was waving his hands and screaming something. We continued to climb around on the backstop. From out of left field, the fat guy came running towards us screaming, "Get the hell off the backstop." Roy jumped off and ran away. However, before I could get down the Parkie came through a gate in the fence carrying one of those sticks with a nail out of the end, which he used to pick up paper and crap. Facing the diamond, while climbing down the fence, the fat guy was standing directly behind me winding up like he was going to hit a baseball with his stick, but instead he was aiming right at my ass. As the stick came around, I lost control and pissed my pants. It seemed like a gallon of hot liquid discharged in a split second. BAM-SQUISH he made contact. Letting go of the fence, dropping the rest of the way to the ground while running like a bat out of hell leaving a yellow stream behind. Upon catching up with Roy, my pants were soaking wet.

Roy got a big kick out of the incident but all I got was a black and blue mark on the ass and a pair of pants soaked with urine.

Since walking around with wet pants was not an option, the next thing to do was get into the house without my mother seeing me. If she knew what happened, I was sure to get another whack from her. Parents in those days did not protect their children as they do today. If an adult hit you, it must have been for a good reason. By letting mom know, what had happened would never result with her showing any pity? So, I changed clothes and hung the wet ones out the back window to dry. I felt like I just outsmarted my mother and avoided another smack in the ass, which I could not afford at this moment. It was already sore.

Foul Balls: Behind the concrete seating area at the park was a big old abandoned brick building. It had something to do with city water because everyone called it the waterworks. There were also large empty lots with loads of tall weeds located outside of the park grounds. A kid could get lost in these thick weeds.

Mostly every Sunday in the summer there were baseball games played on the diamond. People gathered to watch the games. Fathers brought their kids, dudes brought their girlfriends and all of the people related somehow to the ball players were there too. Before game time, my friend Philly DiMaio and I set ourselves up to collect foul balls. One of us sat on top of the concrete stands while the other person planted himself in the weeds. The umpire yelled "Play Ball" and the game began.

Whenever a batter hit a foul ball outside the park, the fella up on the concrete silently pointed towards the ball. Meanwhile, the person in the weeds would pay close attention to the person on the concrete, so that he did not have to yell anything and bring attention to anyone else. The Ball players immediately sent someone out to look for the baseball, but we already had the jump on them. The weed guy already retrieved the ball and hid it in the waterworks. After a couple of innings we switched positions because it became too hot just standing in the weeds. When the game ended or when we had already collected enough balls, we picked up our stash from the waterworks. One thing we had to remember was not to be greedy because if these ball players could not find any of their baseballs they would become suspicious and we will have ruined a good thing. Besides, we never wanted to catch a beating from some big ballplayer, not at our age; we were only about 10 years old.

There were always people in the neighborhood looking to buy balls at a discount. Between baseballs, spall deens, handballs and softballs my pals and I always had coins in our pockets.

Sidewalk Games: Children were outside every day weather permitting. None of the kids had or needed expensive toys. There were so many sidewalk games, which we played. The girls jumped rope while singing different songs. They jumped alone or with a few of their friends. Some of the girls were very good. They were able to jump with two people while two other girls worked the ends of the rope. They called it Double Duchies. I do not know where the name came from but it was neat to watch. My cousin Elaine was always involved in all of these games.

The girls also played Pottsy, Hopscotch, Red Light Green Light and a variety of other games. The boys stood clear of the girls at that age in fear of the other boys making fun of him. If a boy tried jumping rope, or was seen speaking to them, the other boys called him a sissy.

Living in Brooklyn, everyone learned to take teasing very lightly. No one took anything seriously. It was known as a Ranking contest when two guys squared off on a street corner or in the schoolyard with a bunch of people standing around them, they would start saying bad things about each other. Some of the things became raunchy while everyone began laughing at the poor soul on the losing end of the contest. A few of them were very good at it. They must have kept notes on what bad things to say. As time went on everyone developed thick skin, no matter what anyone said, we brushed it off with no remorse, just like water off a duck's back.

Johnny on the Pony: The boys played many rough games, like "Johnny on the Pony." Depending upon how many kids were available, we made up teams of about five to ten people on each a team. The first person acted like a pillow. He leaned his back against a solid wall. Everyone else on the team bent over and held onto each other forming a line of people known as a pony. The first person from an opposing team ran very fast, then jump and leap frog onto the backs of the pony people. The next opponent did the same thing, and so on until everyone jumped. The idea is to make the pony cave in. Therefore, the harder the landing the better chance of a cave in. When everyone finished jumping they began bouncing and kicking while the person playing pillow yelled out very loud "Johnny on the pony one two three". He said it three times. If there were no cave in, the pony team now became the cowboys. This went on for hours. Everyone was in good shape. There were no fat kids in our neighborhood.

Ringalevio: Another popular game named Ringalevio. One person being considered' IT' and all the other people were potential Jail Birds. We used chalk to draw a box, which is the den or jail. The IT person closed his eyes and counted to fifty, while everyone else ran to hide somewhere. The idea of the game was to capture everyone and put him or her in jail. To capture someone, the IT person must tag him. This went on until he captured everyone. If someone came out of hiding and placed, his foot into the box while yelling "*FREE ALL.*" This automatically freed everyone and the poor IT person had to start all over again. It was a hectic game. Occasionally towards the end of the night, while the IT person was counting, everyone ran home and was in for the night. The poor chap could not find anyone and would eventually go home himself.

Ice Cream: Each evening after supper, all the kids would be playing outside when the Bungalow Bar truck arrived and stopped at the street corner ringing a bell. The truck looked like a little house. It had Ice cream including cones, pops (Ice cream on a stick,) ice cream sandwiches, and Dixie cups (Ice cream in a cup with a little wooden spoon.) The Dixie cups had a picture of an actor or a baseball player on the lid, which we traded. Usually each kid had money in his or her pocket that their parents gave to them. Occasionally, if we were lucky, one of the men from the neighborhood sprang and bought all the kids ice cream. He had probably won a few bucks shooting craps or playing cards that week.

OHH GOTZ

The street corner: It was always lit up from the lamps on the wooden poles. The candy store was on the corner. It had a newspaper stand, which sold out by evening, making the empty stand a good place to sit. In the evenings, kids always hung out in the store reading the magazines free until the owner complained. The store had a soda fountain with high stools to sit on. You could always get a nice, cold, freshly made soda or an Egg Cream. "Only New Yorkers know what an Egg Cream is."

Four Corners Baseball: We played four corners Baseball under the lights. The game required two teams. The street was the court. Each corner was a base. The positions were the same as in Baseball. The pitcher stood in the middle of the street and pitched the ball on one bounce to the batter who used his hand as a bat to hit the ball. He then ran the bases. There was no center fielder because behind second base was a Protestant church.

People gathered to watch the game. If you were lucky, you got a seat on the newspaper stand. These games went on all night. Intermission was when the ice cream truck came and stopped at the corner. After the game, most of the people went into the candy store for a cold drink. Once again, we needed nothing to play this game besides a Spall Deen. "I hope by now you have observed the point that I am making. No one in our neighborhood had expensive toys. However, everyone enjoyed a vigorous childhood."

Old man Koch: A church bell rang every Sunday morning at the Protestant church on the corner.

The caretaker was an elderly man by the name of Mr. Koch. He kept the grounds nice and clean, planted flowers and did all sorts of repairs. All the kids liked him. We all knew him as *"Old man Koch."* Just outside the church fence on Doscher Street was a large dirt area between the concrete sidewalk and the church fence. This was one of the best places to play marbles because old man Koch kept it manicured. He was a good old guy.

The Tough Guy: I must have been 10 or 11 years old. Doscher Street was a good place to play. Many of our friends lived on the block. The houses were all single-family dwellings. The grocery store *Bohack* was just one block from our house at the end of the street. Mom had me go there several times a week to pick up two quarts of milk, a loaf of bread, and two packs of Pall Mall cigarettes.

One afternoon on the way home from the store, I stopped to play with some friends. Along came this big fellow with a brief case filled with schoolbooks. This fellow was attending college. His name is Steve. He lived in one of the apartment buildings on Glenmore Ave. Anyway, he stopped and said something nasty to us. I asked him, "Hey what are you a tough guy or just a guy with a big friggin mouth?" He shoved me and said he was a tough guy, so I punched him in the eye. A very nice shot, Bam! Steve grabbed his face and started to scream, "I can't see, I can't see I'm blind, I can't see." After giving him a good kick in the ass, he began running toward Glenmore Ave. with me on his tale. Not realizing it, Mom was standing on the stoop outside the house. This fellow was still screaming. Mom came running to see what was going on. She stopped him and looked at his eye. The friggin thing was bright red. "What happened?" she asked. He yelled just as a big sissy would do, pointed and said; "he hit me." I started laughing. Just then, Mom gave me a whack across the face.

"Where are the groceries?"

"They are down the block."

"Go get them and get your ass in the house I will deal with you later."

She took the crybaby to his house, and then came home. Man, mamma was pissed off. I just could not convince her that the blind dude started the fight. In good conscience, I never started a fight with anyone. It just was not in my nature to do something like that.

Bohack: We knew the men at the Bohack Grocery store very well. As a young boy 8 years old, I asked the manager of the store if he would inform his customers that he now provided a delivery service for their groceries. I promised to check in occasionally to see if there were any items ready for delivery. Eddie, the manager, agreed to do this. Therefore, a routine had begun for generating some cash.

This little operation went on for a long time. The store had these skimpy carts with very small wheels. They used them inside the store for the customers. Each day I used one of the carts to make the deliveries. Eddie packed the groceries into cardboard boxes and placed them on the side of the store with the customer's name and an address on the box. Pushing the skimpy cart through the streets was easy except when the damn thing would hit a rock or some other foreign object. The wheels were so small, it caused the cart to tip and the friggin box fell off the cart. This happened several times causing eggs and glass to break. Each time this happened, I bought new items to replace the broken ones. Mother taught us to be responsible for anything we broke.

As time went by, friends noticed me constantly pushing the cart. They also noticed that I always had money. Therefore, common sense told me that eventually one of them is going to try to weasel in on the gig. Sure enough, one of the twins that lived on Doscher Street horned in on my operation. The little service was growing slowly but surely. The customers figured it was better to have a kid carry all the groceries home for them instead of carrying them home themselves. The average tip was about ten cents a delivery. Often making trips up and down several flights of stairs but it did not bother me one bit. Sometimes I received a quarter for a tip; this was like winning the lottery. Eddie did not want the orders hanging around the store too long. Therefore, he allowed one of the twin brothers to begin making deliveries. The twin was like a little twat. He could have just done what they told him to do and kept his mouth shut. Nevertheless, he would mouth off in a teasing way like, "Ha-ha I took away some of your orders." The twin was a real pain in the ass. It was not bad enough that he was horning in on my turf, but he had to break my chops besides. I had to think of something to eliminate him.

One day I approached John, another store worker. He packed the shelves, brought up items from the cellar, organized the fruit and vegetable stand and kept the store clean. I told him that if he talked with Eddie and told him to be a little more patient with the timing of the deliveries, I would work a little faster, to get them delivered, and to show my appreciation I will sweep out the store for him each day and do whatever else I could do to help him. Besides, this makes me available for deliveries.

Bingo! The little plan worked. Not only was the twin gone, all the orders were mine to deliver once again. Each Saturday evening John allowed me to take home a bunch of the fruits and vegetables that would probably look bad after the weekend. Mom was very happy. It was like being on the farm again every Saturday night.

The men also taught me some of the lingo that they used in front of the woman customers, Eddie would yell out to Johnny, "Bring up some more manhole covers." None of the women knew what that meant. However, I did. On his next trip up from the cellar, he would have in his hands a case labeled, KOTEX. "Gee, it was nice being one of the men."

Newspapers: While continuing to deliver orders at the grocery store, I always had money in the pockets. I bought gifts for mom. It was nice whenever she made a fuss over the gifts she received. The things I gave to her were not expensive, but she appreciated the thought and the effort.

On Saturday mornings, I got up early. Mom never allowed us to sleep late anyway. She always said to us *(The early bird gets the worm.)* After building a wagon from scrap lumber that was lying around the empty lots, and picking up some wheels from the city dump, the wagon was ready to roll. The early bird (me) picked up another boy to help. We went through every garbage can in the neighborhood collecting newspapers and cardboard. They were stacked on the wagon while we worked our way to the junk yard.

The man at the yard had a scale at the front of the building. "OK, roll your wagon on the scale." The big dial on the scale read one hundred pounds. The man looked at us with an evil eye then said, "Unload it." We looked at each other for a moment then the guy yelled "Hurry up, I don't have all freaken day." When the bricks fell off the wagon, the fellow started screaming at us "I knew it looked too heavy." We removed the bricks for an honest count, collected our money and high tailed it out of the junk yard.

Mongo: Mongo was a slang word used by all the kids. It was short for scrap metals. At a young age and still in elementary school, I kept abreast of all the current prices for metals like Iron, Lead, Aluminum, Copper, Brass, newspaper and cardboard.

Whenever going any place I kept an eye out for Mongo. The city dump down by The Old Mill was a great place to go looking for good stuff. I usually went with a friend. Many of the Old Mill kids were very sharp when it came to Mongo. It was often that we found nice pieces of metal there. People threw away short pieces of copper pipe and old fittings. We found lengths of electrical wire that had copper in it. We removed the insulation from copper wire with our pocketknives. Smokers usually tossed their empty cigarette packs in the street. We always picked them up, remove the silver paper wrapping, which was actually aluminum and roll it into a ball. Eventually the ball became big and heavy enough to cash it in. Whatever else we found we hid in the backyard on Glenmore Ave. until we saved enough to make it worth wild and the price was right to make a trip to the junk yard to trade it in for cash.

Deposit bottles were always a good find. You could trade them in for cash instantly at just about any store. When collecting newspaper from the garbage pails we came across many deposit bottles, we had an extra bag to carry them. Whenever there was a construction job in progress, I waited until lunchtime to sit and talk with the workers. When the whistle blew and the men went back to work, that was the time I gathered all of their soda bottles. The same people sometimes drank a cold beer after work. I returned once again to pick up the beer bottles too. Mongo was also an easy find at the job sites.

The Bohack fellas generally stacked their empty milk bottles in grates outside the store so, each time I went in to get the refund for my collection of bottles, it was easy to pick up one or two more from the crate and cash them in for a second time. "Yo, What the hell?"

The Twins: The twin brothers George and William who lived on Doscher Street were the same age as me. The father's name was Murray. They had an older brother Franklin who went to school with my cousin Anthony. They also had a younger sister. The father was a roofer by trade. He did all his own work around his own house. Murray was quite a handy person. One day he poured a concrete sidewalk leading up to the back door to his house. The family used this door most frequently to enter the house.

It was their suppertime, when I called on the brothers. The whole family gathered around the kitchen table eating. I had never seen wet concrete before. Nonchalantly, I walked thru the freshly finished job up to the back door. Knocking on the door and asking, "Can the twins come out to play?" At an instant, Murray jumped up from the table and looked at my feet, which were covered, in wet cement. "Jesus Christ" he yells and makes a lunge at me. I spun around real fast, jumped down the flight of stairs into the wet concrete again and took off like a Jack Rabbit. Murray never caught me that day but the word was out on the street that he was after me and I was due for a good ass whipping.

The Tar Truck: It was not until sometime later that Murray did work on the front of his house. He constructed a brand new front entrance with a nice, white door and a big glass picture window looking into the porch. He did a real nice job, and he was proud of himself.

For some reason, the twins and I were at odds with each other. While chasing them down the street, they ran into the new porch and locked themselves inside. I stood outside the house daring them to come out and fight.

However, the two sissies just stayed inside making funny faces and flipping me a bird. The father had his roofing truck parked out in front of the house where he always parked it. The truck contained roofing materials including an opened can of black roof cement. (Tar) A bright idea came to mind. Maybe I could flush them out of the house if I threatened to spread this black tar over the new door and the glass window. The friggin twins would not budge, so I began to follow thru with my threat. Tar was all over the window and the new door when who appears and starts screaming? It was the older brother Franklin. This dude was big. His feet must have been a size thirteen. Instead of Franklin, he looked more like Frankenstein. He went to grab me, I wacked him in the face with a load of tar that was on the stick. He stopped in his tracks. While dropping the stick with tar on the clean brick stoop, adding insult to injury, I turned and ran down Doscher Street towards Glenmore Ave. with Frankenstein close behind with tar hanging from his face. Upon reaching the corner at top speed, there was mom sitting on the stoop. Never stopping, I ran past her, hopped over a fence and out ran the monster. Franklin knew mom and told her what had just taken place. Upon returning home, she was waiting with a belt in her hand. What a beating she bestowed for that episode. It took a long time before finally making restitution with the roofer and his family.

Rainy Days: Believing, wholeheartedly that mamma was happy when it rained. We usually stayed inside the house on rainy days; therefore, we were less liable to get into trouble. Billy and I played together on the living room floor. It did not take too long before I became bored playing with the toys. Although I was much bigger, we often wrestled. I over powered him with ease, pinning him to the floor while pinching his cheeks and kissing him on his cute little face. He did not like it so, he started screaming until mom told me to get off him and leave him alone.

When it stopped raining, it was time to go out to play. As the water ran down the street along the side of the curb towards the sewer, I made little boats from ice cream pop sticks. They floated until they reached the corner, then swirling around like a sinking ship in a whirlpool until disappearing into the dark smelly sewer. It was a neat thing to do until the water stopped running.

The sanitation department sent out large trucks holding many gallons of water. The trucks had a large spray nozzle on each side that enabled them to spray water that washed the dirt to the curb, then eventually down the sewer as the truck moved along the street slowly. During the hot summer months many kids ran alongside the trucks to watch the water spray and to cool off with the splashing water. This was not a very healthy pass time. By the time the water truck finished washing the street that we lived on, we kids were filthy. Mom could not believe how dirty we became. She would say, "Throw everything in the hamper and jump in the bathtub you little ragamuffin."

One afternoon at a very young age, during a hot August day, one of the water trucks was making its way down our block with water pumping from its nozzles like a jet stream. Alone that day while running alongside the truck, becoming engrossed with the spraying water, I continued to follow the truck. After going quite a long distance, the truck finally ran out of water, and then sped faster down the street to fill with water again at a fire hydrant. Standing there dripping with dirty water, a face full of dirt, filthy clothes and looking like a ragamuffin, bewildered as to where my house is? I was lost. As I wandered through the streets, a woman approached me asking questions. After telling her that my house was located across the street from the brickyard, she took me home. She could have dropped me off on our block. However, she insisted on knocking on the door and making her delivery directly to mom. Need I say more?

Train Set: One-year pop got the idea to fasten train tracks to a sheet of plywood for a set of electric trains. He had just the right spot for it too. Our apartment had fancy moldings on the walls along with a chair rail. He cut the plywood to fit on the rail inside an alcove in our living room. Now we had a platform for our railroad trains. It was a real nice thing that pop did for us. We received a set of Lionel electric trains that Christmas with different types of cars. One was a milk car. A little man shot out to deliver milk cans. Another one dumped coal. The coal tender had a whistle and the locomotive bellowed out puffs of grey smoke. This thing was terrific; everyone loved it, especially Billy. He could play with it for hours.

Dad noticed that I lost interest in the trains very quickly. He asked,

"Do you like the train set?" I replied,

"Yes I dink it's great."

"If you like it den why don't you play wit it?"

"Well pop I get bored watching the train do the same ding all the time. I appreciate dat ya did all dat work and spent all dat money but I would rather play ball outside. I hope ya aint mad at me?"

I will always remember the disappointed look on his face as he said.

"I understand son, go out and play ball, you can do whatever makes ya happy."

"Ya gotta love the guy."

The Landlord: A Jewish family named Solaway owned the building that we lived in. The woman's name was Sadie and her husband's name was Nat. They had one Gorky son named Sidney. Jewish people had a reputation for being cheap but the Solaway family topped the cake.

Our parents rented a one-bedroom apartment from the Solaways. It was located on the first floor in the front of the brick building facing Glenmore Ave. Mom and dad slept in the bedroom. We kids slept on a convertible sofa.

The buildings were under rent control. According to law, the property owner could not raise the rent amount whenever they felt like doing so. The amount went up periodically. Surely, if the Solaways had their way, our folks would have been paying more than they could afford. We understood that renting apartments was a business, and if you did not turn a profit or break even monetarily, you would not be in business too long. However, when it was cold out, is it unreasonable to expect that the property owner provide heat to the tenants? As the law read, the property owner was not compelled to provide heat for their tenants until a certain date which was sometime during the month of October. The Solaways abided by that rule then even stretched that ruling some.

The heating system in the building was steam. Each room had its own steel radiator, which became hot while the steam passed thru it. The heated water, generated by a boiler in the cellar connected to a stove, which burned coal to heat the water. Every so often, the coal man came with a truck. He used a barrel to transport the chunks of coal from his truck to a cellar window. The coal man dumped the coal down a chute until the storage area was full. It was neat to watch the man roll the barrels with one hand. He was a pro at it. I tried doing it with my grandfather's wine barrels, but could never get the hang of it as the coal man did. Besides, it would always piss off the Old Geezer when he caught me trying it with his barrels.

During the cold winter months, mamma lite up the gas oven in our kitchen and placed our underwear on the door to heat them up. She then brought them to us while we were still under the warm blankets. We got dressed while still lying in bed. Mom had a warm breakfast waiting for us before sending us out of the house into the cold. After we left the house, the friggin steam came up. The same thing took place each night. Mom had a metal pipe, which she used to bang on the radiators sending the sound thru the building while yelling, "Send up some steam." The landlord lived above us. Mom also banged on the ceiling with a broom to get their attention while yelling the same old thing. It was like a broken record. Mamma always made sure we were in bed early because Solaway shut off the furnace to save the cost of burning coal. The same thing began all over again the next morning.

It must have been rough handling coal every day, placing it into the stove. We could not really blame them too much. Later on, they changed the heating system to oil. We said good-bye to the coal man. Bring on the Oilman. This seemed like a much better way to heat the house. The steam still came thru the radiators but now it burned oil instead of coal.

The Solaways never changed their routine with the heat. Mom kept the pipe and broom going. She continued heating underwear along with the hot coco and breakfast each morning. It was our way of life, we never knew any better.

A large portion of the brick building in the alleyway had no windows. It was a good place to play handball. Old lady Sadie often stuck her head out the window yelling, "Stop throwing the ball against the wall you're gonna loosen the bricks". Gee, it was only a Spall Deen.

The cellar door had at an angle to it so we used to slide down it like a sliding pond. "Get off the cellar door you're going to break it." The back yard had weeds. "Get off the grass you're going to kill it."

If she came home in time to catch us playing stoopball in the front of the house. "Don't throw the ball against the steps you will break the concrete." Woo! Occasionally a ball went up on the roof. There was a scuttle with a steel ladder going up to it. By lifting the cover, it gave access to the roof. The only time I went, there was when none of the Solaways was home. I was always careful not to go near the edge of the building. It was not because I was scared of falling off, but because one of the neighbors saw me one time and told Sadie. Sadie told my mother and I got another ass thrashing.

Old man Solaway wore a pair of eyeglasses as thick as coke bottles. The poor guy was half-blind. When parking his car he would get out, bend over on his hands and knees to feel just how far the tires were from the curb. He did this repeatedly until he felt the car was close enough to the curb.

As he walked away, he kept turning around looking at the car four or five times before going into the house. I often wondered if he thought the car was going to move away from the curb.

Nat had something to do with the Green Bus Lines. Maybe he knew someone at the licensing bureau who helped him keep his driving license because he could have never passed an eye test.

His son was a real Geep. He was much older than I was. One afternoon while walking towards the house, smoke was coming from the cellar steps. I began running to find out what was burning, and hoping our house was not on fire. Upon arriving at the cellar steps, there were flames right near the entrance. I jumped over the stoop, ran down the steps and trampled out the fire. Who was standing there with a broom in his hand? It was the son Sidney. He began to yell,

"So, what are ya doing?"
"I am putting out the fire."
"Why? I'm burning leaves."

"What are ya crazy? What the hell is wrong wit you, do ya want to burn the freaken house down? Who starts a fire in the cellar to burn leaves?"

"So, you shouldn't worry" he says.

This was only one of the reasons why we considered him a "Geep."

The Movies: There were three movie theaters within walking distance from our house. Saturday was usually the day we went to the Earl Theater down city line. When we came home from the movies all our clothes went directly into the hamper for washing.

The afternoon show was a matinee. The movies went on for hours; half the kids never paid attention. They were too busy grabassing (A slang meaning to fool around.) with their friends.

Cousin Anthony and I timed each other to see who could run around the movie house the fastest. The runner takes off while the other person keeps time by counting, until the runner returns to his seat. The movie screen was very large but you could always see the person running across the stage while the movie played.

Another game was to crawl under the seats, climb up to the stage, touch the screen, then crawl back to your seat while being timed once again. The games were a lot of fun, that is, if Mary the matron did not catch you. Mary was a fat old woman who wore a white dress, for her uniform, and she carried a flashlight. If she caught you, Mary made you leave the theater.

It was common for the kids to throw food, chewing gum, candy wrappers and spill drinks on the floor. We use to bring our own lunch to the show in a brown paper bag. After leaving, the theater there was no telling what you had crawled thru. We came home filthy.

Anthony was chewing a large wad of bubble gum in the movie one afternoon. I kept asking him how many pieces he had in his mouth. He could not talk with such a mouth full but he was able to blow real big bubbles. I eventually became interested in the movie when he spit the wad into his hand and rubbed it all into my head. The gum stuck to the hair like glue. Trying to remove it made it worse. The bubble gum was over my entire head and clothes. "Oh, what the hell might as well watch the movie? Mom will get it out later."

On the way home, all of us kids made believe that we were characters from the movie picture. If it was a western, we were cowboys, a war movie we were soldiers. I would always find something to jump off pretending to be Superman. I loved Superman.

Upon our return home that day, I rather forgot about all the chewing gum in the hair. When we entered the house mamma said

"What in the hell is that all over your head?"
"Oh, its bubble gum."
"How did it get there?"

What could I say but the truth? I surely did not put it there. Mom walked me across the street to her sister Mary, Anthony's mother; together they rubbed my head with all sorts of things trying to remove the gum. They tried using soap and water No good. Next, they tried

Olive oil, No good. Even turpentine. Nothing worked. Finally, they took a pair of scissors and cut the hair off. It was like the worst haircut I ever had.

Poor cousin Anthony, there was absolutely no friggin way he could talk his way out of this one. Aunt Mary told him "Just wait till your father gets home. (That was Uncle Louie.) He'll take care of you." Mom never said that to us. She whacked us herself. She was tough. Pop never once hit us. He had a way of explaining things to us. I guess that is because he was not around us all day.

One-day mamma told him about an incident that occurred and that he should give me a good beating. "OK Lucy I will take care of it. Go get the belt mommy uses to whack you guys with." After bringing pop the belt, he told me to go into the bedroom. He then took the belt, folded it double. He said, "When you hear the crack of the belt yell then make believe that you're crying." Crack! Dad snapped the belt, I screamed Ouch he did it again. "Now cry," he said. Guessing, we were not very good actors, because when we came out of the bedroom momma said, "You two morons did not fool me one bit." She grabbed the belt, smacked me in the ass with it and said. "That's for trying to make a fool out of me." Momma never asked pop to do her dirty work again.

The Lumber Yard: I was still a very young boy only about eight years old after the farms were all gone. The empty lots became a big play area for the neighborhood kids. The elevator train ran over the unpaved streets for two blocks. There was a lumberyard on the block just opposite our house. One morning the fire alarm rang. Smoke and flames filled the air and I could hear the fire burning with the sound of crackling wood. The lumberyard was on fire. The firehouse was just across the street but the inferno became outrageous in minutes.

There was a large mess after the fire, which destroyed the lumberyard. This was a bad thing for the owners of the lumberyard but it gave us kids another place to play and in addition, search out the place for good stuff.

Lumber and nails were gathered and hidden for the construction of our future clubhouse. Meanwhile the burned out building will serve as a great hangout until they knocked it down altogether.

Watermelons: Just about fifty yards from the lumberyard was a watermelon stand, which someone built on the corner where Liberty Ave ran into the Sunrise highway. Lots of traffic ran along this road. As a result, the person sold many melons at this location.

The stand, constructed of wood with a slanted roof for protection from the weather. Occasionally a bunch of us gathered at the lumberyard. We elected one person to go steal a watermelon and bring it back to the crew. The sales person stacked up the melons each morning to make a nice presentation for the passing cars to observe. While he carried a watermelon to a customer's car, it was the opportunity to grab a melon and run back to the crew waiting to indulge in an afternoon delight. All the guys had a pocketknife, and were eager to cut his share and chow down. This always wound up with a pit-spitting contest to see who could spit a watermelon pit the furthest off the second floor of the remains of the burnt lumber yard building.

The Bully: Not every day was a good day, especially when Angelo came around. Angelo was part of one of the Italian families with many kids. They lived on the next block from us on Glenmore Ave. This fella was an animal. We all swear that he had a few bolts loose in his head. He had a few sisters that were also Botz (Means Crazy in Italian.) His sister Mary nicked named *B-29* because she resembled the bomber plane that dropped the Atomic bomb on Japan. She was obese. Whenever she went off her rocker, you could hear her scream a mile away. When she screamed, we knew that there was a fistfight going on with her and some other poor slob.

Angelo always had it in for me. He'd think nothing of walking over saying "Hey Boobie, I heard you hit my brother Mikie." He would begin whaling on me. Bam-Bam delivering punches to my head. When trying to defend myself, it would make him angry. He'd say, "Oh, trying to hit me Hah?" Then throw a few more punches at me. This guy was like "Godzilla." There was no way I could match up to him. This was not by any means a onetime incident. This went on for years. Besides, I never laid a hand on his brother Mikie.

While walking down the street one afternoon, Godzilla had come out of his cage. He assaulted me as usual. Deciding to pull out a pocketknife to help protect myself, Angelo grabbed my arm and snatched the knife, stuck it between two boards in a fence and broke the blade right off the freaken handle. "You tried to stab me," he said. Then gave me a good beating right there in the middle of the street. When entering the house, mom asked,

"What the hell happened now?"

"Angelo beat me up again."

"Not again?"

Mom spoke to dad that evening she said,

"Frank; you have to do something about this."

"Just what would ya like me to do?"

"Maybe you should go over there and talk with them or do to him what he has been doing to our son."

"Come over here son. Sit down."

He always had a nice way to explain things to us.

"It is obvious that mommy is upset because this big kid has beaten ya up many times but ya must learn to defend yourself. I cannot go out in the streets to fight your battles for ya. If I do go out and help ya, tell me, what are ya gonna to do if I am not around someday to protect you?"

Sitting there, not knowing what to say to him. I knew he was right but I could not speak.

"I'm gonna to tell ya what ya can do to protect yourself from him." Sitting there attentively listening to him, he said.

"The first ding dat ya must realize is dat this person is a bully. Do ya know what a bully is?"

"No, what's a bully?"

"A bully is someone dat will pick a fight with anutta person dat he knows he can beat. Dares no doubt in a bully's mind dat he will win, or else he will not pick a fight."

"So, do ya dink Angelo is a bully?"

"Of course he is why, do ya dink he keeps picking on ya? Because he knows dat, you are no match for him. This will go on forever as long as ya let him get away wit it."

"What can I do?"

Mom just stood there and listened. She never said a word.

"This might not be easy but ya have to make your mind up first dat you're not afraid of him and ya can beat him, OK?"

"OK."

"Now; the next time he comes at ya do not turn your back on him, wait till he comes close then kick him in the balls as hard as ya can. He will go down. Look for a 2x4 or anything ya can get your hands on and beat him wit it. Beat him to a pulp, do not stop until he starts to cry or runs away. After that Angelo will never touch ya again."

"Wow! Do ya really dink dat will stop him?"

"Yes I do."

Mom looked surprised but still did not say a word, then walked away.

"Do ya understand?" pop asked.

"But, dad, dats not fair to hit someone like dat."

"I know it's not right but he is doing the same thing to you each time he gives ya a beating. He does not care one bit about how he hurts ya. What ya doin is equalizing the playing field."

"Now, dink about what I told ya."

OK I will."

A couple of days later, a few guys and I were up on the second floor of the burnt out lumber yard splitting open a watermelon when all of a sudden who arrives but Godzilla himself. I sat there eating a piece of watermelon anticipating what was about to happen. Sure enough, he opens his big fat mouth and says to me "My brother Mikie told me that you hit him. Get over here." I stood up, everyone watched in anticipation. All that my dad told me began to go through my head. ---- Let him get close enough before you kick. OK, do not be scared, you can do it. This should be the last time I go through this torture. I looked around real fast for something to whack him. I spotted a piece of partially burnt 2x4 lying on the floor. Ok, here it goes, remember kick him in the balls very hard then run for the 2x4. You will have time to get it while he falls and grabs his nuts. The moron came at me. He was at just the right distance when I swung my right foot up at his nuts as hard as I could. I missed. I kicked him in his thigh. "WHOO! You tried to kick me in the balls you little piece of shit, now you are dead!" Before I could say Yogi Berra, it was déjà-vu all over again. I thought he was going to toss me off the second floor. I managed to stay up there but I took such a beating. What am I going to tell my mother when she sees me looking like this? Everything settled down at the lumberyard, Godzilla left. He had gotten his rocks off, and once again filled his yearn for power.

That evening when my father came home, he took one look at me and asked, "What the hell happened to you?" I told him what happened, I gave him a blow-by-blow description and I told him how I swung my foot but missed his balls. My dad chuckled and said "Son, next time don't miss." My mother turned once again and walked away. I knew from that day on that I would have to fend for myself or become a chump!

Eventually they removed the remains of the lumberyard. We had enough wood and nails stored away to build our own clubhouse. However, we had time for that.

El. Over Liberty Ave. & Sunrise Hwy.

Elevated Train (The El): Meanwhile, we continued playing under the elevated train tracks, also at the forts and tunnels we had dug out in the empty lots that once was a farm.

The train tracks of the El are similar to the tracks on the ground except that they were about 30 feet in the air with Steel columns and beams. The trains made lots of noise, especially along Euclid Ave. It made two turns, one turn from Pitkin Ave. and one from Liberty Ave. The train wheels made a screeching sound as the cars rolled along the tracks. The noise never seemed to bother anyone. After hearing it for so long, it became a second nature.

The El was a great place to play. The firehouse was nearby in case we needed a drink of water and no traffic on the dirt road. Everyone was a good climber, especially Billy and me. We could climb anything including fences, roofs, trees and billboards.

There were two advertising billboards on Liberty Ave. that faced the Sunrise highway. Both framed of lumber in a diagonal manner. It held up the big sign that stood about 25 feet high. This was a good place to do tricks and practice jumping. We climbed to the top, stood up, jump off then roll on the ground pretending that we were paratroopers. We became real good at it and conquered any fear of heights.

Any time we found pieces of rope, we tied them together with knots until it was long enough to reach the El. We then hurled it over one of the steel beams with the help of a brick. This gave us access to get on to the train tracks. All one had to do was climb up the rope which became easier with practice. It became so easy that it that it was not necessary to use our feet. Once on the tracks, we waited for a train to come barreling down. Standing up while waving our hands, we could hear the squeaking brakes of the train. When the train got close enough to see the motorman's terrified face, this was the time to slip down between the railroad ties on to the rope, slide down and run like hell. Shortly afterwards someone came to inspect, hoping to find the culprits. They never caught us doing this because by the time an inspector arrived at the scene we were already hiding in our foxholes and tunnels camouflaged with plywood and grass. We could not pull off this stunt too many times. Eventually the inspectors will catch us. If it were one of us brothers, it would be a sad day in hell once, mom found out about it.

The foxholes and tunnels were places where we sat, told jokes or stories with candles burning. We always received a lecture from mom about how dangerous it is to go into a tunnel. We listened to her then we went back into the tunnel. I remember one of the humorous questions that a new guy would be asked:" "How do you get into a fox hole?" He tried coming up with a good answer but it was always wrong. Finally, he'd ask well, how do you get in? "Simply lift his tail and crawl in."

Potatoes: There was always a fire burning. It was never a problem gathering wood, between what was still laying around from the lumberyard and the old Ginny fences. A couple of days a week were Mickey Days. Everyone brought a potato from home. When the fire was good and hot we placed all the potatoes on the burning wood. While they cooked, we chose sides, all the people split up into two teams. We played a game called: "A Dirt Bomb Fight." Plenty chunks of dirt lying around from the dugout tunnels made excellent dirt bombs. The idea was to hit a person with a bomb to knock him out of the game. Last man standing wins.

Sometimes we ran out of dirt bombs so everyone began using whatever rocks they found. When the mickeys were cooked, it was chow time. Everyone returned to the fire and conversed over his wounds while eating a burnt potato.

After eating the hot mickeys, everyone's face was black. Some of the lads looked like the singer Al Jolson, who put boot black on his face for makeup. Soon after that, you could hear the different calls from the mothers or the whistles from the fathers. It was something every kid knew well. It was dinnertime. Upon arriving home, we stunk like fire and our clothes were filthy. Some of us even had a little blood on our heads where a rock or a dirt bomb hit us. Mom asked if we were eating potatoes (There was always a good dinner waiting. She did not want our appetites ruined.) I said.

"Who me?"

"Yeah you. Whom else can I be talkin with? You are the only one here."

"No"

"OK, go inside look in the mirror then washed up."

After gazing in the mirror and looking like Al Jolson, thinking, *"SHIT"* I just told her a lie and there is no way to go back to the kitchen and explain this. Dam it she out foxed me once again.

Duel & Wrestle  Dueling was always in season. After school, at three o clock, everyone went home, dropped off their books, changed clothes and headed for the lot. Wrestling was an everyday activity. No one actually tried to hurt each other but the idea was to have your opponent give up or say uncle. (Uncle meant I give up) Therefore, twisting someone's arm or leg until he was in pain was a good way to get an *UNCLE* out of him. The old headlock was also good. You squeeze the hell out of a person's head until he could not take the pain any longer and he would give up.

We used swords for dueling. It was easy to make a sword. You took a piece of wood about three foot long carved a point at the end with a pocketknife, nailed a hand guard to it and you were ready for action. "Hey! On guard!"

Crew Cuts: When summer time came around most of the kids got a crew cut. Almost every boy had a scar on his head from a rock, stick, falling from a fence or something else. Like a knot on the head given by "Godzilla the Bully." The evidence was obvious. They were in battle. Everyone looked like a warrior; it is part of growing up in Brooklyn.

The New Kids: When I was about 8 years old a couple of new families moved into the neighborhood from the European country of Lithuania. They moved one block away on the corner of Chestnut Street and Glenmore Ave. This is where Godzilla and the other Italian families lived. Johnny was my age and we became very good friends. He had two older brothers and they were quite tall, just like the father. The other family had two boys, Raymond and Gerry. Their father was a soccer coach. All of these kids were exceptionally fast runners. The fastest runner was Johnny. This fellow had Platinum blond hair that felt just like silk. Everyone wanted to touch his head.

These new kids knew very little English but they all got by with what they knew. New York is the *Melting pot of the world.* We met many immigrants. I remember a new kid who enrolled in our elementary school. He came from Germany and could not speak a word of English. I came home and told my mother, "There's a new kid in my class, the dummy can't speak English." My mom said to me. "You just wait, in six months he will be speaking English, he will also be speaking German and he will be able to converse with twice as many people as you can. Then come and tell me who the dummy is." Once more, my mother was right.

Bad Day at Black Rock: At a young age while still attending elementary school, Euclid Ave. was where we spent most of our time playing. We still swung from the ropes that we had hanging from the train tracks. We also built a clubhouse with the wood and nails we had stored away from the burnt out lumberyard.

It was common to find good stuff along the dirt road. While running thru the grass one day I found a small shotgun. I played with it during the day then brought it home because it looked like a good thing to keep. When my father saw it, he asked, "Where did you get this?" I told him that I found it in the lot. My dad told me it was a sawed off shot gun and asked if I found any bullets. I told him "No." He said he did not want me playing with it and decided to bring it to the police station. He thought a criminal might have used it as a weapon.

Another time I found a bunch of bullets. I do not know what kind they were but instead of bringing them home, I threw them into a fire we had going, then hid in a hole we had dug waiting for them to explode.

Someone had dumped several boxes of fruits and vegetables on the side of the street. Like tomatoes, heads of lettuce, and peppers amongst other things. Finding this stuff, turned out to be, what the cowboys on TV would say: *A bad day at black rock.*

My little brother and his friends Sandy, Eddie Boy and Bobby were swinging from one of the ropes under the El when my friends and I gathered them up and told them to come with us. "Where are we going?" they asked. "You'll see."

Mr. Ricardi owned a garage, which was located behind his house. It faced the dirt road. We told the youngsters to line up facing the garage door with their hands held up and to lean against the door. The same way they did in the Saint Valentine's Day massacre in Chicago. Billy asked "Why" I gave him a pinch on the cheek and told him not to run away.

The kid named Bobby, who was a cute little lad liked to sing. We told him to sing aloud the song "Old soldiers never die." The kid began to sing and we started throwing everything we found at them. We pulverized the poor little dudes. When it was all over, they looked like part of a tossed salad.

The little lads scattered shortly after we ran out of things to fire at them. Billy ran home and Mr. Ricardi came out to see what had caused all the commotion. My friends and I ran like hell. My brother told my mother what had just taken place. She quickly came out to see what Ricardie's place looked like. After surveying the situation mom went to the Ricardi home. She apologized for what just happened and assured him her son Louie would clean up the mess. When I came home, she beat me with a broom. She then told me to go clean up the mess at the garage. "When you get finished, go apologize to the Ricardie's for what you did. I will be out later to inspect." I took my lumps then cleaned up as she told me to do. Like I said it was, *a bad day at black rock.*

P.S 159: Was the name of the public school we attended. It was an elementary school, which started from kindergarten to the sixth grade. The school was four blocks from our house. Everyone walked to school.

The teachers were all down to earth. Every one of them took a special interest in teaching their students. Let me give you an example: Several mornings of each week, there was an inspection. All the students placed their hands on the desk palms facing down. The teacher looked to see if the fingernails were trimmed and clean. The ears were next. Each child had to have a clean, fresh folded handkerchief in his or her pocket. If your hair was not neat and clean and cut properly, she would mention it to the child. "Tell your mother that you need a haircut."

The school's rule stated; no one can expect to be promoted to the next grade, unless he or she turns in a completion note from the dentist. If a parent could not afford to pay a dentist, the school provided one for them. It was very unusual to see anyone with missing teeth. Besides, we never saw anyone chewing tobacco until we came down south.

The East New York Savings Bank worked with our school. Every child no matter how poor had to open a savings account. Every Monday morning the teacher collected money from each child. The money went to the bank for a deposit. The minimum amount to deposit was a nickel. The teachers all demanded that one hundred percent of the students in each class make his or her deposit.

As a reward, a photographer came to the school periodically, to snap a class photo to give to each student. Each student had to bring their bankbook to school so the teacher could show us how the deposits were adding up. This encouraged each child to save money. Any money that we received for a birthday or any other gift, we deposited in the bank. It began to accumulate.

The teachers taught etiquettes. We learned table manners. Setting a table, place a napkin on your lap; wipe your mouth before taking a drink while eating and the proper way to pass a pair of scissors or a knife. They allocated time to allow us to practice holding a door for each other, the way to say thank you and you are welcome. Very few of the kids, including their parents, now days would not ever think of holding a door for someone, nor say thank you if it were held for them.

How do you think a person under the age of fifty would answer if I asked? "Is there is a handkerchief your pocket? Chances are good, that they will not have one. Then ask what they would do if they had to sneeze or blow their nose. Do not be shocked by the answers you will receive.

Students throughout their lives used the basic lessons taught at P.S. 159. I would like to see more teachers and guidelines used similar to what we had, in the schools today.

No jeans, (we called them dungarees.) sneakers, shorts, or tee shirts were allowed in school. Each boy had to wear a shirt and tie. On assembly day which was on a Tuesdays, the boys all had to wear a white shirt and a red tie. The girls also wore a white blouse with a red ribbon or bow. We learned songs and sang along together. The music teacher had us sing different types of songs. To make it interesting she had a student knock two-coconut halves on the stage to produce a sound of a horse running while we all sang western songs.

This is about the time I began laughing and disrupted the class. I made the other students laugh too. The music teacher picked me out as the instigator then sent for my mother. The teacher told my mom, "He thinks everything is funny." I heard my mother tell the teacher "I have the same problem at home with his father, always laughing." The poor teacher did not know what to say.

Safety Guards: Part of the school's structure was to provide safe crossing at each street corner within a block of the school. The teacher in charge-selected special students for this choir called Safety Guards. Each guard wore a white belt similar to an automobile's safety belt when standing on a corner directing the students' crossings.

Instructions on street crossing became a routine subject in the classroom. It was always the same old thing; cross at the green not in between, before crossing look left then right then left again. We all knew the rules, but every so often someone jay walked. This gave the safety guard an opportunity to report the student, who in turn received some sort of punishment from the teacher.

One day a safety guard walked into my classroom to report someone for jaywalking. He stood in front of the classroom looking over all the students, he pointed to me and said, "That's the boy." I replied, "who me?" "Yeah you, you jaywalked this afternoon." The teacher called me out in the hallway and began to lecture me about street crossing. The truth of the matter was I did not remember jaywalking. I took my lumps from the teacher. I had to write *I must not jay walk* about two hundred times on paper then turn it in.

This pissed me off. I said to myself what kind of a candy ass would report someone in the first place. The next time I saw the fellow I confronted him and told him just what I thought of him. The fella did not take what I had said to him too well, push came to shove and I wound up in a fistfight on the street corner. The safety guard wound up with a shiner. The next day he was in front of the class again telling the teacher what had happened. He had the black eye to prove it. The teacher called for my mother and I wound up with black and blue on my ass.

In my senior year, I became a safety guard. My post was on the corner of Glenmore Ave and Crescent St. There was a bar and grill on that corner. Two brothers owned and ran the place named, Benny and Abbie Shultz. I recall the baseball games on the television. I observed the games in early spring while standing outside the door watching the Brooklyn Dodgers play. I enjoyed it because there was always a bunch of men yelling during every play. It made the games exciting to watch. I ate it up. Late in the season, I stood there watching the World Series. It was always between the Dodgers and the N.Y. Yankees. Everyone went nuts over each play; the Shultz boys always had peanuts or pretzels on the bar for the customers. Occasionally a customer invited me in and gave me a hand full of peanuts. It made me feel like one of the guys. Little did I know that one day in the near future my dad would own the joint?

I'd return to school just before the bell rang, and then returned to the bar after school to watch more baseball. I never reported anyone while I was a safety guard. I just was not that kind of dude.

The Principal: At school, I continued to get into trouble with the teachers. It ticked them off whenever I laughed, or just give what my mother called *a smirk* while getting a scolding. One of momma's famous expressions was "Wipe that *smirk* off your face or I'll wipe it off for you." Whenever mom was extremely mad at us and, it was quite often, she would demand our undivided attention, while the veins in her neck swelled up. When she was extremely angry, her clinched hand went towards her mouth while showing her teeth over the knuckle. This was never a good sign. She began with a lecture, before she finished I usually give her one of my *smirks* then Bam! She wiped the friggin *smirk* off in one second flat. I always knew what the result would come to, but somehow the *smirk* always appeared.

At the age of seven, one of my teachers sent me down to the principal's office. I cannot remember what her reason was. While standing at attention in front of Mrs. Delaney she began to lecture me. She then told me,

"Stand up straight."

"I am."

"Relax,"

"Now stand at attention again." so, I did.

Mrs. Delaney finished her lecture; I remember giving her the famous *smirk*. She then told me that she wanted my mom to come to her office *A.S.A.P.* The first thing that came to my mind was, O boy! This is going to be a big one.

The following day mom and I were in the principal's office. I was ready for something huge to come down. Instead, she told me to stand at attention again. Mrs. Delaney told my mother to take a good look at my head. She then asked,

"Do you notice how his head tilts to one side very slightly?" Mom said to me.

"Stand up straight."

"I am! Why do youse guys keep telling me to do the same ding?" My mom said;

"Go wait in the hallway while I speak to principle Delany."

She thanked the principal for being so observant. She told her that she could never notice such a thing because I never stood still in one place long enough for her to catch this problem. It turned out to be a serious condition.

The Hospital: Shortly afterwards mom brought me to a children's hospital (Saint Giles.) There I was standing in my underwear in front of about ten doctors at the age of seven, each one checking out my neck, telling me to turn left, turn right, and a bunch of other things. They informed my mother that I had a Rye Neck or another name for it is Torticollis. If am not operated on soon, it would eventually become worse. They told her that as I became older my head is going to tilt further downward. It is necessary for the removal of a growth of muscle in my neck. Not too long after that, the doctors scheduled me for an operation. They told my parents it would be necessary to put me in a cast. After the operation, I remember waking up in the hospital bed and feeling very cold. My mother was sitting there crying. I told her I was freezing. She continued to cry. She could do nothing to warm me up. They had me in a cast, which covered my head completely, with only small cutouts for my face and ears. The cast also provided a small hole on top on my head for air circulation. It covered my body from my shoulders to my waist, past my belly button. The plaster was still wet when they told my mom, "Once it dries he will warm up." The cast dried and I warmed up. I looked just like a freaken *MUMMY*.

A few days went by before I was able to move. My mother came to see me every day. My dad was always working. I never knew how they paid for all this. Maybe my father had insurance from where he worked at UPS.

The Mummy suit must have weighed fifty pounds, but I managed to maneuver myself around the room, then eventually around the hospital hallways. There were many other kids in there with all different kinds of problems. This was a good thing for me because I never once felt sorry for myself.

ME IN MY CAST 1947

One-day two baseball players from the Brooklyn Dodgers came to the hospital making a surprise visit with us kids. I remember sitting and talking with Bobby Bragan and Hugh Casey. They signed a few baseballs and gave them to the kids. Unfortunately, I never got one. However, it did not matter. I was just glad to spend time talking with them. I could not wait to tell my father about it.

The Nurse:  Someone brought me one of those plastic guns that shoot darts with black rubber tips.

I remember lying in bed while shooting the darts at the ceiling. If I wet the tips, the things would stick up there for a while. When the darts fell down, I tried to catch them. I made up a little game keeping score while amusing myself. The darts left a black ring on the ceiling. A nurse was at my bedside when a dart dropped down; she looked up saw all the little black rings on the white ceiling. She scolded me and told me not to shoot at the ceiling anymore. I said, "OK I won't." As the nurse left the room, I shot her in the ass with a dart then gave her a *smirk*.

Well, it was not long before I became bored hanging around the hospital. I did not know what to do with myself. Therefore, I traveled through the hallways. I recollect entering a room where they had a television set. They told me I could stay if I behaved myself. Therefore, I agreed to behave. Groups of kids were watching TV when a nurse brought in a bed with wheels. A boy was laying in the bed with his leg in a cast in the up position hanging by a pulley. His name was Joe. I had seen him before in my travels. When the nurse left, I walked over to Joe's bed. He was tossing one of the baseballs up and down, which the Dodger players gave to him. He let me look at the ball. I then chose to hang out close to the fellow with the ball. I decided to jump onto the edge of his bed. All of a sudden, due to all the extra weight, the friggin bed fell over. *"OH SHIT!"* Joe and I fell out of the bed. He was lying on the floor screaming in pain with a broken cast. All the other kids were horrified. I did not know what to do. After getting up from the floor, I said, damn it! I was in trouble again. I thought it is best to run and hide somewhere. I knew the layout of the hospital pretty well from my strolls through the hallways. I headed for a broom closet opened the door and stood in there for a while. Eventually, I had to come out to pee. They found me and restricted me to my room. I laid there in my room and thought "holy mackerel wait till my mother hears about this."

About a day or two went by when a doctor came in and asked me if I was ready to go home. I was so excited! I yelled, "Yes! I'm ready. I'll show you." The room I was in had two twin beds. I stood up on my bed, jumped up and down a couple of times then leaped to the other bed. The cast was just a little too heavy and I fell short of reaching the other bed. I hit the side of the bed with my chest, bounced off and landed on the floor. I now had busted not only Joe's cast but also my own. The doctor was amazed, he stood there horrorstruck. He told the nurse to schedule me for a cast repair, and then he told me that there was no way that he would allow me to leave the hospital now. I tried to relax and think about the dumb stunt that I had just pulled off. I prayed that they would not tell my mother what had happened.

After a couple of weeks, they sent me home. I recall them asking me for a telephone number that they could call, so that someone can pick me up from the hospital. I told them that we did not have a telephone but my aunt Millie had one and the number was Michigan 2- 8888. "It is funny how we remember some things." My dad picked up a bag of plaster, which he used to mend the cast every time I broke it. I wore the cast for a little over five weeks.

The Television: In 1947, very few people had a television in their home. Because of my condition, my parents decided a television would be something that could possibly slow me down. They purchased a ten-inch TV. We were now the only people in the whole neighborhood with a television. "Talk about the Ritz!"

There were all kinds of things to watch. Billy and I stood glued to it. We watched Cowboy movies, Howdy Doody, Pinhead and Houdini. We were kings.

Mom had to stock up on more milk and cake for all the kids that came to watch the new TV. Our home was like a clubhouse. The only thing we did not do was burn candles. Everyone was reading comic books too. My parents were pleased that I had settled down for a little while.

The teachers at the school were always concerned about all of their students. My teacher had made a class project. Everyone had to make a get-well card for me, Louis Borek. Most of the kids knew me by my nickname Boobie. After arranging with my mom, the whole class came to my house to visit and hand me their self-made get-well cards. Mom set a little folding table with a chair right out there on Glenmore Ave. It was for me to sit at, receive the cards and talk with all of my friends from school. I still remember that bright sunny day and I still have those cards. "The day the class came to visit with the *MUMMY*. Man, I loved my mother."

Television was a good thing to have. Not only did our friends come over every day, many of the neighbors came in the evenings. The hottest show on TV was

Milton Berle. (Uncle Miltie) The name of the show was The Texaco Star Theater. It came on at eight o clock on Tuesdays.

The folks piled in to watch. Beatty, who owned the candy store across the street, brought a bag of candy for everyone to eat. Mom made soft drinks. After a while, the television was not such a good thing. Mom became annoyed with the continuous crowds in our house. The couch and chairs began to sag besides all the cleaning up after the guests left. It was getting old.

Pop and his pals enjoyed watching sports. I recall the Joe Louis fights against Jersey Joe Walcott and Ezzard Charles. Joe Louis was my Idol. *His nickname is the Brown Bomber.* I tried to imitate him. I also had dreams of Joe and me walking down the street together as pals. I once dreamed that Angelo (Godzilla) saw me with Joe and just walked past without hammering me, he would not try it with the Champ at my side. That was just a dream, because the next time I ran into Angelo, he did hammer me.

The championship fights were a big deal back then. Dad saw how annoyed mother was getting from all the company. He got the bright idea to place the TV on the windowsill facing the alley on fight nights. This seemed like a great idea, because now, no one came into our house. The neighbors brought their own chairs and the crowd began to grow. The whole neighborhood, including people who were just walking by stopped to watch the fights. Everyone was yelling one night, the police stopped to see what was going on. They wound up staying until the fight was over.

As I think back, I could have sold peanuts or popcorn but I would have missed the fight. Could you imagine so many people attracted to a ten-inch black and white television? Times certainly have changed.

The baseball season started. The Brooklyn Dodgers were our favorite team. Dad, Billy and I watched just about every night game. Gil Hodges was my favorite baseball player. He started as a catcher then switched to a first baseman. Dad always talked about the big hands Gil had. When he died, I attended his funeral in Brooklyn, and took notice of his hands while he lay in the casket.

After the removal of the cast, I was able to go into full action. It does not take long for a young body to heal. Momma took me to the clinic once a week on Fridays for a checkup. We took several buses to get there, and then waited a long time to see a doctor. It was the same old crap each week. They told me: turn your head all different ways. Stand against the wall. Now stretch your neck. "Give me friggin a break." After a while, we had to go every two weeks, then once a month. Later it became every six months. This went on for four years. When I reached the age of eleven the doctors told my mother "The operation was not a success. He needs another operation." I stood there and watched my mother cry.

I tried to console her. She cried all the way home. My dad felt just as sad as mom did. They just could not bear to go through that whole ordeal again. I remember my aunt Viola telling my mother to snap out of it and come to your senses. She told her to stop thinking of herself and think of that poor child. If he grows up hunched over you will never be able to forgive yourself will you? My mother consented to allow them to operate once again. However, she pleaded with them not to place me in another cast. They operated without placing a cast on me. I healed up well again and went about my normal routine. To this day, I thank my parents for the operations because I have lived a normal life. God bless both of them. I caused my mother a lot of heartache.

Tarzan: My mother had a cousin who we all knew as Tarzan of Brooklyn. His name is Johnny Ciampa. This fellow was great. The difference between him and the Tarzan in the movies was the movie Tarzan used a vine to swing through the trees. Johnny could do it without a vine. He jumped from one branch to another like a chimp.

I recall mom reading the newspaper. She'd say, "Look, my cousin Johnny is in trouble again," while looking at a picture of him on his way to the police station. Tarzan did many wild things. Sometimes he'd perform for a charity, but most of the times just for fun.

With a long rope attached between two high-rise buildings in Manhattan, he swung from one end to the other like a monkey doing tricks. This drew a large crowd.

My Uncle Frank had a 16 mm camera and often took pictures while he pulled off his stunts. Afterwards, my cousins and I sat in awe while watching the films. Naturally, my brother and I wanted to try some of the things he did.

Yankee stadium was a set for him. One afternoon Uncle Frank and Johnny went to the ball game. Johnny began walking up the steel columns like an ironworker until he reached the top, and then did some tricks on the high beams. The authorities tried to apprehend him but he was too fast for them as he ran across the rooftop. Both may have had to leave the ballpark. However, my uncle had plenty of good footage in his camera. Johnny was always in trouble especially when he performed tricks in the public parks. He'd fly through a tree jumping from branch to branch doing flips, once again drawing a crowd. The cops came and once again hauled him off to the police station. I never could figure out why they did not let him do his thing. I guess it was some ordinance on the books, which he was violating.

The T.V show called, The Olsen and Johnson Show contracted him to appear on television dressed in a gorilla suit and run across the backs of the seats. He made it look so easy running and jumping through the audience. Everyone was screaming while the lights and cameras followed him. I remember watching television that evening. We all were anticipating Tarzans entrance. We knew in advance what to look for. After all, we knew the gorilla himself.

It was always fun when Johnny came to Glenmore Ave. He did many stunts with Uncle Frank who was also athletically inclined. We were amazed to watch them leap over car hoods with such ease and perform tricks on the wooden table in the alley while the crowd watched.

Johnny ran across the street while my uncle leaned against the large brickyard sign with his hands clasped together as though he was ready to give someone a boost. When Tarzan jumped into his hands, he threw him straight up. Somehow, he continued to run up the wall. He then grabbed onto the edge of the roof and climbed up. Billy and I tried that trick for years afterwards, but neither one of us was ever able to jump high enough to grab the roof.

I asked mom why her cousin was not Tarzan in the movies. She told me that he had auditions but he was too small and skinny to play the role of Tarzan. Just to piss her off, I asked. "Why doesn't he play the part of Cheetah"? Tarzan always had on a pair of sneakers He was like the Lone Ranger, always ready for action. Billy and I got a kick out of watching him eat a banana. It made him look more like the part monkey that he was. We loved Johnny Tarzan.

The Fedora Hat & the Patch Pocket Suit:
Another Easter was just around the corner. It was time for another new outfit for my brother and me. As usual, mom dragged us down to Jew town into one of the clothing places for a fitting. We were ready for some new duds. Billy got a suit that made him look very dapper. I got a tan colored suit with patch pockets; made of that tough material they called sharkskin. We looked like the two Dapper Dan's of the neighborhood.

When we came home, my mother told us to put on the new clothes so her sister Mary could see how nice we looked. We changed into the new suits and the women made the usual fuss. All of a sudden, my aunt Mary pulls from a large paper bag, a Fedora hat. This hat was popular with all of the men back in those days. She looked at me and said,

"Put it on."

"Who Me?"

"Yes, you, who the hell else do you, think I'm talkin to?"

"I aint warrin dat ding."

The sisters insisted, and then placed it on my head. That is when the fuss thing started all over again. I sat there with a frown on my face.

Sunday morning my father told me to get ready; "we are going to go see grandpa." Little did I know that he wanted me to wear the hat? I told him right out.

"I'm not warrin dat ding." We went back and forth arguing about it.

"You will!"

"I won't!"

Finally, daddy put it on my head picked me up, threw me on the couch, and told me,

"You will wear the damn hat."

I got scared and left it on my head.

As we walked to the train station, he kept telling me how good I looked and how my aunts and uncles were, going to love the hat. However, I was thinking of something else. We proceeded up the long stairway to the train platform and then waited for the train to arrive. Just as the train pulled into the station, I removed the Fedora from my head and tossed it over the fence like a Frisbee. The friggin thing took off like a bird flying down Pitkin Ave. My dad turned around and asked,

"Where's your hat?"

"The wind from the train blew it off my head and it flew over the fence."

Pop leaned over to see it rolling down the street.

"You little shit! Stay where you are I will be right back"

He ran down the stairs then chased after the hat. When he got back upstairs, he jammed it on my head pulling it over my ears. We waited for the next train. I saw how pissed off he was so; I sat there looking like a dunce. However, I would not attempt to remove the Fedora again.

The Patch Pocket Suit: Easter morning was upon us once more and it was time to get dressed for church. My mother took out the new patch pocket sharkskin suit from the closet and told me to get dressed. I went to the gizmo we had hanging on the closet door to check out what color tie I should wear with the suit. After picking out a matching tie, I made sure all my other colors matched. Shoes, socks belt, shirt, OK I am looking good.

Mom said; "go downstairs and wait, as soon as I get your brother ready we will come down." "OK mom, I'll be on the stoop." Most of the times when I left the house I slid down the banister instead of walking down the stairs, today was no different. As I reached the bottom of the stairs, my ass hit the newel post signaling that my trip had ended. As I slid off the railing, the patch pocket of my brand new suit caught on the post and it ripped off leaving a nice size hole in the coat as the pocket hung by a thread. "Holy Shit" mom will be down in a minute, how am I gonna hide this? Too late, here she comes. Prior to walking to the church mom gave us a once going over to make sure we looked OK. "What the hell? Get over here look at that suit. How did you do that?" I told her what happened with a little *smirk,* Bam! I got a crack in the back of my head. "Go back upstairs," Mom pulled out her sewing kit and began to do her own alteration. She warned my brother not to move off the stoop until she came back down. We wound up missing the mass and had to wait for the next one. It seemed like a long Easter morning but mom cooled off while we waited for the next mass to start. After church, we went home and had a nice dinner then changed our clothes. The sharkskin suit was not that tough after all.

The Trolley Car: The trolley car ran along Liberty Ave. It passed by the firehouse located a block behind our apartment. The cars rolled on steel tracks similar to a train. They ran on electric power that came from an overhead cable, which ran along the street. Some gizmo sticking up from the roof of the car, attached to the cable, which feeds it the electric power. The car ran on a schedule just like a bus. The difference is the trolley stopped in the middle of the street for passengers to get on and off unlike the bus which pulled to the side of the street at each stop.

 I was still in elementary school when I told a couple of my friends that I could knock the trolley off the track and stop it dead. "How the hell could you do dat"? I asked if they were willing to bet that I could not do it. They agreed. I had been thinking of this for a long time so it was not a spur of the moment idea. I told them to go sit on a nearby stoop and to keep an eye out for the next trolley car. I went to the lot behind the firehouse where I hid a chunk of steel that I intended to use for my little trick. I jammed the steel into where the metal wheels engaged the track. When it ran over the chuck of steel, the friggin car ran right off the track. "BINGO!" It derailed right in front of the stoop. Naturally, I was gone like a flash, only to return awhile later to see my friends sitting there wondering how the hell did he do dat? The city sent out a tow truck to lift the car back on the track. Therefore, there were no other problems besides a little aggravation to all involved. My friends thought I was a magician.

The Fast Ball: My father and I continued to catch baseball every week. My reflexes and agility became sharper as time went by. One day, pop contacted one of the older Italian fellows who lived on the next block. His name was Johnny Casio. He played baseball for an organized team along with a brother Joey. These two brothers were exceptionally fast runners, and both of them were good ball players.

Johnny was a pitcher. This fella could throw just about every kind of pitch very fast. Pop asked him if he would pitch to me across Glenmore Ave. He agreed to do it. Johnny knew I could catch whatever he wanted to throw at me because he had been watching dad and me catch for years. He told me he would let me know what kind of a pitch he was going to throw at me prior to throwing it. The distance across the street was much less than the normal distance of a baseball diamond. The official distance from the pitcher's mound to home plate is sixty feet. We got our signals set and Johnny began to pitch to me. He started at a slow pace then began to pick it up. Pop told him not to hold back. After a few minutes, he was throwing as hard as he could. The balls were coming in fast. He could throw a curve with a break of about two feet. His fastball had a rise to it, he also threw a drop pitch; today they call it a sinkerball, and a screwball, which broke opposite a curve ball. The guy was awesome and I handled every pitch. He signaled to me a curve, but instead, threw a fastball. The friggin ball came at me so fast that I could not move my glove fast enough to catch it. The baseball hit me on my wrist then fell to the ground. I stood looking at the stitches of the ball engraved on my wrist. After that, we stopped for the day. Pop put ice on my wrist and the swelling went down. We all went to the corner candy store for a cold drink. I had my usual cherry soda. I made my father very proud that day. I could see it in his gleaming green eyes.

The Fiddle: My dad tried to teach my brother how to play baseball too. He gave him a glove and began throwing a ball to him very easy. Billy missed more balls than he caught. Dad tried to explain to him why he was missing so many balls. My bro said to him "I know how to do it." Dad continued playing catch with him and he kept missing most of the balls. Again, pop tried to coach him on the way he was holding the glove. "I know how." Well, this went on for quite some time. Pop was getting nowhere with Billy. Each time he tried to correct him, Billy would tell him the same thing, "I know how to do it."

My poor father was starting to get pissed off when he grabbed the glove from my brother and told him to go in the house. "Damn that kid. How the hell could he know, no one ever showed him." I told dad not to get excited because he is always that way. He says the same thing every time I try to show him how to do something.

"Come wit me."

"Where are we going?"

"We're going to my father's house on Miller Ave."

"Why?"

"You'll see,"

I knew he was angry. Off we went on the elevator train to grandpa's house. When we got there dad took me down to the cellar. He said,

"My brother Willie has an old fiddle in here somewhere."

After moving a lot of junk around, dad found a small black box with a fiddle in it. I asked him,

"What are ya gonna to do with dat ding?"

"If that kid aint gonna play baseball, he's gonna play the fiddle."

Pop took the fiddle home and told Billy,

"You better take a good look at the fiddle because with the smart ass attitude ya have, this is the only thing your ever gonna play."

Well, that went over like a pregnant nun in a convent. Billy never attempted to play the thing but we all got a good laugh out of the drama. To this day, we still talk about it.

Later, Billy wanted to play the guitar because he saw Roy Rogers and Gene Autry playing on television. Pop got one for him and then set him up with music lessons from Jimmy the music teacher who lived just across the street. I believe the only thing he ever played was the "Polly Wholly March." After that, he tied it on his back like the cowboys do, and ran around the neighborhood with it.

Lindenhurst: I spent a lot of time with my cousins Anthony and Elaine who lived across the street from us. Their father, my Uncle Louie, included me in just about everything he did with his kids.

He belonged to a bowling league, which met once a week. Anthony and I always tagged along. We sat at a table with cokes and pretzels while the men bowled. There was a fellow named Babe on my uncle's team. Babe had a weird approach before he threw the ball. His ass moved just like a model as she walks along the runway. We giggle each time it was his turn to bowl. When Babe went to the men's room, I ran out on the bowling alley shaking my ass just as he did. All the men laughed, then my uncle yelled, "sit down God Damn it don't let Babe see you." Babe returned and asked what is so funny? Someone told him he missed the joke.

My dad brought home a snow sled one day. He got it from someone while making a delivery for UPS. The sled needed some repair, however Uncle Louie could fix just about anything. Elaine and I went down to the lot with a slope and played with the sled along with a bunch of other neighborhood kids. Somehow, she missed her turn to ride the sled and went home crying. When I came home dragging the sled behind me, my Uncle approached me and began yelling. His Ginny temper began to get the better of him. He grabbed the sled from me and said, "If you cannot share the rides equally with Elaine then you do not deserve to have a sled." He then smashed it against the tall wooden pole in front of the house breaking it to pieces.

I got scared; however, I managed not to show him. I gave him a good *smirk* and went home. "What the hell, I never had a sled before, and I do not have one now!" However, it was good while it lasted.

My uncle bought property in the town of Lindenhurst out on Long Island. On weekends, he began building a house. I recall riding there with them. We'd stop at the White Castle hamburger place to eat. The hamburgers were small but tasty and cost only about ten cents each. My uncle often bought a bag full for us to eat during our trip to the lot.

The trip was about forty miles from our house. When we were a few miles from our arrival on Montauk highway, we could see a big black pole up ahead in the distance. All the kids watched closely to see who could notice it first. My uncle gave the winner some kind of a prize. He was always good to us.

The property is just a block off the water. There is a small beach, which had a concession stand called "Charlie's Beach." As youngsters, we developed a friendship with the undeveloped songwriter "Marvin Hamlish." His mother rented a house on the same block as my cousins and often took Marvin and his sister to the beach. Across the street from the beach is a building with a carousel. We called it the "Merry Go Round." Each time it went around, we reached out to grab a metal ring. If you get a brass ring, you get a free ride. The place was neat.

My Uncle continued to work on the house. There were always people around to help him besides us kids. We mixed concrete and carried stuff for the men. Uncle Louie built a concrete fireplace. He burned scrap wood in it. My aunt used it to boil water to cooked spaghetti and sauce. Once the roof was on, we were able to stay for the whole weekend.

My uncle bought a small rowboat with a motor. He'd take a break from work and bring us kids out to the bay, which was about three or four foot deep. He taught us how to dig for clams. There were thousands of them just below the sand. All we had to do was feel around for them with our bare feet, dive down and grab them. One person stayed in the boat while the rest of us tossed the clams to him. We filled a couple of washtubs with clams.

Uncle Lou taught us how to catch Killies (Small Fish) off the beach using only a milk bottle, a string and small pieces of bread. On the way back from clamming, we threaded the Killies onto a piece of wire called a Killy ring. We lowered the ring into the water while the fish tried to swim, therefore, attracting the crabs. The blue claw crabs tried to eat the fish. We pulled it up slowly and my uncle netted all the crabs and placed them into another bushel. Upon our arrival at the house, my aunts had everything cooking on the fireplace. The men took the crabs and boiled them in water. They opened the clams and baked them on the grill with different seasonings. They also ate some raw on the half shell. Others made into a clam chowder. It was like a feast.

The men drank beer while listening to music. We played different games in the yard. There were always numerous people, mostly family. This was a typical Italian gathering.

It was about 1949 when my cousins moved from Glenmore Ave. Soon after their house was completed, they all moved in. Not long after that my folks bought a 1947 dodge coupe. Now we could drive out to see them on a Sunday. My uncle commuted daily to Brooklyn for work. My cousins enrolled into a new school, my folks had a set of wheels and things went on as usual in Brooklyn. You could not ask for more than that.

My Cousin Nick: My cousin Celia began dating a fella from the Old Mill. His name is Nick. Most of the fellows from the Old Mill were interested in cars and hung out around the junk yards. They enjoyed tinkering with auto parts, buying, selling or trading vehicles.

Nicky was no different. Every few weeks he came zooming into the city with a different car. He picked up Celia and off they went. My uncle Tony, Celia's father, thought this fellow was too wild for his daughter, but what father is ever satisfied with any boy who dated his daughter. No one is ever good enough. Celia was always very close with my brother and me. When Nick showed up we all knew he was in town. Between his noisy cars and all the commotion he made, no one could miss noticing him. Celia and Nick put me Billy, and my cousin Joann, in the back of the automobile. Nick started the loud motor and off we went. My uncle sat on the stoop shaking his head.

Nick took us to Rockaway Play land, they paid for all the rides; bought us hot dogs, cotton candy and drinks. Each time we went to Rockaway parking was a problem. There was a lot of rental vacation homes filled with many people having a good time. Nick pulled into someone's driveway to park the car. The tenant came out and asked,

"Just where do ya dink you're parking mister?"

"Well," Nick told the fellow,

"This house belongs to my Uncle and he gave me permission to park here whenever we could not find a parking space. Do ya have a problem wit it?"

"Oh it's OK as long as ya Uncle said that, it's fine wit me."

Off we went to play land. Nick was a different kind of a fella. We thought he was cool. When he came speeding down Doscher Street making lots of noise with his mufflers and tail pipes he pissed off numerous people. As the parents of my friends grew to know him, they eventually linked my brother and me as an associate of his after seeing us in his car. When I went later, to call for my friends I received a lecture about the wild man, and all the commotion that he caused while driving down their street. Uncle Tony was getting to know Nicky as time went on, he realized that he was a good person and always had either a job or something else going on with the automobile business.

When my parents went out for the evening, they asked Celia to watch us. Naturally, her boyfriend accompanied her. They entertained us for a short while then told us to go to bed. The two lovers wanted to make out and they did not want us to watch. My brother fell asleep quickly. I laid in bed for a short time and then got up using the excuse that I needed a drink of water or, I had to go pee. This annoyed them. Nicky had his own technique on how to put a kid to sleep. He told me scary stories. At that time, the war had ended and I was quite familiar with the enemy from Japan. I recall mom reading to us from the newspaper, about how the Japs tortured the American soldiers. I also watched newsreels about the war and saw many photographs of the Japanese soldiers; I had a very bad image of them. Nick told me that if I lay in bed real still, and went to sleep I would be safe. However, if I moved even a little bit a Jap will get me. He told me that a Jap will be sitting in the chair in our room and he will watch me very close to see if I move, so if you do not want the Jap to get you, you had better lay still.

I recall lying there sweating bullets without moving, not even an inch, waiting for my parents to come home. This kind of crap went on for a long time until one night my parents went out with my Aunt Mary and Uncle Louie who lived across the street from us. That night my cousin Elaine stayed at my house. Nick started in again with the scary stories and frightened Elaine almost to death. When our folks came home, Elaine started to cry. She stood there soaking wet and told her father what Nicky did. WOW! My uncle became extremely angry, he said to Nicky "You God damn idiot what the hell is wrong with you?" He threw Nicky out of the house and that was the last time they ever babysat us.

Celia married him and he became part of the family. They lived on Glenmore Ave. across the alley from us. Nicky grew to know the Old Geezer and his stingy ways.

He also knew where he stored his homemade wine. On occasion, Nick broke into the locked area to steel some wine. The Geezer had so much wine that he never missed what Nick stole from him.

One evening, Nick and my Uncle Danny invited the old man in for a glass of wine. They told him that it was a special import from Italy and they wanted to know what he thought of it. The Geezer took one taste and began cursing them out at the top of his lungs. "You son of a bitch this is my wine, I know my wine when I taste it." The old man carried on like an imbecile. They finally had to push him out of the apartment.

It was not long before my cousins moved into a house, which they purchased from Slim, who had the two hunting dogs and the fabulous peach trees. Billy and I thought this was terrific because now it was like having our own peach trees. Nicky spent a lot of time with us. He was like a big brother.

It was a hot summer night; my mother was down in my grandmother's cellar with a few of the neighbors. Grandma had a kitchen built in the cellar. It was a good place for them to hang out, eat and drink. Nick and Celia were also there. I was outside playing in the street when along came Angelo. (Godzilla) Once again, he went through his normal routine of bullying me. I tried once again to kick him in the nuts but he was wise to me. I took a pounding from him. When it was over, I walked into the cellar where everyone had gathered. Mom looked at me and asked, "What happened now?" I told her. She became furious. "Not again" she said. "Where is he"? I told her he was outside in front of the house. Mom turned to Nicky and told him how long this had been going on and how her husband would not do anything to help me. She asked Nicky to go out and try to put a stop to this continuous harassment.

Nick went outside and approached Angelo. He asked him why he was always picking on me. Angelo told him that it was none of his business so Nick told him that he would make it his business. Angelo threw a punch and the brawl began. Angelo tried to crack a bottle over Nicky's head. Nick grabbed his arm, they fell to the ground, the bottle broke and a crowed began to gather. All of a sudden out of left field comes Angelo's Sister Mary (B-29) screaming at the top of her lungs. Half the neighborhood was out there. Finally, they broke up the fight. Godzilla and B-29 went back to their cages and we went down to the cellar. Poor Nick was all beat up. He gave Angelo a good fight but it was not enough to tame the monster. When my mother saw what had just happened she was amazed to see how powerful this animal was. When my father came home, she spoke to him about it. My dad stood his ground. He told my mother that it would be up to me to protect myself.

Red Furman & the Haunted House:

My brother and I continued to bust everyone's balls. We did anything for a good chase. A short distance from the watermelon stand under the El there was a Jewish man by the name of Red Furman. He sold dinette sets that he made inside his shop. Each day he would set up all his tables and chairs along the Sunrise highway on display. Most of his sets were made of chrome. People stopped to look around while Red hung out with a smelly old cigar sticking out of his ugly face hoping someone would buy something.

Billy and I watched him until he was a good distance away from us. While Red was talking to a customer inside the shop, we knocked over a table along with a few chairs then yelled "Hey Red." He took off running after us. Old Red could never catch us.

Each time we were in the area we did "the old Red Furman trick," and then out ran the old guy. This went on for a long time until one day as we went passed his place to knock down some chairs we found that the creep hired two big dudes to catch us. We knocked over a table and these two goons came running after us like a bat out of hell. "Feet do not fail us now."

I told Billy to follow me to the old garages. It did not take us but a few seconds to climb up the wall to get onto the flat tar roof. The two dudes were right behind us. I told Billy to keep running to the end but do not stop. Jump off like a paratrooper then roll. (People rented these garages for workshops. They repaired automobiles and various other trades. They were attached and ran almost a block long.) Billy did exactly as I said. We landed on the ground together, made a roll, jumped up ready to start running again. With a quick glance behind, we saw the two dudes stop short. It was too high for them to jump. We laughed at them then ran back to Red's place to finish knocking over the rest of the chairs. Poor old Red never caught us.

Behind these garages was an old house with a pointed round roof that resembled a steeple. It looked like a Victorian style home. It was painted dark gray. All the kids knew this place as the haunted house. An old man lived there. His last name was Kinney. The poor old man must have had a stroke because his face was twisted and he dragged one leg as he walked.

None of the kids went near the house, they were afraid of Mr. Kinney. One day my brother and I climbed over the garage roof and went down towards the haunted house. We were on the lookout for old man Kinney and hoped he was not home. At the rear of the house was a cellar door and it was not locked. We pushed open the door. Billy asked,

"Do ya dink we autta go inside?"

"Sure we should, if we don't, how the hell will we ever know what's in dare?"

I then gave him a pinch on his cheek. Billy did not think twice as we entered the cellar of the house. The place was very dark and difficult to see anything, but we kept going in deeper but slowly. We almost tripped on a five-gallon bucket of pure black carbola marbles. (Big marbles) We began to see well again, as our eyes adjusted to the dark. Not only was there one five-gallon bucket, but there were about four of the friggin things. I said "Holy Mackerel! We found gold." Never had we seen so many marbles and to boot, they were all carbolas. We kept on looking. There were also bags of cement and lots of other crap. Wow, we thought, how are we going to get all this stuff out of here? Let us start with the marbles. We cannot let anyone, not even the other kids see what we found. When the coast was clear, each of us carried a bucket to our backyard and hid them behind the cellar door. By the end of the day, we had all the marbles and a couple of bags of cement. The old Gimp never showed up and we made a clean get away.

Why were there so many marbles down there, and what in the world are they used for? Upon another trip passed Red's place we noticed black marbles under the legs of all his tables and chairs. Red installed them there so the tables and chairs could slide. I am sure that if Red Furman ever found out that we had all the marbles he would go berserk and put a hit out on us.

What the hell are we gonna do with all these friggin marbles? We decided to trade some of the big marbles for regular size marbles. Nevertheless, just how many marbles do we need? After a while, I came up with an idea. Everyone in the neighborhood had a sling shot and was always looking for rocks to shoot. Therefore, we sold them to the fellas as ammunition. Before you knew it, everyone was shooting out the windows on the passing trains. By the time the cops came, everyone hid in the tunnels we had dug out. No one ever caught us and God only knows how many train passengers we hit with a black carbola.

Amongst all the good stuff, we found, there were cases of pink hand cream. We could not bring them home because momma would want to know how we got them. Now what could we do with these? They had to be good for something. We decided to choose sides, instead of dirt bombs and rocks we would use jars of hand cream to throw at each other. This seemed like a good idea at the time. We made up two teams. One team took a position in front of the concrete wall of the old garages, while the other team gathered under the El. We began firing the glass jars at each other. They smashed into the wall making it look like an explosion, with the pink crap splattering and glass flying. While running and dodging flying jars I stepped on one of the broken containers. The cover still screwed on to part of the broken glass that laid flat on the ground with the jagged edges sticking up. The glass went through the side of my sneaker right into my foot. I could feel the blood filling up inside my sneaker. I called time out to remove the glass. I then removed my sneaker and poured out all the blood. Now it was time to use what we learned in school. (Always carry a handkerchief.) I wrapped it up and hobbled home.

"What the hell happened to you now?" asked mom. "I was running through the lot and stepped on a piece of glass," Which was partly true? She patched up my foot then told me to stay off it for a while. Therefore, I did, for a little while. I chalked the whole thing off by making believe I had stepped on a land mine. That game was over for the day.

My cousin Nicky showed us how to make barbells using a steel pipe and two old paint cans. We mixed the cement that we took from the haunted house, filled the cans and then stuck each end of the pipe into the wet cement. When it got hard, we had our own barbell to start lifting weights. Nick taught us a lot of good stuff.

My Friend Otto: Otto was one of my classmates in elementary school. We hung out together for a few years. He came from a large family consisting of about seven or eight siblings. The family lived right next to the El, which ran along Pitkin Ave. You could see the passengers in the train from his window, and I am sure they were also able to see into his house.

Their apartment was located one floor above a Chinese laundry. The owner's name was Ho Bing Fung. The Chinaman Ho Bing had a wooden counter in his store, which he used to conduct business. He also kept a metal bottle filled with water sitting on the counter. The bottle had a spray nozzle on top of which he used to dampen the shirts while he ironed them. Each time I went in to call on Otto, I would stop, go into the laundry, pick up the bottle of water and squirt the Chinaman with it. I still cannot figure out why the dumb Chink never kept the bottle on the other side of the counter.

Across the street from Otto's house was the Chestnut Street train station. This is where we got on the train to go see my father's family on Miller Ave. The train station had a long stairway leading up to the train. There were a couple of platforms in between the sets of steps. Above the steps were steel bars the width of the stairs. Both Otto and I spent a lot of time playing on those steps. Most people would consider what we did a workout.

We started at the top of the stairs swinging back and forth from the steel bar. After gaining enough momentum, we let go and actually flew to the next steel bar. We continued this until we reached the street level below. God forbid if either one of us ever missed the bar; the other fellow most likely would have called an ambulance. We both worked at this for quite some time before we were able to complete swinging down all the steps. We thought we were cool because none of the other kids could do it.

When they opened the new subway stop on Euclid Ave. the neighborhood began to change with congested streets, consisting of public transportation and parking lots. Otto came up with a good idea. He noticed the people getting off the bus had a small piece of paper, which resembled a movie ticket called a transfer. All they had to do was go down to the turnstile of the train station, drop the transfer into a glass box and they had a free ride on the train. Otto picked a couple of old matchbook covers and gave one to me. We deposited them into the box and went for a free train ride. When we arrived at a station with a double platform, we walked across and took the next train back home. From that day on whenever we felt like taking a train ride, we did.

The 5 & 10 Store: My brother and I had a bunch of little toy soldiers, which we played with on the floor. The other kids labeled us as the "Ritz." The reason being, they did not have real toy soldiers, they painted faces on the end of a clothespin and made believe they were soldiers.

Otto came to school one day with a couple of real toy soldiers. I asked him where he got them. I knew that his family was poor. He told me he got them at the five & 10-cent store down at City Line. He asked me to go with him after school and he would show me how he gets them. After school, Otto and I went to City Line. He told me before we entered the store to watch how he does it. Therefore, I did just that. He walked up to the toys, picked up a few and put them in his pocket. We then walked out of the store. Otto showed me the new toy soldiers. He then told me to try it because it is so easy. I said, "OK I'll try it." Upon entering the store, I began to think. I do not need any more soldiers. We have enough at home. I began to look around the store, when I noticed those little rubber stoppers that are used in the sink or the bathtub to stop the water from going down.

I recalled mom always wrapping a piece of rag around the old worn out stopper. That is what I will take. I approached the counter and did just as Otto did with the toys. I had it in my pocket. That was easy. Suddenly a big man put his hand on my shoulder and told me to come with him. He brought me into a small cubical. I began to tremble.

"What do ya have in your pocket?" He asked.
"Nothing" I said.
"Empty them." Out came the friggin little rubber washer that cost a nickel.
"I am going to call the police and have ya arrested."
"Oh God!" I thought what my mother might do to me. I pleaded with him!
"The ding only cost five cents, I have a dime. If I give it to ya, will you please let me go?"

The man made me sweat for a while before he released me. My friend Otto was nowhere in sight when I exited the store. I never tried to steal anything from the five and 10-cent store again. "Lesson learned!"

The Bus Stop: Buses always lined up at the Euclid train station. At rush hour people formed lines waiting to get onto a bus. They stood on top of steel gratings, which covered large vents to circulate air in the train tunnels. Occasionally, when digging into their pockets or the women into their purses, they dropped coins, which fell through the gratings into the large hole in the ground. There was a lot of crap in the holes including cigarette butts, gum and paper wrappings.

I always kept a long stick hidden in the back yard so I could fish out the coins. The stick was thin enough to fit down the hole and with a piece of chewing gum stuck on the end of it. By simply pressing down on the coin, it stuck to the gum. I then gently pulled it up. This was a good thing until other fellows caught on. There were only so many coins down there. I decided that there must be a better way to do this without attracting too much attention. I got a padlock that fit in my pocket, or I locked it on a belt loop on my pants. I tied a string to it, took some grease off the fitting of the bus door, placed it on the lock, dropped it down on a coin and pulled it up. This was a better way. No one saw the big stick. I saved on chewing gum, and the lock was an easy thing to carry.

The train stations were the best place to find things however, the gratings ran all along the streets so whenever I walked any place I kept an eye out for goodies. Occasionally, if I were lucky, I would find a piece of jewelry.

The Parking Lots: All the empty lots around Euclid Ave. eventually became parking lots.

People paid to park their car then hopped on the subway to Manhattan.

The parking attendant collected the money, stored the keys on a rack in his shack, and left. They did not lock most of the car doors. There was no reason for him to sit and nurse the cars all day long. That was until we found out that the cars moved if you pushed on the starter button. It was like going to the races every few days. Each of my friends picked out a car, and then we lined them up by continuously pushing the starter to get a jolt. The cars moved a foot or so, with each push of the starter button. The race is on. The first one to the end of the lot wins. When a battery went dead, we went and got another car. It was that easy. By the end of the workday when the people returned and got off the train, their cars were scattered all over the lot. A tow truck came to jump-start each automobile. We never did this twice in the same parking lot. However, there were several lots. A few days later, we held a race in a different lot. This was better than going to the stock car races.

The Gum Machine: Across the street from the 5 and 10-cent, store is a Dentine chewing gum machine, mounted to the concrete wall. It is about a foot wide and three feet tall with a mirror on it. I guess the mirror was a come on item. People looked at themselves then bought a piece of gum for a penny.

One day, while tinkering with the machine, I discovered that if I inserted a penny into the slot and pushed in slowly on the button, the first slice of gum would fall down. If I did not let the button come out too far, I was able to continue pushing it in and out while more pieces of gum dropped out of the machine. The machine had four buttons, which released different flavors of chewing gum. "WOW!" What a great thing to know about. I could have all the gum I wanted for practically nothing. I thought I was very cool while looking in the mirror as the gum dropped down. I could see the *smirk* on my own face. It always gets me into so much trouble.

Each time I went to City Line, I would pop out a few flavors fill my pocket and be on my way. I made sure not to go near the machine when I went shopping with my mother. I was also careful not to take home too many pieces because momma seemed to know everything that I did. How could I ever explain to her why I spent so much money on friggin chewing gum?

The Move Upstairs: There was a Jewish family living behind us on the first floor of the building that we lived in. Their name was Smith. The woman was Margie. Her husband was Bernard, and they had two daughters. Margie was good friends with my mother and Bernie was a regular guy who fit in with the rest of the men. Margie told mom stories about the Holocaust. She had lived in Europe when she was younger. Because they were Jews, they had to hide from the Germans. It was very interesting when mother told us about Margie's experiences at dinnertime. It helped us to understand how much the Jewish people suffered during the war.

Bernie had become an Electrician. He opened his own business. Mom, at the drop of a hat, would send her sons to work along with anyone willing to teach us their trade. Billy learned a lot about electrical work from Bernie at a very young age. The Smiths decided to move to Levittown Long Island. They had a brand new home built, and we were all very happy for them. When they left, so did the family that lived upstairs from them. This left the property owner with two empty apartments.

My folks made a deal, and we moved up stairs. Billy and I now shared a bedroom of our own. "Boy Oh Boy, we were moving up in the world."

Our new place was great. We could see everything out of the back window. The Firehouse, the El, the empty lots even the Sunrise highway. What a view. "Who had it better than us?"

Another Jewish family moved into the Smith's old apartment. The newcomers name was Halperin. My brother and I continued to wrestle on the living room floor. We were getting bigger and made a little more noise. It did not take long before the new tenants were knocking at the door to complain. My mother would yell at us and tell us to stop.

Mom went across the alley occasionally to see her mother or some other relative. As soon as she left, we started another wrestling match. Old lady Halperin or her daughter Rive came up knocking on the door. I guess it was annoying to have all that noise coming from above your head. We were used to living on the first floor with only a cellar below us. No one ever complained.

The Halperins were pretty pissed off at us. Every time they came up to complain my mother whacked us. I guess mom was getting pissed off too because whenever the Halperins came knocking, without any hesitation she started swinging. The Halperins caught on to this whacking business and enjoyed it too. When they heard my mother leave, they waited for her to return home, then come knocking on the door to tell her; "They pounded so hard that the tea cups fell off the shelf, the pictures are all crooked on the walls." Bam! Momma went into action on us.

"Ma, we weren't doin anything." She said,

"If the lady says you did, I believe her."

This became the Halpern's routine.

One day, after all our pleading with my mom, she decided to test the downstairs neighbors. She told us to go down the stairs very quietly then go by grandma's house. So, down the banister we slid and out the door. My mother slammed the door and followed us. About an hour, later Billy and I crept up the stairs very quietly and waited for mom. She came up the stairs making some noise letting the Halperins know that she had returned. Less than five minutes went by before they came knocking on the door complaining to my mother about all the noise we had made. The Halperins had messed with the wrong woman. I never heard my mother yell at any one in our defense. She gave them holy hell. "I've been beating these poor kids all this time for nothing. What the hell is wrong with you people? I should whack you a few times." The Halperins ran downstairs and locked themselves in their apartment. Mom even apologized to us. After that, each time she went across the alley the wrestling matches begun. When we got older, we took Judo classes. I could now smash Billy to the floor without any squawk from the Halperins. Mom had told us the story about *'The boy who cried wolf'*. Now we understood it much better. I wonder if anyone ever told the people downstairs about that boy.

Never Run From The Police: This is something our folks preached to us at a very young age. If you run, it shows that you are guilty of some wrongdoing. If the cop chasing you is trigger happy, he could possibly shoot you.

One evening after dark, my friend Bobby (Nick named Raviola) and I were climbing on a garage roof behind my house. The garage belonged to the neighbor. As we climbed up the roof, we saw the Halpern's daughter Rive taking her clothes off. The light in her bedroom, cast light on the roof. Raviola and I fidgeted around to get a better look at the half-dressed Rive. All of a sudden, Raviola began to slide off the pitched roof and let out a noise. Rive opened the blind only to see him tumbling to the ground. The lights went off instantly. I started to laugh at my friend down below. We decided to hang out for a little while. Suddenly, we noticed a police car coming down Euclid Ave. There were two more cops coming down the alleyway with flashlights. Raviola said,

"Let's run." I thought of what my folks told me and said
"No! Don't run."
Both of us tried to hide between the fence and the cellar door. It took them only a minute to find us with their guns drawn.
"Come on out with your hands up"
"Wow! This is just like the freaken movies."

The cops saw that we were just two kids and put their guns away. They asked where we lived and we told them. I gave the cops one of my famous *smirks* and he asked if I thought it was funny? He brought me upstairs to my mother and told her that I was a Peeping Tom. I started to laugh. BAM! Right in front of the cop, I got whacked. The police officer told mom that there was a complaint of prowlers in the back yard. He told her that it was a good thing that we did not run. A police officer could have shot them. The police took Raviola home and he got his ass whipped from his older brother Mikie. I chalked it off as a check in the win column for the Halperins.

The Winter Snow: Whenever it snowed heavily, the city sent out plows to shovel off the streets. On the corner of Glenmore Ave. and Euclid Ave., there was an empty lot, where they stored the snow. At times, it piled about fifteen feet high. This was a great place to play.

Most of the kids from the neighborhood gathered on the mountain of snow. One of the popular games was, 'King of the Mountain.' Everyone fought his or her way to the top to try to be the king. It was a rough game and some of the kids got hurt. I recall this boy named Michael who I knew from elementary school. He lived a couple of blocks away from us on Pitkin Ave. Michael came to play with the group, things got a little rough and he got hurt. I do not recall exactly what happened but he threw a punch at me. "Whooh! What are you doin?" I asked. Without any explanation, he came at me again. I side stepped him then gave him a good punch in the face. He fell in the snow with a bloody nose. He got up, tried to hit me again so I let him have another shot to the face and he began to cry. He got up and started running towards his house with me chasing after him. Suddenly his shoe came off but he kept on running wearing only one shoe thru the deep snow. I picked up his shoe and buried it in the snow. I then went back to try to become the king of the mountain.

That evening the doorbell rang at our house. It was Michael's mother looking for his shoe. She told my mom that I took her sons shoe. My mother asked if I had his shoe. I told her the truth. "I do not have his shoe." His mother became very upset. She claimed that the shoes were brand new, and began to cry. I gave her a little *smirk*. My mom gave me a crack in the face.

"Where's his shoe?"

"I don't know." Mom asked the woman,

"What do you want from me?"

"I want you to pay for a new pair of shoes."

Mom tried to reason with her, and then asked,

"Why should I pay for your son's new shoes?"

The woman insisted that I had the shoe, and would not take no for an answer. Finally, she left, but she told my mother that her husband would come here to see you. This little episode went on for a while. The father came and my mother told him the same thing she had told his wife. This was the end of the issue. When I saw Michael in school, I told him that he was a little fagot and that he should wait for the snow to melt, then go look for the friggin shoe. After that, Michael stayed away from Glenmore Ave.

Grumman Picnic: I was about eight or nine years old when my family was invited to a picnic out on Long Island. Some relative of my Uncle Louie worked for the Grumman Company, and each year they held a very large picnic for all the workers and their families. I guess they used it as a tax write off.

Everything was free. There were tents set up all over the area. Hot dogs, hamburgers, corn on the cob, soda, beer, you name it they had it. There was music playing and plenty of games for the kids to join in and play. Right there in an opened field they had a big boxing ring set up. My father decided to go and check it out. A few minutes later, he came to get me.

"Come with me" he says.

"Where are we going?"

"You will see."

When we got to the ring, there were a couple of hundred people cheering while two fellas fought in the ring.

Dad took me to where they registered the fighters and matched them up according to size and age. The person in charge told pop that we had come a little late, everyone had already paired off and scheduled to fight. He said there was one other kid that also came late but he is much older and bigger than your son is.

"I could not put them in the ring together."

Without even looking at the kid, my dad tells him,

"It's OK set them up."

"But it won't be fair"

After some persuading, the man scheduled us to fight.

Time came to get into the ring. This dude was thirteen years old and he looked like a tough kid. The bell rang and we began to box. I took a shellacking in the first round while the people were screaming. I went back to my corner and dad gave me the old pep talk.

"I want you to rush into him when the bell rings don't give him a chance to hit you."

"OK dad, I will."

The bell rang; I rushed him, I gave him two good shots and it was all over. From then on, he rang my friggin bell to a tune that I had never heard before. Everyone was screaming and I started to cry like a sissy. The referee stopped the fight and I left the ring.

After the bouts were over, each fighter received a trophy. They were model airplanes replica to what Grumman manufactured. Winners received a large plane losers got a smaller one. I apologized to my dad for what happened and how I had acted. I told him that I was embarrassed in front of so many people. He gave me a big hug and a kiss and told me that he was so very proud of me. I hugged him too and told him. "I love you dad." We did not get emotional very often, but sometimes it is just necessary.

The Grumman model plane sat on our bureau for several years. It is funny how people see things in a different view: To my mother, it was just another thing that collected dust, but to my dad it was a token of a great effort by his son. My brother Billy played with it on the floor along with his soldiers. I liked the plane, but each time I looked at it, it reminded of the day I took a beating in the ring in front of so many cheering people and cried.

There is a Season for Everything: As the four seasons changed, the things we did changed too. For instance, in the summer time when it was sweltering hot outside we opened up the Johnny pump, better known as a fire hydrant to someone who did not live in Brooklyn. This provided lots of flowing water for everyone to keep cool. We cut both ends out of a tin can then held it up against the nozzle of the Johnny pump. This caused the water to squirt out even faster. By aiming the can, it was easy to shoot water at each other and into the window of a passing car. No one wore a bathing suit; we all played in the water in our street clothes. By the time we went home, everything dried from the hot sun.

Carpet guns: We made these guns from sawing the corners off a wooden fruit crate. When finished, it resembles a gun. A homemade rubber band cut from an old tire tube, then nailed to the bottom of the so-called barrel of the gun. To load it, stretch the rubber band around to the trigger part. Ammunition, made from a piece of old linoleum found in a lot somewhere, cut into one-inch square pieces and used as projectiles. The square piece, laid flat on the top of the gun barrel. When we pushed the rubber band up with our thumb, it flew out while spinning like a top. The guns were not very accurate but everyone had the same chance to hit someone else.

Pea Shooters: Looked like a large drinking straw but were much more durable. It worked similar to a blowgun. The only difference was we used peas or beans as ammunition instead of a dart. Mom could never figure out how we were eating so many peas and beans. She never caught us filling our pockets before leaving the house.

Slingshot: Everyone made a slingshot by cutting a Y shape piece of branch off a tree, and then tied a piece of rubber from an old inner tube on with wire. Also cutting a square patch of leather from an old shoe that was easy to find while hunting for newspapers in the garbage cans on Saturday mornings to sell at the junk yard. Next, cut two small slits into the patch, then threaded the rubber tubing through it to form a pocket to put a rock (or marble!) in for shooting.

Water pistols: These things were store bought. They came in all sizes and colors. The name of the most popular gun was 'Wee Gee'. It is very small and it was easy to hide in our pocket when we went to school. The only trouble was that the damn things leaked and it looked like you pissed in your pants.

Off to war: There were always many boys in the neighborhood that joined in when it came to war games. No one was out to hurt each other but getting hurt was part of the game. Every street had its own little clique. There was a bunch of fellows from Pine Street, only a block away from our house. We knew them as the (Clemmy Gang.) It consisted of Clemmy who was the oldest, his brother Gerry, two more brothers, Richie and Charlie, and the Hill boys, Joey and Henry. Henry later became a famous mob member of the Lucchese crime family. His story is in the book (Wise Guy.) They later made a movie called (Goodfellas) that portrayed his life as a mobster. His brother Joey later became part of our crew. We hung out together for many years. He was an exceptionally fast runner. It was no fun playing Football with him unless he was on your team. No one could catch him.

Everyone came out in full gear with a Carpet gun along with a pocket full of linoleum cut squares, a peashooter with a pocket full of peas and beans, and a sling shot with rocks. One gang chased the other gang through the streets shooting everything they had at them. The Clemmy gang chased us down Doscher Street. We ran into an apartment building where another bunch of boys from the neighborhood lived. It was five or six stories tall. My brother and I knew the layout of the buildings well. We could go either through the cellar or over the rooftop to get to another apartment building a block away on Chestnut Street. In those days, people bought seltzer and syrup to make soda. The seltzer man delivered a couple of times a week placing the bottles outside their doorways. On the way up to the roof, we grabbed a couple of seltzer bottles, filled with carbonated water. As the gang approached the building, we threw the bottles from the rooftop. When they hit the concrete below, they exploded. When the Clemmy gang ran for cover, we came down through another building to surround them and open fire with all our ammunition. When it was all over everyone joined together and walked back home. Some of us wounded, while others escaped injury. We were all friends. Maybe tomorrow we will all be playing baseball together. That is how it went on a normal summer day in the East New York part of Brooklyn.

Paper Airplanes: I was progressing well in elementary school. I managed to keep up with all of my studies in spite of my two neck operations. I never fell behind while advancing to every grade and always staying with my friends.

One of the boys in class made a paper airplane and tossed it out the school window. The plane glided over the assembly roof and landed in the schoolyard. Wow! That was neat. Therefore, someone else tried it. His plane went a little further than the first one. When the teacher had to leave the room for some reason, this was the cue to launch your plane. Just about every boy had folded a piece of paper into a plane and tossed it out the window. This went on for a couple of days and became intense. We began to run out of paper. As soon as the teacher left the room, the boys raided the supply closet and started making gliders with brand new paper. Everyone experimented with different types of folds, which created different looking gliders. Each boy was trying to beat the farthest paper plane lying in the schoolyard. Down below on the assembly roof it looked like it had snowed. It was loaded with white paper airplanes.

Class was in session when we heard a loud knock on the classroom door. It was Jimmy the custodian. He had several pieces of paper in his hand. He told the teacher to look out the window at what was laying all over the schoolyard including the roof below. He then started reading a list of names and showing the teacher the test papers he had picked up with our names on them. My name was one of them. Once again, the teacher asked that my mother visit her at the school. It was the same ole same ole thing all over again. I got the lecture, gave them the *smirk,* got my smack in front of the teacher and went back to the classroom. I could not help but think what a dunce I was to throw a plane out the window with my name on it. I will be more careful to check next time.

The Baseball Glove: I was in the sixth grade, my final class of elementary school. I was a senior at the school. Next year I will be going to Junior high school, P.S. 214 but I had to get thru this final term without any problems. "This is easier said than done."

Some fellow named Philly had stolen my baseball glove while I was playing down at Euclid Park. The dummy brought it to the schoolyard one day. It was not hard to spot one's own glove. When I saw it, I picked it up only to see his initials P.D. carved in it. I asked him where he got the glove. He lied to me. Therefore, I took my glove and began to walk away. He called me and told me to give him back his glove. I said to him, "whose glove?" "My glove" he said. I walked up to him and punched him in the face. Before I knew it, we were on the ground wrestling on the concrete. I managed to whip his lying ass and taught him a good lesson.

A teacher brought us into the school, then down to the principal's office. Once again, my mother had to come up to school. There I was standing in front of Mrs. Delany the principal, and mom. Mrs. Delany told my mother that this is not the first time that a teacher brought me to her office for fighting and therefore, "I am going to teach him a lesson. He is going to be put back into the fifth grade." She then told my mother "He is going to be starting in Junior High next year, the school he will attend is not like this school. It will be full of tough kids from other areas. If he does not learn to control himself he is going to get hurt there." I gave the *Smirk,* received another whack from my mother and went down to the fifth grade for two weeks. I considered it as a visit to my old fifth grade teacher Mrs. Cleary. She had always been my favorite. Mrs. Cleary also knew my mother well.

Mrs. Ahearn was my sixth grade teacher, a nice woman and I got along with her well. One day Mrs. Ahearn began to scold me for chewing gum in class. I laughed at her in front of the other students and that must have hurt her ego. She called for my mother to come to the school. She asked me to step out in the hallway while she spoke to my mom. She began to ramble on about how I find everything funny, especially when she reprimands me. I could see the veins in my mother's neck beginning to swell up. This was not a good sign. The teacher began to tell her about the chewing gum incident when I interrupted and said,

"Hey you chew gum in class too."

I should have known better, when I saw the veins but I spoke at the wrong time. I got a crack across my mouth right in front of the teacher. My mother said to the teacher.

"Did you see what I just did?"

Mrs. Ahearn nodded in a yes motion.

"Well you have my permission to do the same thing whenever you feel he deserves it."

"Now go back into the classroom,"

I gave them a *smirk* then hustled my ass from the hallway. I am sure that my mom apologized to Mrs. Ahearn for my behavior. When I got home, I received another smack for the last minute s*mirk*. My mom said, "I saw it."

Public School 214: Not quite a teenager nevertheless, this is the beginning of a new era. The first day in the new school was anything but normal. I am now looking forward to three years of Junior high school. I am now starting the seventh grade as a freshman. The school is about a half mile from our house. Therefore, I walk there each day. I was just a small part of an entire new assembly of students coming together from many different neighborhoods, with many familiar faces consisting of the people from the Old Mill and the Hole who we had attended religious instruction classes with at Saint Fortunata church. There are also many new faces from other areas.

Everyone had a homeroom class. This is where we begin our day before traveling around the hallways, going into different classrooms to study various subjects. The day also ended here. The first morning everyone took a seat in the classroom. Our new teacher introduced himself to the new students. This was the first time I had ever seen a male teacher. It was only natural to look around the room just to see if you knew anyone. When I turned to look at some big dude behind me, he muttered out.

"What the F--- are ya look-in at?"

"Are ya talkin to me?"

"Yeah, you"

"I'm looking at you; do ya gotta problem wit dat?"

Just then, the new teacher came over and broke up the conversation very quickly. I thought to myself, Mrs. Delany our old principal was not kidding this could be a rough friggin place.

The bell rang and everyone went to a different class. It was very important to keep a schedule with you each day; otherwise, you would not know where to go when the bell rang. I know this because I forgot my schedule a couple of times and felt like a stray cat in an alley.

At the end of the day, we all returned to our homeroom. The big dude sat behind me again but this time he did not act like a tough dude. He introduced himself to me as

Tony. We remained good friends for the next three years. My father's lessons were beginning to pay off. Never show anyone that you are scared.

The first day of school ended and I figured that I did well. I looked for what tomorrow would bring. On the way out of the school building, there was a lot of commotion in the street. I followed the crowd to check out what was going on. It was two boys fighting on the ground. All the students were pushing and shoving to get a good look at the fight. I was right there in with the crowd. All of a sudden, this big dude pushes me with both hands, almost knocking me off my feet. I went back at him and gave him a good shove. Without any hesitation, he hauled off and gave me a punch in the eye. Wow! I could not see from that eye. The pushing and shoving went on with the crowd while I managed to walk away. As it turned out the dude that popped me in the eye was a senior. I grew to know him better as the term went on but we were never friends. I went home that day and by evening time, I had a black eye. As usual, my folks showed me no pity. My mom asked how I liked my new school and my dad just shook his head in disbelief.

Everything was going well at the new school. I made many new friends and became closer to all the people from down the Hole and the Old Mill. I met many pupils who were into sports. Everyone indulged in just about everything. The school gym opened at night. Many people met there to play basketball and other games. Some of the new people I became friends with lived near the new school.

There was a teenager called the Cat. His real name was Alfonso but we called him Alley for short. He had a pair of green eyes, which looked like a cat's eyes. Thus, they coined the name Alley, as in "Alley Cat." The Cat had a brother by the name of Charlie who was a year older than we were. This guy looked like the mob worked him over. His nickname was "Chisel Head." The shape of his head looked like some apprentice sculptor was practicing on it. Therefore, everyone called him Chis. This explains how people got nicknames in Brooklyn. The Cat had a pool table in his house, which was located on the enclosed front porch. Mostly on rainy days after school, a few of us met at the cathouse to shoot some pool "No pun intended." When Chis showed up to play with us I could not help starring at his head each time he bent over to take a shot. I was willing to give odds that I could bounce a friggin pool ball off his head and he would not feel a thing.

Another teenager named Joseph lived on the same block by the nickname Cookie. Do not ask me how he got that name. Maybe his father gave it to him just as if my dad gave me the nickname Boobie. Today, (Boobies) means a woman's breast. Back then, we just called them tits. Joe later became part of a well-known rock and roll group called *The Admirations.*

Cookie's mom rented a small store space just across the street from the school. Most of the time it was empty, I have no idea why. Anyway, Cookie had a key to the place and could enter the store whenever he felt like it. Occasionally when it was empty, a few of the pupils would cut a class, meet at the store and play cards. It was a good thing while it lasted. Little did we know that the wood shop teacher, Mr. Flam, was able to look out of his classroom window and watch us playing cards? Mr. Flam never told anyone's mother. He handled the skipping of class his own way. When any of the card players entered the wood shop, he had us bend over the workbench with our head down. This schoolteacher could bend a handsaw back and forth and actually get a little sound out of it, then WAM it snapped and gave you a good smack in the ass. Man did it hurt! He told us that he could see us from the window and we were not fooling anyone. Mr. Flam was a good person. He could have sent for my mother and things might have been a lot worse.

Just about the time I entered Junior High school the New York Transit Authority began work on a very large construction project. The plan is to extend the train tracks beyond the last stop on the subway system at Euclid Ave. further east, towards Queens. The underground train tracks were to go one more station then rise out of the ground and tie into the elevated tracks on Liberty Ave. in Queens.

This construction work took place only a few blocks from PS 214.

The work site became a great playground for everyone with a little adventure in his or her heart. This included my friends and me. Lunchtime was different at PS 214 than it was at PS 159. At the elementary school, most of the kids went home to eat lunch. At the Junior High, we either brown bagged or bought a sandwich at a delicatessen and ate it in the street. This was where and when most of the students started to smoke cigarettes. They all looked cool in front of each other.

When the steel structures began to rise above the ground it was an everyday affair to run along the steel "I beams" with a baloney sandwich and a can of soda playing tag. As the ramps got higher the games became more dangerous, but we all got used to the height because it was a gradual change. They piled mountains of sand at different locations. This was a great place to jump off the beams into the sand. I remember jumping from such high heights that when I landed in the soft sand I sank up to my chest and sometimes my friends had to dig me out. Hanging out at the construction site during school hours went on for a very long time. Eventually, a few of the older pupils became too wild.

One afternoon a big crowd of students gathered on one of the temporary bridges built so that street vehicles could pass over the upcoming train tracks.

The construction workers had a large scaffold made of structural steel. The scaffold sat on wheels that rolled on the finished train tracks. They used this as a rolling work platform as they progressed along the tracks. The construction crew tied the scaffold with a couple of chains and locks to the new track, which was at an angle headed upwards toward the existing elevated tracks. One of the older pupils, a crazy Irish kid nicknamed Quinny, decided to smash the locks, untie the chains and allow the large steel scaffold to roll back down the tracks and crash into a train. The dude was swinging a big sledgehammer, which he found lying on the job site. Everyone on the bridge cheered him on while eating baloney or some kind of sandwich. The nearby construction workers heard the noise and began to run towards the "Paul Bunyan" dude swinging the mighty sledge. As the workers came out from the tunnel, everyone hurled rocks, bottles, cans or anything else they could find at them. You could hear the friggin missals pinging off their construction helmets. The place was a mad house with everyone screaming, the construction workers yelling for the chap to stop, and the pounding of the hammer. It was bedlam! The crowd grew larger. One of the chains broke loose. Quinny continued to hammer on the other chain. Just at that moment of possible disaster, a cop car arrived with the lights flashing and the siren screeching loud. The crowd dispersed in a flash. The Irishman dropped the sledgehammer and ran like hell.

The next morning the school principle held a meeting in the school's auditorium. The big dog of the yard (Mrs. Schwab) laid down the law by saying, "Anyone! And I mean anyone caught near the construction site during school hours will immediately be *EXPELLED* from school." That put an end to hanging out at the job site at lunchtime. Everyone continued to eat his or her lunch in the street or in the schoolyard. However, after things cooled down a bit, my friends and I continued to play there after school. I often wondered if the television sitcom Welcome Back Carter with Gabe Kaplan and John Travolta was not a takeoff from P.S. 214.

The Junk Wagon: On the way, home from school I occasionally saw an old man driving a horse and wagon. His horse was big and brown in color. The horse wore blinders on the side of his head so that he would not become frighten by the vehicles on the road. Behind him, he pulled an old wooden wagon full of junk. They called this a Junk Wagon. The old man sat on a bench in front of the wagon and held a whip in his hand, which helped him direct the horse.

One day I decided to hang on the back and hitch a ride. The old man saw me, reached back and snapped the whip hitting me in the head. I let go and fell off the wagon. The horse continued pulling the wagon and I walked home. A few days later, the wagon was passing the school once again. I tried the same thing only this time I was a little more careful of the man with the whip. I tucked my books under the wagon and positioned myself in a spot where the junkman could not reach me with his whip. When I reached my destination, I grabbed my books and as I got off the wagon, I waved to the old man and went home. This went on for quite some time. The old man realized that he could not clip me any more with the whip.

One afternoon at three o'clock, school let out. As I came out of the building, I saw the wagon parked on the corner and the old man was sitting there on his bench. When he spotted me, he began signaling to me to come to the wagon. The first thing I thought was that he was going to hit me with the whip. Instead, he told me to climb up onto the wagon and take a seat beside him. The man cracked the whip and the big brown horse started pulling the wagon up the hill. When we reached the top of the hill, the old man handed me the reins and let me drive the wagon. When we reached, the place where I usually got off he stopped the horse and I climbed down. The man became my friend. Each time he passed the school at about three o'clock he waited for me He was a nice old man.

"PERSISTANCE" paid off.

The school term progressed and so did the extracurricular activities after school. I did not see the old man as often as I use to, but every once in a while we met and I would ride home with him. I spent a lot of time hanging out on the corner of Crescent Street and Pitkin Ave. This was across the street from my elementary school. One afternoon while walking on my way home from school, I saw commotion on the street corner. As I got closer, I saw the Junk Wagon standing there. Alongside it was the old man. The poor man was crying while looking over his big brown horse lying dead in the street. The police were there directing traffic around the scene. A tow truck came to pick up the horse and place him into a sanitation truck. Another tow truck took away the Junk wagon. I stood next to the old man as he watched his whole world come tumbling down on the street corner. The crowd dispersed. I never saw my friend again.

Gambling: Just about every kid growing up in Brooklyn learns to gamble one way or another. It comes with the turf. Baseball cards were always popular. Every kid carried a few in his pocked at all times. There were several different games played where the winner won the loser's picture cards. "Flip" was the game played most of the time. One lad would say, "I'll take you five." His opponent flipped five cards along his side, dropping them to the ground. The card landed showing either a head or a tail. Just like flipping a coin. The other lad had to match the same combination of heads and tails. If he did, he won all the cards on the ground. Another game we called "Wallsie." We played it with several people. Each person holds a card against a wall and lets it drop. The next lad does the same thing. The Idea of the game is to have your picture card land anywhere on a card that was lying on the ground. If it did, you won all the cards. You could always hear marbles clicking in every kid's pocket. Wherever there was a patch of dirt available, we played a game of "marbles" there after school. Winner takes all.

Next to the marble game, you might see a game called "Land" played in the dirt. You needed a knife to play this game and just about everyone had a pocketknife. The idea was to draw a big square box in the dirt with a knife. The first fellow throws his knife into the box, which usually sticks into the dirt. Everyone knew how to throw a knife and to make it stick. He then sliced the box in the direction of the sharp side of the blade, and then erased the rest of the box with his foot. The box becomes smaller after each throw. He shoots until he misses. The next dude tries to stick his knife in the smaller area. When the box became too small to split up, the last fellow who put his knife into the smallest area won all the money. Money is set aside before the start of the game.

"Pitching pennies" was a simple game. The fella who could pitch his penny closest to the wall wins all of the other pennies. Many people were able to play this game.

Just two people often played "stickball" in the schoolyard. There was a pitcher and a batter. The pitcher threw a rubber ball against a wall with a home plate painted on it. If the batter did not swing, it was either a strike or a ball depending on where the ball hit the painted home plate. If it hit the home plate, it was a strike. If not, it was a ball. We kept score in our head. A nine-inning game sometimes took all afternoon to finish, but you could always pick up some loose change if you were a good ball player.

"Craps" was played but not in the open areas. If a cop saw you playing, he took away the dice. Losing your dice is bad enough. However, none of the people wanted to look bad to the neighbors. Most every game that we played involved the winning or losing something of value. Everyone took the games seriously.

Christmas Trees:

While attending Jr. High school, after Christmas everyone threw his or her dried out trees outside. I do not remember anyone that had an artificial tree. Therefore, trees were lying all over the streets. It was a common event to burn a tree in the street. They went up into flames in a split second along with a nice crackling sound, a bright blaze of flame and a sweet smell of pine.

On the way home from school one day while walking with my Lithuanian friend Johnny, we picked up about three trees, piled them up and set fire to them. What a blaze. We stood there and watched until the fire went down to a small flame while inhaling the sweet fragrant.

Suddenly Johnny started to laugh. I asked him, "What's so funny?" "Look" he said, pointing to the trees "someone's books and sneakers are under the trees." I looked and then realized they belonged to me. The pages were turning as they burned. The sneakers were completely gone, the only thing left were the rubber soles and the little metal rings for the shoelace.

"Wow!" Now what, I have not a clue as to what I could tell my mother, much less the teachers from every class who issued a textbook. In addition, all of my class notes were gone. I later managed to get new books from the school with some cockamamie excuse for the disappearance of my books. I had to tell my mother the truth because I needed new sneakers for gym class the next day. Need I explain what took place in our house that night?

It did not end there. The Christmas season is over and there are plenty of trees out there ready to burn. I came up with what I thought at the time was a great Idea. I gathered a bunch of neighborhood dudes and told them that we could have the biggest Bon Fire ever if we all pitched in to collect as many trees as we could find. We will pile them up in the empty lot until we get enough to celebrate the big day. Everyone agreed it would be a blast. I tugged on my brother's cheek and told him to gather his friends to go find trees.

The idea was working like a charm. There were so many trees coming in that we needed a ladder to pile them higher. That was no problem. We always could find wood to build one. We piled them up very high. We were ready! All the boys were there for the ceremony. Now all we had to do was light them up. This pile was not only high it was wide, so it would take several people to start the fire. Ready Go! Before you could say Jack Flash, the friggin things looked like a burning inferno. The flames shot way past the El. tracks. The noise was terrific. It became more overwhelming that anyone of us had expected. I began to worry, what if the wind blows and the wooden railroad ties that hold up the train tracks catch on fire. "O my god!" The train will fall off the tracks and come tumbling down to the ground. Just then, a siren went off in the firehouse, which was right behind the fire. RUN!

Everyone took off. I ran up to my house and knelt down to watch out our back window. The noise was very loud, not to mention the fire trucks and the glaring blaze. Abruptly, who was standing behind me? It was my mother. She took one look at what was taking place and said "You're behind this, you son of a bitch. I just know it." What could I tell her? I stunk of smoke. I will never forget that day. I received one of the worst beatings ever from my mother that afternoon. However, as I said, I thought it was a good Idea at the time.

Mom took no crap from my brother and I. Raising two boys in the neighborhood we lived in must have been quite a task for her to endure. Today as I look back, I never think she did wrong when she punished us physically. Someone had to keep us in line and she did! I realized that mom had many things she had to contend with besides us. Therefore, she sometimes became extremely angry quite rapidly. As I grew bigger, she hurt her hands a couple of times when hitting me. I'd start laughing at her. From then on, she did not hesitate to use a belt or a broom to whack me. I'd be in a corner while she'd be swinging. I'd give her the *smirk* and she swung harder. My brother would start to cry and then she'd stop hitting me. I noticed each time he cried she stopped. So I took my little Bro aside one day, gave him a nice pinch on the cheek and told him that each time mommy starts to hit me, I want you to start crying a little sooner than you usually do. As a reward, I will pay you money. He asked, "How much money?" I told him not to worry I will pay you lots of money. This was a good thing because I always had money in my pocket, and from then on every time my mother hit me, my kid brother had money too.

The Sales People:
Something unique about our neighborhood was how so many people made a living doing different things. In the warm months, you could always hear somebody selling something in the street. A man pushing a cart down the street packed with fish covered with ice yelling at the top of his lungs!

"Ou-Pesce-Ou Pesce." (It means fish in Italian)

"Ou Pesce Bacala." (Cod Fish.)

"Fresco Pesce." (Fresh Fish.)

People ran down to buy fresh fish for supper.

Another man followed yelling!

"Pomodoro rosso." (Red tomatoes in Italian.)

"Fresco Gagootz (Slang meaning fresh squash.)

Sometimes a horse pulled a wagon or the man had a truck. When we heard a bell ringing in the alleyway, we knew the person who sharpened knifes and scissors was setting up his stand, which had a stone wheel that turned by pumping on a pedal with his foot. The man sharpened everything for the folks. The women never had to go anywhere else to get things sharpened.

There was always the man selling shaved ice doused with different flavors of syrup. All the kids liked when he came around. Every kid had a different colored mouth indicating the various fruit flavors.

Many people in the neighborhood did not have an electric refrigerator. They had an Ice Box. On the top of a large box, there was a compartment, which looked like a freezer, but it held a block of ice, which kept everything cold. We had a regular electric refrigerator in our apartment. After all, we were *THE RITZ*. Every day the Iceman came by with an open backed truck filled with big blocks of ice. Before climbing up the stairs to deliver the ice he placed a piece of a burlap bag over his shoulder then, with a pair of ice grips he'd grab a piece of ice and place it on his back to make the trip. As soon as he was out of sight, we jumped up on the truck to grab some of the small pieces of ice that he left behind after chopping off what he needed. This was always a treat in the hot summer days.

Trucks came by with different kinds or rides for the kids. They parked alongside the curb and everyone waited their turn to get on the ride. Meanwhile, the ice cream man came. This was always a delight for everyone. There was never a dull moment in our Brooklyn neighborhood. I would not wish to have grown up in any other place.

Orange Beaut: Behind our house, lived another family with two kids, a boy named Johnny and his little sister Ann. His father was a police officer. This Johnny character loved to imitate his comic book idol Straight Arrow. He was also good at catching butterflies with an old window screen. Whenever he spotted a Monarch butterfly, which is the color orange, he'd yell out "There's an orange Beaut." Still, until this day, my brother and I yell out the same ole thing every time we see an orange butterfly.

Catching butterflies was one of our favorite pass times in the hot summer days. Everyone used a discarded window screen. It was easy. When you spotted a butterfly, you ran after him until he landed, then pounce on him with the screen. The best looking ones, we mounted on to a piece of cardboard with a straight pin. Every boy in the neighborhood had a butterfly collection.

There was a fence separating our yards. However, most of the time we climbed up to his dad's garage roof then jumped into Johnnie's yard imitating Tarzan or soldiers. It was also a short cut to Slim's peach trees in the next yard.

This fella was slick; he would tell a few boys to meet him in his back yard behind the garage then he brought his younger sister back there. Johnny said for three cents each I will have my sister pick up her dress and pull down her underpants so you all could all peek. Naturally we all coughed up a few cents apiece to see the show. Little Annie strolled in and do her thing. We all peeked then gave a handclap congratulating her on her performance. OK, Johnny would say, the show is over for today. Everyone then climbed over the garage and went about their business until Johnnie needed a few more coins. I often wondered if he ever became an adult pimp.

After those people sold the house, a new family moved in. Another kid named Jimmy lived with his grandmother and his Uncle Patsy. This kid was a real character, spoiled rotten by his grandmother but took an ass whipping from his uncle Patsy. It was not odd to hear the grandmother screaming, "Jimmy please don't hit me I'll buy you anything you want." Jimmy stopped hitting his grandmother and then they went shopping. You could not blame Jimmy for how he was. You must blame his grandmother. If she had whacked him a few times when he was younger, it would have never come to this nasty situation of blackmail.

This Uncle Patsy fellow did not take much crap from his nephew or any of the other kids in the neighborhood. He'd just as easily kick you in the ass or give you a good smack as to look at you. One of his most popular victims was my brother Billy. I do not know what he did to piss the chap off but Patsy was always chasing him.

One afternoon I was sitting on the stoop talking to with mom when my brother appeared, running around the corner with Patsy right behind him. Up the stoop he ran, thru the hallway, down the cellar steps and thru the cellar. The cellar door went flying opened and Billy came running up the concrete steps. He jumped over the fence while telling mom and I "see you later." A few seconds went by before Patsy came out from the hallway asking if we saw that little son of a bitch. Mom said "NO." She then chalked it off to just someone else looking to whip my brother's little ass.

While playing ball in our alley, my Spall Deen bounced over the back yard fence and landed in Patsy's yard. I simply climbed over to get my ball. There was a car parked in the yard and the ball had rolled under it. I got down on my hands and knees to crawl under the car. To my surprise there was a big German Sheppard dog laying there. The dog must have been asleep but as I began to crawl towards him, I must have startled him. The dog growled and charged at me. I backed up as fast as I could and jumped to my feet as the dog lunged at me with an opened mouth and sharp looking teeth. The dog was faster than I was because as I backed up his paw put a scratch across my chest, and his opened mouth was coming at my throat. I fell backwards while the dog was flying thru the air, suddenly like a miracle his head just snapped back as I hit the ground. I got up to run but the big German Sheppard just laid there on the ground. There had been a chain tied around his neck, which stopped him in midair.

My chest was bleeding from his paw but the dog laid on the ground grasping for air. I climbed back over the fence and went into my house to tend to the wound that I had just received. After I cleaned up, I went back to look at the dog. He lay there dead as a doornail. The chain must have broken his neck. I thanked God that day for looking after me. If there was not a chain and if it was a couple of inches longer, I probably would have been laying there and not the dog. I was also glad that Uncle Patsy was not around at the time. If he had known what had happened he probably would have done to me what the dog failed to do.

I think back and wonder what ever possessed us to climb over a barbed wire fence. What was so important on the other side that caused us to go there and risk being cut up? Behind the two buildings across the street from ours were two fences with several rows of sharp barbed wire running across the tops. If we climbed over one of them, it would get us into the brickyard. The other got us into the next yard where there was absolutely nothing, but we all had to climb over. I cannot remember how many times we went home all cut up from climbing over those fences. My folks patched us up and we went back to climb over the same friggin fences again. Kids can be stupid sometimes.

The Boy Scouts: One of the boys in the neighborhood came up with the bright idea that we should all join the Boy Scouts. It sounded good at the time. I became a Tenderfoot at troop 229; the meeting hall was located in Queens, located just over the Brooklyn Queens boarder line. Every few weeks all the boy scouts met at the troop-meeting hall. They divided us into different patrols. Our crew elected the name Beaver patrol. They had flags made up for each patrol, which we mounted to a pole. After a couple of weeks, we had Boy Scout uniforms with troop 229 on one arm and a patch of a beaver on the other. We had the hats to go along with the new suits. We were all set to venture on trips to learn how to survive in the woods and take various tests to receive promotions.

Once a week each patrol met at some one's house to go over the future tests and practice various things like tying different kinds of knots, becoming familiar with hand signals and other scout things. I met a bunch of new people from Queens and some of them were in my patrol. Things started out OK. I was glad to be a Boy

Scout and was looking forward to doing many different things with them.

At one of our first patrol, meetings we gathered outside a troop member's house dressed in our uniforms. This fella Bobby was holding a lighted punk. (This is a dried decayed wood.) We used them to light firecrackers on the Fourth of July. The punk stayed lit for a long time. The only way you could put it out was by stepping on it to knock the burning tip off. For no reason, Bobby decided to drop it down the back of my shirt. It went down to my waist and stuck there burning a hole in the back of my new uniform and my back. I tried like hell to remove it by jumping and wiggling while it kept burning my back. I finally got it out from my shirt while the moron Bobby was laughing. I walked up to him and punched him in his face. That put a stop to his laughing. It also put blood all over his face and his new uniform. We never became good friends but we both stayed in the Beaver patrol.

After a troop meeting several weeks later, a few of my friends and I were walking down Liberty Ave. in the City Line area heading home. We were dressed in our Boy Scout uniforms. One of the scouts was carrying the Beaver patrol flagpole when three tough fellas approached us. They began calling us bottle suckers and names like fagots and sissies. That was all right with me because all I had to do was ignore them and go about my business. Well, it did not end there. They pulled off their Garrison belts and began swinging at us with the buckles. It was common for the gang members to file the edges to sharpen them up for fighting. A couple of my friends ran away after they were whacked with the belts. I grabbed the flagpole from one of the scouts and began to swing it at the attackers. The pole was much longer that the belts, so I had the advantage. I hit one of them in the face and he started to bleed. I stuck another one in his neck with the point of the pole and the third person took off running. The fight ended and the tough guys left. Meanwhile, the other Boy Scouts were gone too. Damn, I thought, one of the things they teach us at the meetings is "A Boy Scout must be brave." Bullshit, I thought to myself, I am standing here all alone.

The summer time came and the troop leaders planned a camping trip in the mountains. Everyone was excited and could hardly wait to go. I kept going over a list of things that I had to bring with me. The day came and I was prepared like a good Boy Scout.

The twin's father took part in the excursion too. He had emptied his pickup truck of roofing materials and tools and loaded it up with backpacks and tents. We were on our way to the campsite.

Upon our arrival, the troop leaders shouted out orders of things for us to do in order to set up a good campsite. I thought that this was going to be a great experience; I looked forward to learning new things about living in the wilderness. I also expected to pass a few tests along the way, which comes with a promotion to the next rank above a Tenderfoot. It was a long ride to the mountains from the city but no one seemed to mind. We all did our share, and in and in no time, the site was set up. We pitched our tents and set up our bedrolls while some of the other boy scouts started a fire. We are now ready to start our first cook out in the wilderness.

Before we put anything on the grill, it started to rain. The troop leaders told us to get into the tents and we will all sit out the rain. As soon as it stops, we will start cooking the food. Therefore, we all sat in our tents waiting for the rain to stop. We sat there for a long time but instead of the rain stopping, it came down harder. The rain continued for a long time. The water was coming into most of the tents. The rain also put out the fire. Our bedrolls became soaked and wet while the rain came down even harder. The head honcho of the troop finally made the decision to break up camp, pack everything back into the trucks and head for home. What a mess. Wow. By the time we got our gears back into the trucks, it was all full of mud. We piled into the trucks and cars then headed back to the city. What a waste of time and energy.

Forest park was a large area located along Woodhaven Blvd. in Queens. This park was a few miles from my house in Brooklyn. The troop leaders planned an outing at the park one Saturday morning. There were lots of wooded areas and some campsites. We set up at a site and the leaders began to test us on our skills as Boy Scouts. One of the things the older scouts taught us was how to start a fire by rubbing a couple of sticks together. That went over like a lead balloon. We probably would have been there until Monday before anyone got a fire started. I was glad that I brought along a book of matches.

After practicing how to recite the Boy Scout oath, tie a few knots in a rope and saluting each other we were ready to begin practicing the art of tracking someone in the woods. The idea was to leave two Scouts at the campsite while everyone else took off into the woods. The troop leaders showed us what kind of signs to look for, like footprints, broken twigs and so on. I was one of the Scouts left at the site along with Fat Carmine. His nickname is Fat Carmine because he is fat, but he was a nice kid. We waited about five minutes, which was enough time for everyone to go into the woods before we began our search to find them.

Out of nowhere, this creepy looking man appeared at our campsite. He was much older that any one of us. This man walked up to Fat Carmine and for no reason at all punches him in the face. Carmine was scared to death, and began to cry. This nut job hauled off and punched him again. You had to see the fat ass run. He took off thru the woods like Bambi the deer. The crazy guy turned to me, then he picked up one of the Boy Scout's hatchets and began to run towards me screaming I'm gonna kill you and chop you up in pieces while waving the hatchet in the air. I took off like another deer in a different direction with the maniac running after me screaming. I do not think I ever ran so fast in my life. I came to a clearing, then spotted Woodhaven Blvd. and headed right for it. The man finally stopped chasing me as soon as there were people in sight, but I never stopped to look. I kept on running along the Blvd. until I reached Atlantic Ave. I knew my way home from there and kept on trucking.

My mother asked me why I was home so early, and why are you not with the Boy Scouts? I told her what happened up at the park. I then told her how I continued running almost all the way home. A couple of hours later a troop leader called the house to see if I was at home. Fat Carmine told them what had happened at the campsite.

That night I sat down with my parents and told them that this Boy Scout thing just aint working out. I told them that I appreciated all the effort they had put into my joining the Scouts and the help they gave me to acquire all the equipment, but I had no interest in being a Boy Scout anymore. They told me that they understood how I felt and said that I did not have to do anything that I did not want to do. Therefore, I went into the Boy Scouts as a Tenderfoot and I clocked out as a Tenderfoot. That is my story as a Boy Scout. "Is it not a neat story?"

More Baseball: With the Boy Scouts being put aside I continued to play baseball every chance I got. Word was out on the streets that at Euclid Park, they are forming a neighborhood baseball team, which will play in a league against other public parks in Brooklyn. Tryouts for the best players for each position are going to begin soon. The name of the team is the Euclid Park All Stars. Every other park did the same thing, also naming their team with the name of the park and ending with All Stars. This sounded like a real good thing, if I could make the team, I will get to travel all over Brooklyn to play in other parks and when the Euclid team played at home, I will get to play on the big diamond. "Damn, I gotta get on that roster."

The tryouts lasted for a couple of weeks. Carmine the Parkie was in charge of putting this whole thing together. Hundreds of boys showed up. You would think they were giving out free dinners, I mean dudes came out of the woodwork.

With the tryouts now complete, the manager filled each position with the best ball players. Each position had first string and a fellow in reserve. I made first string in the catcher's position. "Wow" I was so excited; I could not wait to tell my father. I know that he will be happy. Another fella who played the catchers position, his name was also Louie, and I knew him from school. He was a grade ahead of me and got along well together while working hard to help each other at our position.

What a great summer it turned out to be. I played baseball all over Brooklyn and met many nice people. I even played out on the Parade Ground in the Prospect Part section where the Torre brothers played. Joe and Frank both made it to the major leagues. Joe went on to manage the N.Y. Yankees. Joe and I are the same age, born a few days apart. Who knows, I may have played against him back then? Sandy Koufax and Manny Ramirez also honed their skills there. The Park league did not last too long but for the time that it did, I had a great time.

The following year another team sponsored by a local super market called Dan's Supreme started to take shape. I tried out again as a catcher and made first string. Each player received a new uniform. We played against many other sandlot teams in the neighborhood. I will never forget a pitcher named John Dorsey. Johnny was a black dude who could throw a baseball better than anyone I had ever played with. He reminded me of the fastball pitcher, Johnnie Casio, the Italian dude from Glenmore Ave. He was the fellow that my dad had pitch to me a few years back. This Dorsey fellow was terrific, he could throw all kinds of pitches and I handled him well. We had a lot of fun that year too. I traveled around again to different ballparks and met some nice people. I often wondered about Dorsey. The fella could have made the pros. He just had that natural talent. I followed baseball all my life but never saw his name come up.

Pop and I continued to catch every Sunday and Monday on his days off work. I knew he was happy that I made all the tryouts and got to play on the starting lineups of the baseball teams. I loved to see him happy.

I played softball just about every day in the schoolyard at P.S. 214 while continuing to make new friends with many good ball players. I also spent many hours at Euclid Park shagging fly balls in the grass or playing in a scrimmage game with whoever was in the park. Whenever there was going to be a game, I took all my catchers equipment with me. Most guys carried only a glove and sometimes a bat but I carried a catcher's mitt, a mask, chest protector, baseball spikes, a couple of baseballs, a bat and a pair of shin guards, I stuffed everything into an old laundry bag, threw it over my shoulder and off I went to the park, always ready to play the game.

Many of the good ball players wanted to start a baseball team. We often met at various vacant sand lots to play some hardball. Prior to playing ball, it was necessary to clean up the lot, which contained a lot of junk that people discarded. There were not too many groomed baseball fields in those days like there are today. I could go for a drive in any neighborhood and see beautiful fields and parks with no one playing on them. "What a shame."

South of Linden Blvd close to the Old Mill area was an empty lot where we gathered to play baseball. It was not much of a field but it was a place large enough to play the game. On this particular day, a few of us cleared whatever crap was lying around so that we could get started. My friend Tommy was playing left field when a fly ball came to him. While keeping his eye on the ball and running to catch it, he tripped over part of an old burnt Christmas tree and fell to the ground hitting his head. He laid there for a while never getting up to retrieve the ball. When we approached him, he seemed a little strange. We asked him if he was all right. He began to speak in a strange fashion. Tommy did not know anyone's name. Some of the boys thought it was funny and began asking him many questions. The poor kid spurted out lots of incorrect answers. Everyone became worried therefore; we took him to his house on Crescent Street near Saint Fortunata church.

Naturally, his mother became very excited and began asking us many questions about what had happened. That evening his parents took him to the doctor. Tom diagnosed with temporary amnesia, which means (Loss of memory.) This lasted for about a week until he began to regain his memory. The kids today do not know how lucky they are to have nice clean places to play baseball. I would love to see more kids take advantage of these empty fields.

The Merchant: After driving the United Parcel truck for nineteen years with a perfect driving record, my father had a minor accident, which involved hitting his head against the truck. Afterwards explaining to mom how it all happened and that he had some pain in his head. I remember my mom telling me "since the accident your father is not the same person that he had been before the accident."

Dad often spoke to mom about packing it in with the United Parcel job. She asked him what he wanted to do instead. He said that he was not sure, but he was tired of hauling furniture for a living. Meanwhile he stuck it out for a while longer.

My mother always did something to make money besides running a household and raising my brother and me. She put together a little business, traveling to the Orchard Street area of Manhattan purchasing various garments for people she knew in the neighborhood. She bought them wholesale at a big discount and was able to add enough of a profit and still sell the items cheaper than the local stores. She did not have to contend with bricks and mortar. One of her biggest selling items was bras and panties. Back then, they called women's panties (Bloomers.)

My brother and I went with her occasionally to help carry packages. It was also a good way for her to keep an eye on us and keep us out of trouble for the day. We took the subway to Manhattan. Mom knew her way about very well. I recall how she bargained with all the storeowners. Most of them were Jewish and she knew her way around them extremely well. While she shopped and negotiated prices, Billy and I ran between the racks of clothes trying to get peeks at the women trying on bras. Most of them never tried to hide; they came right out in the open with a new bra to show their friend or husband, "and us?"

It was a couple of months before Christmas and mom had many orders to fill. One Monday my dad decided to drive to Manhattan with the car to help her with the packages. He asked if I wanted to go with them. I said no and off they went.

Driving in the big city is always a hassle. There is always a lot of traffic and nowhere to park. Mom hustled from store to store making her purchases while dad tried to find a parking space. He spotted a fellow loading his car and figured he would be pulling out soon and the spot would be available for him to park. He doubled parked while waiting for the fellow to pull out of the space. As the car began to pull out, dad began to back up. Suddenly a car from nowhere pulled into the space. Pop got out of his car, walked over to the other car and said, "what the hell are you doin?" He explained that he was waiting for the spot for quite some time and was in the process of backing his car into the spot. The person opened his window all the way and spit in his face. "This was a bad choice!" Dad reached into the window and pulled the dude right through it. He then punched him in the face and knocked him to the ground. Another fella jumped out of the passenger's side to help his friend. Pop picked up the driver and whacked him again. As the passenger came at him, he punched him too and both people were lying on the street. A woman jumped out of the car just as mom was walking towards the scene. The women started screaming at my dad. Mom whacked her in the head with a big role of Christmas wrapping paper, knocking her to the ground. Now the three of them lay there in the street, while a crowd gathered. My parents loaded the car with the packages and left for the ride home. Ever since that day, all of the store merchants treated my mother with a lot of respect. They gave her special attention whenever she entered their shops. When they came home and told us what had happened, I was sorry that I did not go with them. I could have helped my dad.

Horseback Riding: At approximately twelve years old, my friend Philip DiMaio suggested that we go for a horseback ride after school. I told him that I knew nothing about riding a horse. He said, "Don't worry it is easy, I will show you how to ride." It sounded like a good idea; therefore, I agreed to go with him.

We took off after school and headed to Henny Miller's stables, which was located near the Canarsie section of Brooklyn, not far from Jamaica Bay. The cost to rent a horse was one dollar an hour. We chipped in fifty cents apiece and we were ready to ride. Philly suggested that I wait around the corner from the stables because Henny would not allow two people to ride on one horse. I said "OK," then waited for him.

About ten minutes later Philly came sitting on a big black horse named Jet. He told me to place my foot in the stirrup, pull myself up on the horse, and sit behind him. There was no room for two people to sit in the leather saddle. I was actually sitting bareback on the horse. No sooner was I on the horse when Philly kicks him and yells "geddyap." The friggin thing took off like a Jack Rabbit. I thought we were going fast but the horse was only trotting. As soon as we were out of sight of the stables, my friend yells to me to hold on tight. He kicked him with his heels and began to hit him in the neck with the reins. The horse went into a full gallop. Like a friggin Yo-Yo, I bounced up and down on the horses back.

Jet was running through an open field of grass when up ahead I saw a fire. It was the grass burning. Philly tried to stop the horse but he could not. He ran right into the fire. The horse kept running until we reached the beach and then he ran into the water finally he stopped running. "Holy shit!" My ass was sore and the horse was soaking wet from sweat and salt water. We got off the horse and just hung out for a while.

After a few minutes, we climbed back on, only this time it was my turn to sit in the saddle. We ran the horse up and down the beach just to see how fast he could run. We had not realized it but we were out riding for almost three hours. The horse was probably very tired at this point when Philly suggested we head back to the stable.

With Philly back in the saddle and me riding bareback again, the horse knew that we were heading back to the stable and he took off. He ran through the burnt grass at top speed. Philly had accidently dropped the reins and had absolutely no control of the big black Jet. He climbed over the saddle trying to grab the reins. The horse never slowed down. Philly was holding the horse around the neck while I was still on his back behind the saddle holding on for dear life. All of a sudden, my friend lost his grip and swung around under the horse's neck with his back facing the ground. The horse's shoulders were now hitting him as he continued to gallop at top speed. There was nothing either one of us could do but hold on. I was hoping that Philly would not fall off because the horse would trample him for sure. The horse could fall over him with me hanging on to the back of the saddle. I could go into orbit, or be crushed by the falling horse.

Jet never stopped until he reached the stable. The look on Henny Miller's face when we a pulled into the stall with one guy hanging from the horse's neck and another guy sitting on the back of the horse, was not very pleasant, it was rather mean! We thought he was going to kill us. Philly finally let go and fell into the hay. The poor horse was foaming from the mouth and soaking wet from sweat. Residue from the burnt brush was all over him and white salt from the bay stood out like a sore thumb over his beautiful black coat. I jumped off and ran like hell. Henny chased Philly out of the stable with a pitchfork.

A couple of days later we went back to the stable to try to rent a horse. Henny was still pissed off. He told us that his big black horse Jet had died in his stall that night. Then he ran us off.

Philly had another good idea! He said,

"Since Henny aint gonna rent us a horse we autta try to ride the donkey that hangs around the stables."

"Howda hell are we gonna do dat?"

"One of us stands on the hood of a car while the utta guy chases the donkey past the car. As he runs by all we gotta to do is jump on his back and ride him."

"Sounds good to me, let's try it."

Philly climbed on the hood of a car while I chased the donkey down the street. As the donkey passed the car, he leaped onto his back and rode him down the street until the donkey threw him off. "Wow! That was neat," I said; "now it is my turn to ride him." Philly had to run after the donkey and chase him back near the car. As he passed, I jumped on him and took a good ride. It turned out to be a pleasant day and it did not even cost us a quarter.

We let Henny Miller cool off for a while before we went back. When we did return, we brought a few more people with us to rent horses. Henny looked at all of us and figured why turn the two assholes away, and miss renting to all the other fellows, so he gave us all a horse to ride. By this time, I was getting to ride pretty well. This was a good opportunity to play Knights. Each fella found a stick and pretended it was a sword. We charged at each other and started dueling like Knights. My Lithuanian friend Johnny hit me in the face, I fell off the horse and had a bloody mouth but that was all part of the game. We did not stay out too much over an hour because we did not want to get Henny pissed off again.

The Teacher & the Bully: While attending classes At P.S 214, I had a teacher by the name of Mr. Gomez. He was a short bloke with black horn rimmed eyeglasses. He was kind of a nerd. I do not remember what he taught but that is not important.

This little turd had a thing going with none other than Angelo (Godzilla) the bully from Glenmore Ave. The two of them made for a good pair. Whenever someone pissed, Gomez off he would notify Godzilla who was in another class. After school, the chap that pissed off the turd had to take a whipping from Angelo. The students thought twice about messing up with the teacher, while

Angelo got his rocks off doing what he loved to do, bullying the smaller people.

One day I did something to get under the skin of Mr. Gomez. He told Godzilla to take care of me after school, and he did. I took a shellacking from him. After all, I was his favorite punching bag from the neighborhood. I was like a bonus for the big creep.

That night my father ask me how I got the marks on my face, so I explained to him what had happened. He asked me to give him the name of the teacher. I did. Now tell me the number of his classroom. The next morning I was sitting in class when the door opened, and who walks in but my father. He asked the teacher if he was Mr. Gomez. Gomez said, "Yes, how can I help you?" My dad asked him to step outside of the classroom for a moment. They both walked into the hallway. They were not out there for a few seconds before I got up to look in the hallway to see what was going on. My father had his hands around the nerd's throat while lifting him off the ground and pinning him against the wall. He told him.

"If you ever use a bully to keep my son in order, or for that matter, any other student in order, I will come back and rip you're friggin head off. Do you understand me?"

"Yes Mr. Borek, it will never happen again, I promise."

Dad put him down then went to work. Godzilla was now out of a job.

That evening when my father came home from work, I thanked him for taking care of the problem for me. I thought this would be a good time to ask him to go kick Angelo's ass too. My dad smiled at me and said, "I told you before I don't fight your battles for you. That is something you will have to take care of yourself." I remember looking at my mother as she turned a deaf ear and went about her business. Gomez changed his attitude towards the students after that little episode. I just sat there in his classroom and gave him *a smirk* every time he looked at me.

THE BALL: It was the start of another season and the boys of summer came out to play. The year was 1951 a beautiful spring day. My dad had me psyched up from the day before when he told me that we were going to watch the Brooklyn Dodgers play at Ebbets field.

Although I had been to Ebbets field many times before, today was special because it was going to be a day out with my father. I had been going to the ball park since I was 8 years old. In those days parents did not have to worry about their kids like they do today.

During those hot summer days in the nineteen forties a bunch of guys from the neighborhood would brown bag a lunch, generally a couple of cream cheese or peanut butter and jelly sandwiches, a piece of fruit, some candy, a baseball mitt and we were set to go.

The subway station was only a block from my house. It was Euclid Ave. the last stop in the IND line. My mom knew that I would be in good company because most of the guys were four or five years older than me. My cousin Anthony was one of the big guys and he would also be there to watch over me.

We knew that we had to switch trains when we got to Franklin Ave. None of us really knew how to get there. We knew that after Franklin Ave. all we had to do was follow the crowd. I remember going from a subway to the El. (The El was short for elevator train.) The train came from underground then and ran above ground.

We would always get there early so that we could hang out in the outfield bleachers to watch batting practice and try to shag a baseball that came into the stands. All of us had a great time. The thing I remember most vividly was when it was time to go home. No one was sure how to get there. When we came to the ball park we followed the crowd, which was easy because everyone was going to the same place. However, going home was another story; now, everyone was going to a different place. I never worried because I knew that the older guys would find the way home.

Well today I would not have a problem. My dad was a truck driver for United Parcel Service and he knew his way all around Brooklyn. When we arrived at the park my dad found our seats and told me to stay put because he had to go see a friend of his named Babe Hamberger. I remember asking him "Who the heck is Babe Hamberger?" "He's a guy I know, just hang out I'll be back in a while."

It wasn't long when he returned with a brand new baseball signed by the whole Brooklyn Dodger team. I asked. "Where did you get that?" He said that his friend Babe had given it to him. Wow I thought this Hamberger fellow must be some kind of a big shot.

Julius "Babe" Hamberger

Just, who was this guy? For so many years, I thought of Babe every time I looked at the ball. Whenever someone asked, where did you get that ball? I would tell them that my dad's friend Babe gave it to him at a Dodger game.

It was not until recently while looking at the ball. I thought; I will try looking up this person on the internet. It did not take long to find out who this mystery man was. "Click" Brooklyn Dodgers History. Walter O'Malley, and there he was, even a picture (shown above.)

Babe worked for the Dodger organization for 30 years. He was sort of a right hand man for Mr. O'Malley who at that time was the owner of the team. Hamberger did virtually everything for the Dodgers. He would greet and take care of the press and visiting dignitaries, ticket seller, ticket taker, turnstile boy, concessions employee, sweeper, scoreboard operator, groundkeeper, announcer, traveling secretary and clubhouse man. Babe also worked in several front office positions for the Dodgers.

Wow what a nice person to know. It was no big deal for a fellow with this much influence to get a baseball with all of the team players signatures. I still do not know how my father met Babe. Nevertheless, that is not important. The important thing is that I still have the ball.

As of today, many of the players have passed away. The most recent player to go was Duke Snider the center fielder. My dad did not hang around too much longer either. Seven years later he died.

I do not know if Babe is still kicking or if he is with Jackie Roy Duke and my dad. However, I have the ball and it brings back nice memories every time I take it out and look at it.

Brooklyn Eagle: The Brooklyn Eagle newspaper opened a depot on Crescent Street near Liberty Ave. They were looking for people to find new subscribers for a daily delivery. As a reward they were offering a baseball, a bat, or a glove depending on how many customers a guy could sign up for their newspaper.

When I heard about it, I hustled to the depot to get in on the action. I collected a bunch of blank applications, and then took off running to start looking for possible subscribers. I started in the larger buildings because it was easier knocking on every door in the building instead of going from house to house.

I signed up quite a few people on my very first attempt then returned to the store with the filled applications. They gave me a brand new baseball glove for my efforts. The next day I headed back to the store as soon as I got out of school to pick up some more blank applications, then headed for the apartment houses again. I did very well once more. This time I brought home a baseball bat and a baseball. I thought this was easy. It was like shooting fish in a barrel. When the weekend rolled around, I already had the blank applications in my possession and therefore, I got an early start. I worked on a technique, telling the people different crap to get them to sign up. After a couple of weeks, I had more equipment than I knew what to do with. I kept a few bats and balls, one lefty and one righty mitt. I watched my friend Cookie throw with both hands and I knew that if I practiced I could do it too. Therefore, I now had a lefty glove to place on my right hand so that I could practice throwing a baseball with my left hand. I wound up selling the rest of the stuff down at the park. It did not cost me anything but my time so I gave the boys a break on the price and wound up with a pocket full of jingles.

The people at the depot liked me because of all the new customers I signed up for them. I watched the delivery people come in to get the newspapers to deliver on their routes. I noticed there were many workers with bicycles, which they use to distribute their newspapers. They had a big canvas bag with the name Brooklyn Eagle printed on it, which they attached to the bicycle's handlebars. I thought to myself.

"I could do dat."
I asked the head honcho of the shop.
"How old do I gotta be to deliver papers?"
"Thirteen, why do ya want to know?"
"Because I wanna deliver the newspapers."
"How old are ya?"
"I am thirteen and a half, when can I start?"

Before I knew it, I had the job. I lied to the man; I was only eleven years old, but I was big for my age so he believed me. Besides, I knew he liked me. He saw how I hustled to get him new customers.

I had an old bike that my father had brought home. He picked it up while working for UPS; all I needed now was a canvas bag to carry the newspapers. The boss issued me a bag then, Bingo; I was now into another business. I still delivered orders for the Bohack grocery, while saving mungo on the side to trade in at the junk yard. With the occasional Saturday pickup of newspapers from the garbage pails, who had it better than me?

The dispatch fellow gave me a paper route almost a mile from my house. I told them that I knew the neighborhood and not to worry I could handle the route. I watched how the older workers folded the newspapers, tucking them together so they could throw them from the bicycle instead of getting off at every house. It looked simple enough, so I followed along and did what they did with each newspaper.

I loaded all of my daily papers and was on my way. I had a list with the names and addresses of each customer that was to receive a newspaper. When I reached my first house, I stopped the oversized bike I was riding to toss the paper onto the porch. As soon as the friggin thing left my hand, it opened up as if it had wings; the wind took it and blew all of the pages down the street. "What the hell was dat?" I said to myself. It was a good thing I took a couple of extra papers because there was no way I could have gathered all the pages.

I completed the first day of deliveries with only a couple of similar incidents, otherwise everything else went well, I thought! I continued to deliver the papers on my route for the rest of the week. On Sunday, I delivered the paper early in the morning. It was impossible to throw the paper because it was too big with all the advertisements and the funnies. On collection day, everyone hoped to get tips for their service. As I made my collections, quite a few customers claimed they did not receive the newspaper every day. I said, "How could dat be? I brought it here every day myself?" When I got back to the depot, they had also received complaints from the customers about missing papers. Therefore, my first week was a bust. I had to pay for the newspapers and I did not get any tips.

"OK one bad week outta the way, this is gonna be a better week." I learned how to fold the paper a little tighter for throwing it to the stoop. I also delivered the papers to every customer; I was ready for collection day. Then, damn it, the same result. I just finished another week of losing money, instead of making money. What am I doing wrong? I had better consult with my dad he will know what I am doing wrong.

My father took time to go with me on my route with his car. He held the address list in his hand while I tossed the papers. After a few tosses he yelled,

"Stop! Dat's not the right house."

"Watta ya mean, check the address."

"You got the correct address but, you're on the wrong block."

"Ya gotta be kiddin me?"

As it turned out, there were new houses build on two different blocks Milford Street and Montauk Ave. All the houses were identical. I was giving away free newspapers to phantom customers. "My dad could solve any problem."

I continued to deliver the Brooklyn Eagle for some time, but many of the customers were falling behind on their payments. People pretended not to be home on collection day or they came up with some poor ass excuse as to why they could not pay me. After a while, I found that it was not worth my time to do this any longer, so I gave back my ragged canvas bag and packed it in. I knew that something else would come along, besides I still had all my other gigs going for me.

Easter Plants: I must have been 11 years old when this incident occurred: Many people bought potted plants with colored flowers at Easter time. Along City Line on Liberty Ave. was a great place to sell plants because of the many shoppers. It was about a week before the holiday and I had time off from school. I saw this little man named Chickie. He was setting up a bunch of plants in front of a store next to the five and 10-cent store (Woolworths.) I approached him and asked if he needed any help. He said yes and told me that if I wanted to work for him, I could start by helping to unload his truck full of plants and set them in rows on the sidewalk. I jumped right to work following his lead.

No sooner did we have the plants set up, people started to buy them. Chickie told me the prices of the different plants so that I knew how much to charge the customers. The plants were selling like hot cakes. When the stores began to close for the evening, we placed all the plants down in the cellar of the store. Either Chickie knew the owner of the shop or he paid for the storage space. He told me to come back in the morning to set up again and start selling more plants. I told him that I would be back early.

"Wait." he said,

"Take off your shoes and socks."

"Why."

"So I could make sure you didn't hide any money in your shoes."

"What da hell do ya dink I am, a thief?"

"Just do it."

Therefore, I did, he saw I was clean and he let me go home.

I returned the next day and every day after that until Easter. I went through the same routine every day. Each time the boss went for coffee or something to eat, I had to empty my pockets and remove my shoes and socks. I was beginning to feel like a convict, but I stuck it out. We sold many plants. Chickie brought in another truckload of plants and we sold most of them. The day before Easter was the last day; Pay day! The stores began to close but there were still a bunch of plants left. That was not my problem. I told him that I had to go home and that he could pay me now. He told me to help myself to a couple of plants. I thought to myself wow he is a nice person after all, I could give them to my mother besides bringing home a whole weeks pay. I bent over, picked up two plants and thanked him. He looked at me and said,

"Goodbye."

"Watta ya mean goodbye, where's my pay?"

"I just paid you."

"What the hell are ya talkin about I didn't see any money."

"I just gave you two plants, Dat's your pay."

"Watta ya kiddin me? Dat is my pay after a week's work."

"Yeah now get adda here, scram."

"Scram? Who the hell do ya dink you're talkin to?"

I then took the two plants that I had in my hands, and threw one and hit him in the head with it and busted the window on his truck with the other one. I then continued to bust every pot with a plant in it that he had left sitting on the sidewalk. What a friggin mess I made on the street while many people watched. While he was holding his head, I shoved him into his truck and went home with nothing to show for my efforts but a little satisfaction. My mother told me, "let that be a good lesson for you. Before you start working for anyone in the future, make sure that both of you agree on a wage amount. Now get cleaned up, dinner is almost ready." I never told my mother what I did to Chickie or his plants. I knew better than to tell her the whole story. She would have done to me what I did to Chickie. Whenever I went to City Line I would see Chickie selling fruits or vegetables off his truck, I'd walk up to him, give him a *smirk* and watched him twitch. He never knew what I might do next. This gave me a little more satisfaction.

Lemon Ice: A few blocks from where the Easter plant incident took place, was a small lemon ice store. My friend Frankie Lorenzo's father made his own Ices and sold them from over a small counter that he made in his store. The Lorenzo family lived upstairs. The El. train passed overhead and Frankie, just like my friend Otto, could look into the train every time it passed.

The ices that Mr. Lorenzo made were not from shaved ice. He made the real Italian ice. The man was Portuguese and spoke with a little accent. Every time we passed the store, we would yell "Hey Mr. Lorenzo what kind of lemon ice ya got today?" No one called it Italian Ice. To all of us kids it was Lemon Ice. Lemon was the most popular flavor. He served it in a white throwaway paper cup. It had chunks of real lemons in it. He'd yell back, "I gotta Lemona, Cherry, Chocalata and Ou La-La." (Ou La-La was a mixture of everything he had left over,) and it was always a different color. The ice cost a nickel for a small cup and a dime for a large one. We would say, "Hey Mr. L give us the big cup with a little of each flavor and put in some extra, because we are Frankie's friends." He always gave us whatever we wanted. He was a good old man.

My friend Frankie had a nephew also named Frank. They both had the same last name and were the same age. To make matters worse, they attended the same school. Therefore, whenever any of the fellas spoke about either one of the Frankie's, the same question would always arise. Which one do you mean? "Now, this is typical Brooklyn." Neither one had a nickname but they each had a noticeable characteristic. One always wore his pants very high above his waist and the other fellow had a big head. Therefore, during a conversation all the boys used hand signals without any hesitation. They would either hold both hands around their head indicating a big head, or tapping above the waist similar to a salute to indicate the high pants. No one ever had a problem knowing which Frank was the subject of conversation. It was neat.

Roy: Across the street from the lemon ice store, was a corner bar and grill. Above it was an apartment where my friend Roy lived. Roy and I played a lot of ball together. There were all sorts of ball: stickball, baseball or even stoopball. We went to the same school and spent a lot of time together. If Roy looked out his bedroom window, he was able to look into the train just like my other friends Otto and Frankie.

Roy's mother was very strict. She would never hesitate to punish him or his younger brother Georgie at the drop of a hat. For any little reason his mom would not permit him to leave the apartment for several days after school, even on weekends. This made it tough on me too. It seemed that every time we had a game scheduled, the chap could not come out of the house. After a while, this got old. I talked with my friend about all the punishments he was receiving from his mom and how it interfered with our game time. I suggested that he have a sit down with her and ask if she would whack him instead of punishing him. After the licking, we could continue on our way. My friend was not too enthusiastic with my suggestion. He was afraid of having his mother hit him. I explained to him that it is not such a bad thing. "You learn to roll with the punches." Beside, you got a younger brother don't you?" I then went on to explain how his mom would probably stop hitting him once his little brother started to cry. I told him how it worked in my house. After a lot of silly questions that did not amount to a hill of beans, I told him to stop acting like a little candy ass and get with the program. Roy finally decided to have a sit down with his mom the next time she was about to punish him.

I do not remember what Roy did but it was judgment day. Soon after his mother announced sentence, he suggested that he get wacked instead. Well, this idea went over like a fart in a storm. Not only was he punished but his mom gave him a shellacking too. The next time I saw Roy he was rather pissed off at me for talking him into a sit down with his mom. I guess I could not blame the dude. After all, he wound up with a double whammy.

The Club House: My friends and I had built a clubhouse in the lot where the old farms once stood. It was not much to look at but it was a neat place to hang out, cook mickeys (potatoes) and tell jokes over burning candles.

A few of the fellas from Doscher Street decided to build one too. They picked a spot on a lot closer to Pitkin Ave. My friend Joey who lived on Doscher Street was a handy kid. His father was an electrician and was handy too and he taught his son how to build different things. They owned their own home with a tool shed in the yard. Joey lived across the street from the twins, so they were also a part of the new clubhouse project.

Their clubhouse turned out nice. Our crew, white hair Johnny the Lithuanian, Roy and a couple of other fellas and I, would go visit them occasionally. We'd cook a few mickeys, drink a soda and hang out. They in return, did the same thing at our place.

I cannot recollect what happened, but a fight broke out. We went back to our turf and made plans to retaliate. A couple of days later we set fire to their clubhouse and the friggin thing burned to the ground. It did not take a rocket scientist to figure out who did it. Joey came to our place and told us that tomorrow we should meet him at a neutral lot on Glenmore Ave. and we will settle this thing. We told them that we would be there after school at about three thirty.

This Joey dude was quite angry over what we did. He was a year older than we were and he knew numerous people from school. After school, we changed clothes and walked over to the lot, which had a big hole in it. It is the place where we did sleigh rides in the winter. As Johnny and I approached the hole there were about a dozen people standing there waiting for us. As soon as they saw us, Joey yelled out "There they are get em." They came charging up the hill. I could never figure out why, but I started to laugh. Johnny grabbed me by the arm and yelled, "RUN." We took off in a flash, headed down to Chestnut Street, and then turned towards Pitkin Ave. I continued to laugh while being chased. Johnny looked at me and said "I'm not gonna get caught, I'm adda here." This fellow could out run anyone in the neighborhood. He ran at top speed leaving me in the dust. As I reached the corner of Pitkin Ave. and Chestnut Street, they caught me right in front of Cordy's Tavern. Wham-Bam. There I lay on the concrete floor, everyone punching and kicking me. I held my arms over my head to protect my face. I was beginning to feel like a Piñata when an old woman with an umbrella started screaming, "Stop!-Stop." The Good Samaritan even swung the umbrella at them a couple of times. Finally, they stopped and began to walk away. I got up and thanked the woman for her help. To this day, I still cannot figure out why I started to laugh. I received many cuts and bruises and my clothes ripped. When I met up with Johnny, he asked me why I started to laugh. I said, "Who the hell knows." However, payback is a Bitch.

The Court House: Not far from my house was a courthouse. On occasion, I went there to watch court cases. It did not cost anything to get in and it was entertaining. I looked at it as though I was going to the movies with a free ticket. Besides being entertaining it was also educational.

I was outside the courthouse one morning where they brought in the criminals; I was with my friend Red. The police were bringing a criminal into the courthouse for a hearing before the judge. It was sort of like coming attractions. Anyway, this big black dude was in the back of a pie wagon. "A pie wagon is a name given to the trucks that transport prisoners." The truck stopped and a guard told the fellow to come out. The dude was hand cuffed. As he attempted to exit the truck, he smashed his head against the top of the door and fell on his ass while still being in the cuffs. At that point, we started to laugh at what had just happened. The poor fella was in pain and with us laughing, it was like throwing salt on the wound.

When they finally got him up on his feet and out of the truck, he stared at us with a real mean look. I could not blame the fellow. I would have been pissed off too. We watched a couple of cases before Mr. Bump on the head came before the judge. When he came out and saw us smiling at him, once again it pissed him off even more. I do not remember the outcome of his case, but as I said, it can be very entertaining.

The Hangout Corner: The corner of Pitkin Ave. and Crescent Street became a regular hang out for many people. It was across the street from the P.S. 159 schoolyard where we all spent many hours playing sports.

After playing, everyone went to the candy store located on that corner. The proprietors were a husband and wife, Abe and Evelyn. It had a counter with stools and some additional seating in the rear. They made different flavors of soda and egg creams form a tap that dispensed carbonated water. We'd order a chocolate soda, drink half then tell Abe that the drink needs more seltzer. He filled the glass to the top. After drinking about half again, we told him it needed more syrup. He knew we were breaking his balls and threw us out of his store.

This was a busy street. Just diagonally across the street, there stood another candy store owned by Mr. Ratner. Adjacent to the candy store was a delicatessen that sold Hot Pastrami and Corn beef sandwiches, hot dogs and Knishes amongst other good Deli food. Along Pitkin Ave., there was a Jewish bakery. Next to, it was a Hardware store, owned by the Asner brothers. Next, there was a big grocery store also owned by Jewish people. After that, was a bar and grill called Louie Sprung. Louie owned the joint. A pizza place opened next to Louie's bar. The people from the Pizza place also owned the Euclid Taxi, located just around the corner on Pine Street; the taxi stand was a storefront with all kinds of limousines and half ass taxicabs. A Mafia crew from the Lucchese crime family owned and operated the business. It was very convenient because it was only one block from the subway station. This is where Henry Hill got his start as a delinquent. He lived only a half a block from the taxi stand. Pitkin Ave. had many apartment buildings about five or six stories tall. I knew many people from those buildings.

When the weather was nice, you could always find a bunch of fellows standing on the corner or breaking Abe's balls inside the candy store. Everyone always had something to talk about, sports, jokes or some silly ass story, never a dull moment at the corner. When it came to talking baseball, I imagine it was the same conversation as in every other neighborhood. We had three Major League baseball teams in New York. The boys rooted for different teams. There was always an argument when it came to who was the best center fielder: Duke Snider of the Brooklyn Dodgers, Willie Mays of the N.Y. Giants or Mickey Mantle of the N.Y. Yankees.

Some of the fellows were good with the jokes and rhymes, for instance:

There once was a guy named Skinner who brought a gal to dinner,
But Skinner he was no beginner; Skinner was inner before dinner.

There was a young man from Mass, who had two balls made of brass.
When he rubbed them together, it caused stormy weather, and lightning shot out of his ass.

These kinds of antics went on all the time. There were many ranking contests too. When it got late and almost time to go home someone would pull a prank. The candy store always had many people coming in and out. The front door had a heavy-duty hasp for a padlock, for the evening lockup. Some clown would jam a stick through the hasp, which then locked everyone into the store. Abe became very angry. However, what could he do? Everyone left the corner, and the customers could not get out of the store.

Occasionally a new person came to hang out at the corner. He'd try to fit in with all the antics and be one of the boys. All the gang knew of the normal stunt we pulled on a new person, and everyone played their part. After someone told a few jokes and the new fellow chimed in on the laughter, someone told a joke that was not a joke at all. The new fella listened attentively. The joke teller then ended with the phrase, "no soap radio." At that point, everyone started to laugh. The new comer hesitated for a moment then join in on the laughter. This is when it got funny because there was actually nothing funny about the joke. As the new fella looked at everyone laughing harder, he did the same. This made everyone laugh even harder. No one was laughing at the joke, but at the poor sole who didn't know what the hell he was laughing at in the first place.

This little Jewish dude by the name of Manny went to our school and wanted to be part of the crowd. Manny was ready to do just about anything to fit in with us. The poor fellow was a misfit and just did not belong. One day my friend Red told him to come with him across the street to the Deli.

"Look in the window" he told Manny.
"Do you see all those potato knishes lying on the grill?"
"Yeah I do."
"If ya wanna hang out with us ya gotta pass a little test."
"Watta I have to do?"
"You gotta eat a knish then run around the block."
"Dat's it?"
"Well, it's not quite that simple. You gotta eat every one of those things on the grill and run around the block each time."

There must have been at least a half a dozen of those belly whoppers lying there on the grill.

"We will pay for the knishes all ya gotta do is eat dem and run."

One knish is about all the average person could eat but Manny agreed to try it. The rest of the fellows from the corner chipped in for the knishes, they would do anything for a laugh. After about an hour and a half Manny was holding his stomach in pain. Imagine all that friggin potato bouncing around in his stomach while he ran. When he finish we all gave him a hand and congratulated him for what he had accomplished. The Deli owner was happy because he sold all his knishes. Manny was thrilled that he was now one of the guys and we were all glad too because we now had someone to pull more future pranks on.

A few of us were standing on the corner of Euclid and Pitkin avenues just before rush hour. Little Manny was with us, and acting like a nitwit trying to make us laugh. Finally, Red and I looked at each other and together we lifted him up, placed him in a large wire wastebasket ass first, then pushed him down. The little fella folded in half and tried to scream but not much came out of his mouth. All you could hear was a little sound "Help, please help me." The crowded train stopped and the passengers poured out of the cars, ran up the stairways throwing newspapers into the basket on top of the already camouflaged Manny. A couple of people threw chewing gum and one fellow hocked a yogi (spit a snot ball.) on him. Just before he was ready to pass out, we pulled him out of the basket and told him to behave himself. "Imagine us, telling him to behave himself?"

One of my famous hoaxes' was to stand on the corner with the gang and nonchalantly pull from my pocket a box of Chiclet chewing gum. I'd take the top two pieces, throw them in my mouth and begin chewing. As soon as the gang saw that I had chewing gum, they all put out their hands so that I could give them a piece. Naturally I obliged them by giving everyone with his hand out a couple of the little candy coated squares. Little did they know that I had previously exchanged all the Chiclets in the box with FEEN-A-MINTS, (a chewing gum type laxative.) except for the top two pieces, which I was chewing? It took a couple of days until one brave sole admitted that he could not figure out how he had suddenly shit in his pants. Occasionally another fella chimed in and admitted that he also engaged in the mishap. It was entertaining to listen to them trying to back track about what they may have eaten together within the last few days, which may have caused this accident. This was not something I pulled off too often and I have never told anyone what I did. How could I? However, it felt good to knock the crap out of a bunch of guys without throwing a punch.

Suddenly one afternoon Henry Hill showed up on the corner all decked out in a Paratroopers uniform. Spit shined boots, tucked in trousers, the whole Enchilada. I knew he went into the Army but I never expected him to become a member of the Special Forces. I should not have been surprised because both he and his brother Joey were athletic. He was very proud of his accomplishment. I often thought that he should have made a career of the military.

P.S.159 was a red brick building five or six stories high. Each of the corners of the building had a brick design called quoins. Quoins are a pattern in which brick sticks out about one inch from the rest of the brick building. One day my brother decided to scale up the building like Spiderman, using the quoin pattern as a ladder. I do not know if he did it on a dare or he just wanted to see how far up the building he could climb.

It did not take too long to get the attention of people passing by. He must have been at about the third floor when a fire truck pulled up which was summoned by one of the neighbors. The firefighters extended the tall ladder from the truck and proceeded to remove him from the building. I do not doubt it if the firefighter recognized him after getting him down as one of the kids that hung out at the firehouse. As I said, there was always some action going on at the street corner.

A couple of months before the Fourth of July you could always hear firecrackers going off. As the holiday got closer, everyone looked to buy fireworks. I knew that I could purchase them in the China Town section of Manhattan, at a cheap price. I talked to my friend Johnny one day and asked him if he wanted to make a trip to China Town and deal with the Chinks. He said.

"No Way!"

"Tell me, why not?"

"Because I dink it's too dangerous."

"Watta ya mean too dangerous. What are ya afraid of?"

"I heard stories about people going there and getting beat up and robbed." I laughed and told him.

"My mother has been going to Manhattan for years and no one ever mugged her."

"Dat's because she bought clothing and dealt with the Jews, besides we don't know anyone in China Town. We also gotta travel thru Bedford Stuyvesant that bad black area."

"Ahh, dat is a bunch of crap. You don't gotta know anybody, when we get dare we'll meet people, trust me? We will try it once without looking to buy too much and see how it goes OK"?

"Ehh I don't know."

"Come on; we could sell everything we buy, den we go back wit the profits and buy twice as much. We will make some easy money."

Pause.

"Dink about it, if ya decide not to go, den I'll go by myself."

I must have been pretty convincing because it did not take him long to make up his mind.

"OK, count me in!"

Shortly afterwards we pooled our money, dropped a couple of matchbook covers into the transfer box at the subway turnstile for a free ride and we were off to China town.

Buying firecrackers in China town was a piece of cake. We were just two American dudes hanging out. It did not take too long before some Chink asked us if we wanted to buy fireworks. We made our purchase and went back to Brooklyn. My friend was happy and he looked forward to our next trip to Manhattan. We did this a few times before the holiday and wound up with money in our pockets and we had a bunch of free fireworks to shoot off on Fourth of July.

At the corner of Pitkin Ave. and Euclid Ave. was a subway station. There was a set of concrete stairways going down to the turnstiles at each of the four corners. Then, before going down another flight of stairs to the train platform, there was a small booth where an old man sold tokens to deposit in the turnstile.

Several hours after rush hour things got very quiet. I got the bright Idea one night to pull off a great prank. Johnny and I still had a large box of cherry bombs, which we bought in China Town. Cherry bombs are the size of a large cherry, red in color with a fuse sticking out. These things were powerful. One cherry bomb could blow apart a mailbox, and they were extremely loud. We took along a couple of more people to the train station, gave them each a couple of cherry bombs and placed a person at the top of each stairwell. At the signal, everyone lighted a couple of cherry bombs each and threw them down onto the landing where the token both was located. The friggin things blew up almost at the same time causing an enormous explosion. The sound echoed through the tunnel. It traveled to Shepard Ave., the next train station and upstairs into the street. The poor man that was selling tokens had to have shit in his pants. Moments later, he came staggering up the stairway holding his head. He got to the top and just sat there. He did not have a clue of what just happened. Everyone on the street corner spoke about that incident for a long time afterwards. As I think back, it was not really a great idea after all. The poor man could have had a heart attack and died. However, these are stories I remember from the street corner in Brooklyn.

The Feast: Every year at the end of the summer, many of the churches held a feast. Saint Genarro in Manhattan is a biggie. The church always celebrates this feast in the city streets of Little Italy with tens of thousands of people that attend. Food tents are set up on both sides of many city blocks. There was music and gambling too. I recall the statue of Saint Genarro. The folks carried it through the streets in a parade while many of them pinned money on the adorned statue. I guess it made them feel good.

Back in Brooklyn, we also had a feast that was set up in empty lots along side of the Saint Fortunata church. This feast was not as big as the Saint Genarro's was. However, thousands of people attended each year. One of the big attractions was the Grease Pole. A large wooden pole was set up in the ground and then covered in grease. On the top of the pole was a prize for anyone that could climb to the top of the pole to claim it. This was not easy. Many people formed teams who were dressed in old clothes. After many days, most of the grease wore off because of the many attempts to climb the pole. Eventually someone won the prize.

There was also lots of ethnic music played, mostly Italian. My grandmother use to go up on a stage with a pair of castanets in her hands, she sang and danced to the music, while entertaining the crowd. Everyone enjoyed the different kinds of food, like Italian sausage with peppers and onions, Calzones and Pizza. People gambled at the many different booths, and won prizes at other booths while the church raked in the cash.

One night while attending the feast with a couple of my friends, I played a game where if you threw a Ping-Pong ball into a gold fish bowl, you won the fish and the bowl. The game cost about a quarter to play. I played and won. Upon our way home, we ran into this fella named Rizzo. He stopped me and asked,

"Hey, what's in the bowl?"

"Gold fish."

"Let me see dem"

I thought to myself.

Dem? I only have one small fish in the bowl, so I played along with him.

"Rizzo, do ya like dem?"

"Yeah" while starring at the fish.

"I'd like to get dem for my kid."

"I'll sell dem to you for fifty cents each and I will give you the bowl free."

"OK." He says and hands me a buck.

The poor fellow probably had bad eyesight. I am sure that when he got home his wife told him there was only one gold fish in the bowl. After that, every time I saw Rizzo I crossed to the other side of the street. The feast went on for many years until the neighborhood began to change. The good times ended because fights broke out every night. People got hurt while trying to have a good time. Eventually, the church cancelled the feast forever.

The End Is Near. *How East New York Became a Ghetto.*

We the people, who lived in this area of Brooklyn, saw a change beginning to take place gradually, in the mid-1950s. We saw the population from mostly working class Italians, Jewish, and Irish residents, to residents of Puerto Rican and African descent. Property owners and Real Estate agents played a significant role in the downturn of the area. Puerto Ricans were moving in masses to New York City at a time when unemployment rates in Puerto Rico soared to 25 percent, and left their island on the brink of poverty.

The construction of public housing projects in East New York further contributed to its decline. Corrupt managers and contractors built many of the developments. At the time, the city government largely ignored the community when it could have helped turn it around.

Block Busting:
Block by block the unscrupulous mortgage originators scared the elderly Jewish homeowners who lived in tiny, modest, one family home into selling below market. They feared their homes would be worth nothing at all, as the blacks moved into their neighborhood. Neighboring Brownsville "Home of Heavy Weight champ, Mike Tyson," was a good example as the displacement began for the future urban renewal. These

same block-busting brokers then resold these homes at a greatly inflated price to first time black homeowners who believed their American dream had come true. The brokers provided fraudulent documentation on the loans, which were all beyond the ability of the new homeowners to pay given their modest incomes. The brokers made an effort to find the lowest grade in addition, filthiest new buyers they could find, just to intimidate all the other Jewish, Italian and Irish homeowners into selling their homes. In due time, the neighborhood went from 100% elderly Caucasians to 100% black and Hispanic and in no time, the new homeowners were behind on mortgage payments and losing their homes to foreclosure. East New York became a wasteland, row after row of vacant homes in poor condition, in a central four or 6-block area of vacant land, once owned and occupied by decent people.

Life went on as usual. The transformation did not take place over night. However, gradually we saw homeowners leaving the area. It was an uncomfortable feeling to know that a long time neighbor could pull up stakes in a flash, move out and your new neighbor was an undesirable family. This very event was common. Neighbors promised neighbors that they would never sell their house to a black family. At first, we believed them, but after many betrayals, we learned not to trust anyone. As time passed, many events took place in our neighborhood that makes for interesting stories. However, for now, I hung out with my friends and attended school.

The Stroke: My father was a big man with a pair of arms on him that could tear you apart. While still working for UPS pop had a stroke at home. He lost the use of his hand and leg on one side, could not speak very well and his face was twisted. The poor guy was in bad shape. It was very sad to see him in this condition. We had to feed him in bed and help take him to the toilet. He was a very proud man and yet, was completely helpless. Mom tried to assist him to the bathroom but he was too heavy. I heard her crying during the night, I jumped out of bed to find her lying under him pinned against the wall. This happened more than once. As a teenager, I struggled to lift him off her, and then walked him to the bathroom. I knew that he was embarrassed, so I tried to console him and tell him how much we loved him and we are here to help him. The poor fella would just nod. This went on for quite some time. I do not know why he did not go to a hospital.

Christmas time came. My dad signaled me to get a box that he had put away in a closet some time ago. When mom came in, he gave it to her, wished her a Merry Christmas and tried to hug her. She opened the box and started to cry. The present was a bracelet with white stones on it. When it opened, it was a watch. I still have it put away. Somehow, after that day, Christmas to me was never the same. After all these years the Christmas season brings back that sad time in my life. I feel like it was something that I could have done without as a young boy. However, things could have been worse.

Dad was a fighter; he got well again, regaining his speech and the use of both hands and legs. He got a job with a beer company for a short time delivering barrels and cases of beer to the taverns. Pop was strong again, lifting the barrels from the truck and toss them around. We were all proud of him. I do not know why he never went back to work for UPS. However, I remembered him telling my mother some time ago that he was tired of hauling heavy furniture up stairways. Who could blame him?

The Bar & Grill: I guess my father got the idea from delivering beer to the taverns, because he told mom that he would like to own his own place. It was not long after, they purchased the bar and grill business from Abe and Benny Shultz. It was located on the corner of Glenmore Ave. and Crescent Street. They changed the name to F&L Bar & Grill. This was the bar where I watched baseball games when I was a safety guard at P.S. 159.

My mother felt that it was important that she adhere to my father's wishes, after all, nineteen years of hauling furniture up into buildings especially after a stroke was enough for any man to endure. Both my brother and I had managed to save money in our school bank accounts throughout the years. We did not have much according to today's standards, but it had added up as we put away our nickels and dimes and all the odd jobs that I did. My folks told us that they were going to use our savings to help purchase the new business. We said, "Sure mom, take it." She told us that someday she would pay it all back to us. Both Billy and I were glad that we could help them.

The Bar and Grill business was something new for both my parents. My father was the type of person who thought everything that he did in the business, should follow the rules in the book. There were ABC rules, (Alcoholic-Beverage-Control) that issued licenses to business owners. You can only imagine the list of dos and don'ts these people had on the books. For example, In order to allow dancing on the premises you had to have a cabaret license. There was a jukebox in the joint. Occasionally after having a few drinks, someone got up and started to dance. My father would immediately put a stop to it, claiming that he had no license for dancing. When my mother saw him pull a stunt like that, there was always an argument, but not in front of the customers. Mom would ask him "What the hell is wrong with you? The people came here to have some fun don't be a kill joy." She had a completely different business view about so many things. "Let them do whatever the hell they want, they are spending money and that's the name of the game." She was sharp. She always came up with good ideas to draw in customers.

There was a kitchen in the back of the place. She often placed a big sign in the window that read *FREE ROAST BEEF SANDWHICHES SAT. NIGHT.* Most of the local people came in for a sandwich and a few drinks. The place had a license to sell hard liquor too. They played shuffleboard on the long table that was located in the rear of the place. The jukebox played continuously. She did the same thing for various holidays. On Saint Patrick's Day free corned beef and cabbage was on the menu. She had a knack for packing the joint with customers. Mom use to say "Let the good times roll."

The local cops hung out in the bar. They stopped in for lunch and again after work. Therefore, I knew all the cops. They liked my parents very much. I remember this big Irish cop by the name of Eddie Fritz. He usually walked the beat along Pitkin Ave. Fritz was a tough guy. He never took any crap from anyone. All the hoodlums were afraid of him. He thought nothing of whacking them in the ass with his nightstick. When Eddie decided to retire my folks gave him a party at the bar. They presented him with his nightstick, which they had dipped in gold paint. Fritz continued to hang out with his old friends at the bar even after his retirement from the police force.

My Little Gym: The cold kegs of beer were stored in a big walk in refrigerator in the cellar of the bar. The kegs had pipes, which brought the cold fresh beer upstairs through the different tap handles, which signified the brand of beer it would draw. The tap handles were located behind the big wooden bar where the customers sat and drank.

In the rear of the cellar, was an extremely small area, which my father allowed me to set up equipment to do physical workouts. I got the old spring workout set from the bin in the cellar at home. One of my uncles gave it to me when I was very young. I also had a punching bag, but never had a place to use it. I began to teach myself how to work out with the bag. I became very good at it. Dad encouraged me to spend time downstairs getting into good physical condition. I spent a lot of time in my little so-called gym. I was thankful to have something like this for myself; I felt like a very fortunate kid.

I always stopped to see my dad and let him know that I was going downstairs to work out. He usually had a bunch of customers at the bar. He'd tell me OK have a good workout. About an hour later upon leaving the gym I noticed that he was all alone at the bar puffing on a cigar. I asked him,

"Pop, does the punching bag make too much noise for the customers?" He nodded his head and said, "No, you can't hear a ding. They left because they had utter dings to do."

"OK pop, I'll see ya later."

A friend of mine came down to the gym one day. He was punching the bag when I walked upstairs to use the rest room. "Holy Mackerel" I said, "Dat friggin ding makes a lot of noise up here." After that, I rarely hit the bag anymore. I knew that my father did not want to deprive me of using that little space in the cellar. He did not own a home of his own where I would have been able to do these things. I was not naïve. I realized what he was doing. I never wanted to embarrass him, so when he asked me why I do not punch the bag anymore, I told him that the thing does not hold air and one day I will get it fixed. Man, you gotta love the guy!

Odd Jobs:  Wintertime came again and so did the snow. This was always a good time to make a few bucks shoveling the snow off sidewalks and driveways. I would start on my own block first, remembering the lesson I learned from Chickie the Easter plant salesperson on City Line. I made sure to agree on a wage with each person before starting any job. The same thing went for digging a car out of the snow. I always found work at the churches. They had large sidewalk areas and paid by the hour instead of by the job. The people at the church were always good for the money. Although, I always made it clear as to just how much my hourly wage was before starting work. "Thank you Chickie!"

Whenever it snowed, there were always many snowball fights. If I was not throwing a snowball at someone, I was trying to hit a sign or a pole. As it turned out, this was bad for my throwing arm. It became sore from throwing in the cold weather. At the time, I thought nothing of it, but as time marched on, I was doing damage to my arm. Major league baseball pitchers always wrap their arm in a towel and wear a jacket on cool days between innings. They do this for a reason, to protect their arm from injury.

As the neighborhood began to change, some of the stores began to close up too. Bohack, our local grocery was one of the stores that closed for good. This meant that I had to look for something else to keep generating monies. I went to speak with the Jewish owner of the grocery store on Pitkin Ave. where I hung out. I told him that I had been delivering orders for the Bohack store for a long time. I explained to him that I was reliable, honest and a clean cut kid. I told him that I could help around the store if he allowed me to make all of his deliveries. He bought the pitch I gave to him and gave me the job. Bam! I was back in action. This grocery store had many customers that were closer to the taller apartment buildings with no elevators. Many Jewish people did not like walking up all those stairways with bundles of groceries. However, I did not mind doing it. The average tip was ten to fifteen cents. I knew I would not become rich but I always had money in my pocket and I continued to buy little gifts for my mother.

The Buccaneers: As soon as the warm weather returned, I began playing baseball again. My father always found time to pitch to me across the street on Glenmore Ave. The friends I played with wanted to put together a team. This seemed like a great idea. Other teams around the city were always looking to play another new team. It would take a lot of work but if everyone was serious about it, we could do it.

There were many good ball players around and many mediocre players. What we really needed was someone to organize and manage us. I told my dad what we were trying to do. He seemed interested. He told me to let him know when the boys would be getting together to play ball. I told him when and where and he showed up at the field. He just hung around and watched everyone hit, throw and catch. I introduced him to all the ball players. He already knew some of them but there were many that he had never met before.

After that day, my dad invited everyone to meet in the back of the bar. He also invited an older neighbor who lived across the street from us. His name was John. He had a good knowledge of baseball. The meeting went well. John and my dad came down to the sandlot the next time we gathered to play. They got involved right away, hitting fly balls to the outfielders and grounders to the infielders. Things began to take shape. The men worked at picking players for each position. Other people heard what was taking place and they came down to try out for the team. It did not take long before we had booked a game against another team. We held meetings in a back room of the bar. It had many tables and chairs and dad gave everyone nonalcoholic drinks with chips and pretzels.

Pop suggested that we make up raffle books to sell in order to generate money to buy uniforms. We did, and soon after, we selected a name for the new team. They took measurements for a new baseball uniforms. The name of the team written across the front said "*BUCCKANEERS.*" On the sleeve was a patch of a pirate. We played many games that year. Most played on the small field at Euclid Park. Then one day the men managed to schedule a Sunday game on the big diamond. The name of the team that we played that day was the Cardinals. Their uniform was similar to the Saint Louis Cardinals in the National league.

What an amusing day it turned out to be with lots of people in the stands and all of us decked out in our baseball uniforms. We even had a real umpire. We lost the game that day, but it did not matter. We had played on the big diamond. I had previously played on the big field when I made the All Star team. While I played the position of a catcher, the opposing team found it easy to steal second base off me. I realized then, that I had a weak throwing arm. The ball players from the other team were yelling from the dugout "Chicken Arm." I felt hurt, but I could do nothing about it. It is the same thing when it comes to running. If you are not fast, you are just not fast. You can practice all you want. You may improve a little but you will never be fast. However, that is what separates the professionals from everyone else. That is why they make it to the major leagues. Because they have, all of what it takes to be the best.

My father was happy to be a part of the whole thing. He often spoke to me about trying out for the High school team. He had dreams of me becoming a professional baseball player. I must admit he put a lot of work into it too. I tried explaining to him that in order to go Professional; you must be exceptional at four things: Fielding, Throwing, Hitting and Running. I knew that I had a poor throwing arm and I was not a fast runner. However, my pop seemed to overlook these very important things. I believe he was wishing me success.

One evening we had a baseball club meeting at my friend Tommie's house on Crescent Street. After the meeting while walking down the street, a gang of hoodlums approached us. For absolutely no reason they picked a fight with us. None of the ball players was prepared for this. I knew just about all of these hoods and most of my teammates did too. One gang member named Gerry had a piece of 2x4 lumber about six feet long in his hand. He began swinging it at us. Everyone scattered in different directions. Gerry decided that I would be his Piñata. Blow after blow he continued to strike me. He hit me in the back of both my legs then across my back, across both my arms and then in the stomach. I was defenseless. When he thought that, he had done enough damage he stopped hitting me and ran after someone else.

One of my teammates, a little fella by the name of Joey stayed with me. He helped me up from the ground and assisted me to walk towards my home. I was in a lot of pain I could feel swelling everywhere; Joey managed to get me to my house and up the stairs. As I entered the apartment, my parents were sitting in the living room waiting for me to return home from the meeting. My father asked. "What the hell happened to you?" My friend explained to him what had just taken place. "Take your shirt off and drop your trousers," my dad said to me. As he looked at my body all beaten and bruised with big lumps he became outrageous. "Who did this to you?" he asked. "I will kill the son of a bitch." He used other curse words, which I had never heard from his mouth before. "Joey, are they still out there?" I had never seen him this mad in my life. Here was a man who never came out to defend his son in a battle, and now he was so furious that he was ready to kill someone. This scared me. I told Joey not to tell him who did this to me. I knew that I would heal but what my father was prepared to do would be awful. Things would become a lot worse than they were now. After a while, both my parents calmed down. Joey left the house. My parents packed ice on the swells to try to bring them down. My father questioned me about that night many times, but I never told him anything more that he had learned the first night.

My Analogy

There is something valid about the *NEED TO BELONG*. For different reasons a lot of people, have to join a gang. Some needed to belong because there is a lack of love in their home and they desired someone to want them. Some just have to belong to something. It could be a club, a team or a gang. People like power, some feel joining a gang gives them power. They find that there is power in numbers. Others have to build a reputation. This is extremely important to them. They need to stand out from the rest. It is a 'must' to be in the lime light and always be at the center of attraction. There is a drastic need for attention. In addition, some will seek this at anyone's expense. Hurting someone, causing physical damage in front of other gang members and bystanders builds their reputation while it fills their ego. Going to gang fights against other gangs are a big part of their life. Imagine going to another neighborhood to fight with people that you do not know. They do serious damage to strangers just so they can talk and brag about it.

Then, there are the "Wannabe's." These little turds will hang around and kiss ass just to be near them. They are mostly weak and spineless but they feel that power in number. It is very important to the wannabes, that other people see them with the gang members. It gives them the feeling of being important.

The Schoolyard: Was always busy with people playing sports since they did not lock the gates anymore. During a game of softball, a bunch of gang members came running into the schoolyard. They threw all kinds of weapons over the fence into an adjacent empty lot. There were knives, chains, clubs and zip guns. The ball players knew these people from the neighborhood and went to school with them. Therefore, they tossed them a glove allowing them to infiltrate with everyone in the schoolyard. When the police entered the yard searching for them, it was hard to tell them apart from the ball players. This was a common occurrence.

One fellow that played baseball with us on the Buccaneers decided that he wanted to quit the team and become a gang member. I tried to talk him out of it but he insisted on leaving the team. He was a tough kid and was one of those people that craved a reputation as a tough guy. It was not long after joining the gang that they all went to a gang fight in another neighborhood. While we stood on the street corner doing the usual crap, a bunch of the gang members came running down the street. My friend ran up to me and said, "I've just been stabbed in the back." I pulled up his shirt to look. Sure enough, there was a hole in his back from a knife wound and blood was coming out dripping down into his paints. "Come on" I said, "I'll take you home."

I tried once again to get him to quit hanging out with these crazy dudes and come back to playing baseball. "Forgetaboutit" It was like talking to the friggin wall.

This was like a feather in his cap, He was becoming notorious and this was more important to him than any baseball team.

Another one of my good friends, Roy, decided that he also wanted to become part of the gang. He became impressed when they all got a tattoo on their arm of a crescent moon with a star. This was to signify that you were an official member of the Crescents. They took the name from Crescent Street. This is where they hung out. At the schoolyard one day, Roy thought he would show them that he had what it takes to become a part of their crew. Roy got into a fight with a short stocky gang member by the name of Georgie. The fight took place on the concrete at home plate. Roy literately got his ass whipped. Georgie had him down on the ground and punched the living daylights out of him. Roy was full of blood. Georgie got up from the ground and continued kicking him, in the back, the head and his stomach. I just stood there and watched. It hurt to see my good friend take such a beating. I later asked him if he still wanted to belong to the gang, and do, you want to inflict on other people the pain Georgie just gave to you. "If you do then you are a bigger jerk than I thought you were." Roy made up his mind right there. "No!" he answered. I helped him get up and wash the blood off.

Eddie Fritz: On occasion Eddie Fritz the cop walked into the schoolyard looking for this person named Robbie. Robbie had the reputation as a ruthless fighter. He was truly a tough person. He'd think nothing of grabbing a fella in a headlock and running him head first into the corner of a brick wall and splitting the poor fella's head open. His biggest aim in life was to become public enemy number one, and he was well on his way. Eddie would corner Robbie against a brick wall and beat the shit out of him, then ask him if he still thought he was a tough guy. Robbie took his lumps then left the schoolyard.

The police became familiar with all of the gang members. Besides, they were easy to spot with the crescent tattoo. On occasion, the cops blocked the entrance to the schoolyard with their police cars. If I were in the schoolyard, they would tell me to leave immediately. They would gather the gang members and question them about something they thought they were involved. Who knew what they had been up to prior to the shake down? The cops roughed them up, later they met at my father's place for a few beers.

In the hot summer, we went to Rockaway beach for a swim. I usually hitch hiked to the beach. There were always many people driving there, so if you held out a towel and a thumb someone was sure to give you a ride. Gangs were everywhere. One day at the beach a fight broke out on the boardwalk between two rival gangs. It did not take long for the police to arrive and to break it up. I saw a fella running when a glass bottle went flying and hit him square in the back of the head. It was nothing like in the movies. His head split open and blood flew everywhere. I also watched a cop run a fellow down and crack open his head with a baton. Another name is Blackjack. This is a piece of lead covered with leather with a handle on it. The dude fell in his tracks. The cop knocked him out cold. After a few minutes, the cops had everything under control. "It was just another day at the beach."

Street maps were easy to get. You could pick one up at any gas station free. Sometimes a couple of my friends and I looked on a map for a blue spot. This indicated water. We'd brown bag a lunch and hitch hike to our destination. When there were a few people, we'd stake a wager and race to see who could get there first. It was nice to get out of the city and always an adventure how we got there. Occasionally we hitched a ride from a fag. All the fellas were street smart and knew how to handle situations like this. Therefore, no one ever got involved with the gay dudes. We found lakes and waterways in lots of different places. By the time, we got to where we were going we could not wait to jump in the water and go for a swim.

The New Bicycle: Upon receiving conformation, at the age of thirteen, "Which is a Catholic milestone," my parents bought me a brand new Schwinn bicycle. It had a bright red frame and chrome fenders. It was a beautiful bike. I thought it was the greatest thing since sliced bread. I was elated. "Man, who had it better than me? I am now officially THE RITZ."

My parents asked the landlord for permission to keep it down in the cellar. I parked that bike in the cellar each night and kept a fresh coat of polish on it. It also had whitewall tires. I kept them bright white. I could not believe that I owned such a great bike. I rode that thing just about every day except when it was raining. I pedaled it everywhere; I even went to Ebbets field. I found out that if I got there at the seventh inning, they would allow me to go into the ballpark free. I bought a chain and a lock then Brooklyn Dodgers here I come. I rode the bike up the ramp chained it to a column, grabbed a seat and watch the last couple of innings. Then off I went for the long ride home. "Boy O Boy, what a great thing to know about."

Highland Park: Was up around the Cypress Hills section of East New York. It got this name because of its high elevation. At the top of the park was a reservoir that supplied the local areas with water. This was predominately a German area. Each morning you could see women washing down their stoops and front walkways. They were very clean people.

There were baseball fields and picnic areas among other park facilities. It was always a good place to hang out. Across the street from the park was a YMCA. This was always open, they welcomed the kids to join in on all of their activities and it was all free. In the winter after a snowfall, kids ride their sleds on the steep hills. When it was warmer weather, we took a bicycle ride to the top of Snake Hill. It was always a job getting to the top, but it was worth the effort because the ride down was terrific. I had put a speed odometer on my bike and clocked the ride down at fifty miles per hour. "Dat's friggin fast on a bicycle." As you approached the bottom of the hill, it was imperative that you begin braking in time to prevent going into Jamaica Ave., which is a cobbled stone street and heavy traffic. My friend Johnny and I began riding down the hill together. He was slightly ahead of me. I began braking, anticipating

Jamaica Ave. when I heard him screaming, "My chain fell off." In those days, the braking system applied with the pedals and not hand grip type brakes. No one wore a helmet. I said to myself "Holy Shit what the hell is he gonna do to stop?" As the distance between us grew larger, I could not take my eyes off him. So many thoughts went through my head all at one time. Would this be the last time I see my friend alive? What am I going to tell his parents? I could not imagine what was going through his friggin head. All of a sudden, he turned into a big bush. BAM! The bike came to a stop and the white-headed Lithuanian went into orbit. He flew a good distance before landing in the grass. When he finally stopped rolling, the poor fellow had a load of bruises and cuts. It was a lot better than a bus hitting him on Jamaica Avenue. Thank God, nothing was broken. We put the chain back on the sprocket and rode home.

Drugs: I was a teenager when my father sat me down one evening in our living room to give me the scoop on drugs. He asked me; "do you remember the talk we had about smoking?" I said, "Yes I do." "Well you must know by now what's going on out there with drugs." "Yes I know that some guys mess around with them." "I want you to keep an eye on those guys and see what happens to them." "Watta ya mean," I asked. He explained to me that drugs were worse than smoking. Usually they will start out drinking alcohol then they will try smoking marijuana because it will give them a high much faster. After a while, they will not be satisfied with that and will progress to something stronger like cocaine. Each time they will try something new and stronger to get a high. Eventually they may go to shooting heroin into their veins with a needle. As they reach that stage, their quality of life goes downhill. The drugs will have taken over their life. They call it, *HOOKED.* The drugs will become more expensive. They will not be able to afford them so they will turn to stealing things in their home, which belong to their parents. They will sell everything that they could get their hands on. When there is nothing else to sell from their house, they will have to start stealing bigger things in order to feed their habit. You will not be able to trust them anymore. Everything they say will be a lie. At this point, their life will be in danger from either overdosing or spending time in jail for committing a crime to support the habit.

I sat there for a while thinking of what I just heard. My dad added a little more. If you ever become involved with drugs, forget about playing sports. You will never have time. You will have to spend most of your time stealing something that you can sell, then looking for someone to buy what you stole, and then shop for drugs. People, who are hooked, lose their normal senses, and do not know whether they are coming or going.

Trust me; one day someone will ask you to try it. It will be something I just told you. They will tell you that it will make you feel good and give it to you free, go ahead try it. That is when you have to stop and think! *WHAT WILL HAPPEN TO ME IF I LIKE IT?* If you do like it, *YOU ARE HOOKED.* Now you will become one of their customers. "I want you to always be alert about what is going on around you. Your brother is young now; but I want you to set a good example for him and always keep an eye on him. Get to know all of his friends and keep an eye on them too. If you ever see any of them becoming involved with drugs, be sure that you talk with your brother as I am talking to you now! OK?" "OK pop I'll always watch after him I promise."

As time went on, I did watch my friends and other people I knew. I can remember bringing a boy named Philip into my house for milk and cookies while we were still in elementary school. My mother warned me about him. She told me he was destined for trouble. You can stay friends with him but never allow him to influence you into doing bad things.

Years later Philip became involved with drugs. He fell dead while sitting on a garbage can on the street corner where we hung out. My parents seemed to be able to look into the future.

Pool Rooms: Besides shooting pool at the homes of a couple of friends with pool tables, the local poolrooms were great places to hang out. Many fellas from our neighborhood and fellas from other nearby neighborhoods went there.

A large Poolroom is located on Fulton Street at the corner of Logan Street, named the "Logan Street Pool Room." It is a loft on the second floor of a commercial building. The proprietor's name was Vick, a short, fat man with a deep voice. Vick ran a tight ship, never taking crap from any of the patrons. Many rough people shot pool up there, and if he tolerated nonsense from them, surely they would have taken control of his place. Everyone respected him.

The El train ran along Fulton Street, passed right in front of the large casement windows, which Vick left wide open during the summer. A dude could throw a pool ball into a train window that is how close it is. Gambling is big amongst the players. Some of them were exceptionally good pool shooters and eager to hustle anyone with a few bucks. The big money games always took place on one of the front tables. You always could tell by the intensity of the game, the amount of onlookers and the particular people engaged. No one talked during these games besides the shooters. You could hear a pin drop and an occasional Woo or Ahh from the spectators.

There were also other poolrooms located in Queens. My friends and I made a point of visiting all of them. We scoped out all the joints just to keep abreast of what was going on all over town. However, we spent most of the time at Logan Street.

Poolrooms did not have a good reputation. It was just an axiom that bad people frequented the places. Both my parents knew this and did not like the idea of me going to these places to hang out. Therefore, I never mention it at home when I went to shoot pool. I recall coming home for dinner and my mother asking me

"Were you up at the pool room today?"
So innocently, I would answer,
"Who me?"
"Yeah you; who the hell am I talking to besides you." "No"
"Oh, OK go inside and get washed up, dinner will be ready in a few minutes."

As I washed, I looked in the mirror and damn if I did not have blue Cue chalk all over my face. Shit! I should have known better than to lie. She saw the blue chalk on my face and she was testing me. How can I look at her now? She had just set me up. I thought to myself, maybe if I do not say anything it will be better. Therefore, I just kept quiet and sat down to eat. I must have looked like the cat that swallowed the canary. I knew she was looking at me but I kept quiet. She never said anything. I knew that she knew I was in the poolroom and I lied to her. However, I got to hand it to her; she was sharp, very sharp. She just let me stew without saying a word.

Mom never forbade me to go to the poolrooms. She trusted me and believed I would use my best judgment if the time ever came to do so. When we were, alone she'd remind me that I was her oldest son and she wanted me to set a good example for my brother. "He will follow and do as you do. Do not make me ashamed of either one of you. Remember, set a good example." "OK mom I will."

Vick hired a man named Michael Eufemia to help him run his establishment. This was no ordinary person. As legend has it, Mike holds the world record for the biggest run. "A run is shooting consecutive balls without missing a shot." He was a true champion. The word on the street is that he ran 625 consecutive balls. I do not know why he decided to work at a local poolroom, but he was up at Logan's quite often. Large posters of Mike decorated the walls. Everyone knew him and treated him with respect. Vick and Mike were up there together one night when my friend Red and I went to shoot some pool. We clocked in at the counter and set up a rack of balls on a table. Red and I were always ready to have some fun no matter where we went. We took one shot then removed the eight ball from the table and hid it behind a radiator. Both of us began milling around the table without taking a shot. We bent over and began looking under the table when Eufemia approached us and asked.

"What's goin on?"

"There's no eight ball,"

"Watta ya mean no eight ball I just gave you guys a full rack of balls."

"Maybe you can find it."

He began looking all through the tunnels that the balls ran through after dropping into a pocket. He was on his back knocking on every tunnel hoping that it was stuck and he could get it to roll down the chute. Red said to him.

"Hey Mike, maybe ya should ask Vick for a flashlight?" "Dat's a good idea," he says, then yells.

"Hey Vick, bring me a flashlight will ya"

Before you could say Little Boo Peep, both of them were crawling under the table. This got everyone's attention. I started to laugh. I must have had the biggest *Smirk* of all times on my face. Here we were two local yokels making the world champ look like a chump, or better yet a chimp crawling around under the table. Finally, I picked up the eight ball from behind the radiator and quietly placed it on the pool table. Red yells out under the table "Hey here it is we found it." The two men crawled out from under the table, took one look and knew right away that we had made fools out of them. Everyone in the joint began to laugh which only added salt to the wound. Vick threw us out of the Pool Room and told us never to come back. I continued to go to the Pool Rooms but I never made a habit of it. I always made sure to wash my hands and face in the men's room before going home. We stayed away from Logan's for a while giving Vick and Mike time to cool off. We hoped they had forgotten the incident.

I must hand it to my folks, when it comes to smatz (slang for smarts.) They were right once again when they told me that something bad could come about when you hang out around undesirable people. It was a few years later when they found Vick the owner of the Pool Room laying on the tall stairway leading to the room. Vick was dead. Someone had put a bullet in him. I never told my parents about it. I figured it would only give them something else to worry about when I went out with my friends.

Spin the Bottle: We grew to know some of the girls around the Pitkin Ave. area. On occasion, we gave them a ride on our bicycles. The girls began to look better as I got older. Someone came up with the idea of playing spin the bottle on Doscher Street. It sounded like a good idea, so I said OK count me in. Everyone gathered in a big circle to spin the bottle. We later went into a hallway to kiss the girls. It was a fun game and brought us all closer together.

My friend Ronald began dating Mary. She was an Italian girl good looking with a nice personality. Mary had a friend by the name of Martha. The two of them were together all the time. One Saturday Ronald asked me to go to the movies with them. He said that he would take Mary and I could go with Martha. It will be a double date. I thought about it for a while then agreed to go with them.

We went to the Earl Theater on Liberty Ave. This was the same movie house where my cousin Anthony rubbed chewing gum in my hair several years ago. However, this time was different. I am a little older now and on a date. I remember Ronald telling me that we must get seats way in the back of the theater. Therefore, we sat in the last row.

The movie started and the lights became dimmer. I looked over and saw Ronald putting his arm around his girlfriend. He then began to make out with her. Martha just sat there staring at the movie screen. I knew that she saw her friend kissing Ronald and probably was waiting for me to do the same thing. I placed my arm around the top of her seat and just sat there. I began to have second thoughts. What will happen if she does not want me to kiss her? This aint spin the bottle. What should I do if she pushes me away? Damn! It seemed like hours went by and I never made a move. I started to think; the longer I wait the harder it will be. All of a sudden, I could not feel my friggin arm anymore. It had fallen asleep. I thought, I better excuse myself and go to the toilet. I did not have to piss but I wanted the feeling back in my arm. I told her I'd be right back. I turned and looked and my friend still all snuggled up with Mary. I began to think what a wimp I am. Martha must be thinking the same thing. I will take a few minutes to get the blood circulating in my arm again then make my move. The hell with it if she don't want to make out with me I will watch the freaken movie. I returned to my seat and she looked into my eyes. At that moment, I put my arm around her and gave her a real good kiss. Wow! She responded and began kissing me. She had been waiting for me to start the ball rolling. I had it made! I broke the ice and was in charge now. Who was better than me?

I do not know what the movie was about and neither did any of my friends. We took the girls home and from that day on, I became one of the guys.

The Bowling Alley: On the corner of Atlantic Ave. and Crescent Street was the Lucky Strike bowling alley. Having previously gone with an Uncle as a young boy, I was familiar with the joint. My friends and I decided to give the game of bowling a try. We did not need any equipment of our own because all the equipment needed was available at the lanes.

We thought that bowling was a nice game to play. I went there with friends on occasion, but just like the poolrooms, we searched out other bowling alleys in both Brooklyn and Queens. I began to play the game quite well however, each game cost money to play. In those days, there were no mechanical automatic pinsetters. It was a person stationed in what they called the pits and he set the pins up by hand. The pinsetters worked for a small wage and therefore, depended on tips from the bowlers. The job seemed simple. A pinsetter had to know the rules of the game in order to do the job correctly. Thinking, this is something else to make a few bucks. I went to talk to the manager of the alley. He asked, "How old are you?" I lied to him by answering,

"I'm eighteen years old." After a few questions, he gave me the job.

Weekends were the best time to work because many people went out on dates or came to bowl with their friends. I set pins for the league games too. It was hot in the pits so the pinsetters wore a bandana around their heads to prevent the sweat from going into their eyes. Sometimes on the weekends, I worked until the alley closed which was early in the morning. My folks did not worry. They knew it was a better class of people who frequented the alleys, not the like the tough people at the Pool Rooms.

Each pinsetter worked two alleys at one time. A little wall separated them so we had to jump back and forth all night long. It was good exercise. However, it is essential to be very alert, because a flying pin or a bowling ball could easily hit us. At the end of a set of games, the players usually tossed tip money down the gutter, which landed in the pit. Occasionally some jerk would throw a bowling ball down the lane to try to scare the pin boy when he was not expecting it. The first time we considered it an accident. However, when the same person did it more than once, we'd throw the ball back at him on the alley instead of returning it by way of the return rail. As soon as it crashed into where they were sitting, they got the message and never tried it again. Once again, I devised another way to make money. I continued to surprise mamma with little gifts. I loved to see her happy, and she always made a big fuss, which made me happy too.

Crazy Joe & the Shit Canal:  Giuseppe was one of the people that live in our neighborhood. Giuseppe meant Joseph in Italian. He was a few years older than I was and a real nice person. Joe always acted as if he had a few bolts loose in his head. One day he told a few of us fellows to come with him because he had a
great place, which he wanted to show us.

"What is it?"

"I can't tell ya. Ya gotta see it."

"How far is it?"

"Ahh it's a ways down the Sunrise Highway."

"How do we get there?"

"We could either hitch a ride or walk it's not dat far away."

"OK lead us there."

We must have walked about two miles while listening to Giuseppe's crazy stories. When we arrived, he pointed at this big opened canal, which eventually emptied into Jamaica bay.

"Dare it is, Watta ya dink?"

"Wow! It stinks." I told him.

"Of course it stinks; it's the Shit Canal."
A pal Vinnie asked him.

"How the hell did you find dis place?"

"What's the difference how I found it, don't ya dink

it's a great place?"

"Yeah" Vinnie said, "If you like the smell of shit."

We began looking around and discovered all these beautiful pieces of colored rocks and glass, which was scattered on the ground.

"Hey look at this stuff" I said, "its great stuff." A friend Richie said.

"What the hell are ya gonna do with dat crap?"

"Crap?"

"Do ya know how great this would look in a fish tank? There's so much of it, we can sell it to the Tropical fish stores."

Meanwhile, all the raw sewage was running out from this tunnel from under the ground and you could see it and smell the vial odor of raw sewerage. Alongside the canal, there are some long weeds called punks that grew about eight feet tall. Giuseppe pulled one out of the ground then reached down into the canal and snagged a floating condom. Like a whip, he snapped it and the friggin condom went flying across the canal and wrapped around Vinnie's neck. It did not stop there. Everyone pulled out a punk weed and started flinging condoms at each other. No one could have ever imagined that there were so many of these things floating in the canal. This explained why it was so common to see them floating in the water while swimming in Coney Island or Rockaway beach.

Literately speaking, it turned out to be a shitty day, but we all filled our pockets with the colored rocks and glass. Later I set up a fish tank at home with a Gold fish. Sometime later, I showed the place to Billy but never hit him with a condom. There were so many rocks and glass just lying there for the taking. Billy came home with a load of it too. We could not help but sell some of it.

Giuseppe joined the Army. He left the neighborhood for a while. He showed up one day at the street corner all dressed up in a Paratrooper's uniform, boots and all. He had many stories to tell us about how he jumped out of airplanes. While he was on leave, he told us to meet him at the Earl Theater on Saturday afternoon. There was some army movie playing and he wanted us to watch it with him. "OK, what time and where should we meet you?" He told us "just get into the theater and I will do something dat will get your attention. You will definitely know where I am." So one person paid to get into the theater, he opened the fire exit and the rest of us ran in without paying. About ten minutes went by when all of a sudden fire shot up from within the rows of seats. The voice of Giuseppe rang out "I'm over here." He had brought the newspaper with him to the movies so he could set it on fire to let us know where he was sitting. This was one of the reasons he was alias Crazy Joe.

Joe returned to duty. He was not gone for long when he appeared on the corner again with a pair of crutches. He broke his leg jumping out of a plane. He hobbled around the neighborhood for quite a while. He also hung out in the schoolyard breaking everyone's balls. They finally gave him a discharge and we had him back in the neighborhood for keeps. "God help us."

The Good Humor Truck: A few blocks from our house behind the East New York

Vocational High School, the city built a new park, but this one was real close to our house.

Just outside the park, the Sunrise Highway ran into Atlantic Ave. There was a sharp curve and a high hill in the road. The park was always busy with kids playing. On one typical summer day, a man driving a Good Humor ice cream truck took the turn too fast. The truck turned over on its side making a loud noise, which got the attention of everyone in the park. The truck came to a screeching halt right in the middle of the highway. The poor driver could not move because he was pinned beneath the truck. Everyone ran to the scene of the accident. My first thought was to help the driver get out from under the truck. While running with the crowd, I thought to myself, what a nice bunch of people, all responding to help the injured driver. Boy this was the furthest thing from the truth. The first kid to reach the truck went right for the door in the back of the refrigerated truck and helped himself to some ice cream. The rest of the mob followed his lead. Before you could say Jack Flash, everyone was eating ice cream. It was unbelievable. Other motorist assisted the driver while the mob stuffed their faces with the poor man's entire inventory. The truck was empty while they took the driver away in an ambulance. Our neighborhood was certainly going through a transition.

As time marched on the neighborhood continued to go through a gradual change. However, not everything changed. Some of the things never changed. Angelo (Godzilla) still lived on the next block and continued his assaults on me whenever he felt like getting his rocks off. While never managing to kick him square in the balls, he continued to whip my ass.

Good people continued to move out of the area while the undesirables moved into their place. There were a couple of black families now living on the next block from us. They were filthy, obnoxious people who cared about no one but himself or herself. They collected welfare money, food stamps and everything else they could squeeze out of the government, while they sat on their fat asses all day long dangling from the porches. We had a name for them *"Porch Monkeys."* I recall coming home one afternoon and talking about the niggers on the next block. Aunt Viola and mom were present at the time. When they heard me call them niggers, they both scolded me. I always remember a little poem my Aunt recited that day:

God made the Negro; he made him in the night.
  He made him in a hurry and forgot to paint him white.

Both my Aunt and mom explained that we were all God's children and should not discriminate. Momma went on to say that the black folks migrated from the south where they are treated very mean, and became slaves. When they come up here to the north, they feel a sense of freedom and therefore, they tend to do things that we see as being wild. Give them time and they will adjust to the proper ways. I listened and had no comments about what they had said. Knowing that mom was right about everything else, she was probably right about this too.

Movin Out: It was not long after, that my Aunt and her family, along with her daughter Celia and husband Nick moved. They bought a 2½-acre property in Moriches Long Island. The place was about fifty miles from us. The people from whom they purchased the property moved into Aunt Viola's apartment just across the alley from ours. Their names are Bill and Bertha. Both turned out to be very nice people and fell right in with the crowd on Glenmore Ave.

The property where my aunt moved to had a chicken farm and a gas station on it. The newcomers had a lot to learn about chickens, but Nick was good at just about everything and learned the business quickly. He ran the gas station with Uncle Tony and they became chicken farmers.

Billy and I spent a lot of time with them at their newly acquired venture. We pumped gas at the station and made tips by cleaning windshields and checking oil for the customers. Nick taught us a lot about raising chickens, picking eggs, candling eggs, feeding, and cleaning out the chicken coops. We also learned how to slaughter, pluck, cut and pack fresh meat for sale. There was a large piece of property that needed tending. It gave us our first opportunity to operate a lawn mower. Nick taught us how to plant a garden. Both of us loved to spend time out there, while learning many new things, which made mother happy. We also had a lot of fun with our cousins.

One morning Nick drove both of us further out on Long Island to visit the potato farmers. They showed us how they operated their large farms and how to harvest potatoes. After gathering, all of our tip money from the gas station and investing it into buying 50 LB. bags of potatoes; we loaded them onto Nick's pickup truck and then deposited them on the side of Montauk Highway in front of the gas station. After selling all of our potatoes, we reinvested the money again and bought more. Nick kept us busy all the time. We loved the man! He had a knack of turning work into fun and profit. Momma was glad to get us out of the city during the hot summer. We earned our own keep. However, we do not know if our parents ever sent money to our relatives to cover some of the cost of keeping us with them. If she did, it was not very much.

My Uncle Louie: Uncle Lou opened a gas station that was only about thirty miles from our house. He was an auto mechanic by trade. He did major repairs on trucks and automobiles. Momma saw this as an opportunity for me to learn something else. She'd say to us "we must take advantage of every chance to learn from someone who is willing to teach us something." She made sure that we did just that.

At the age of fifteen, I worked with Uncle Louie for a whole summer. Mother knew that it would keep me out of trouble. I got up very early each morning to open the gas station with him and worked until closing. It was a lot of work but my uncle taught me many things. I learned a little about how to operate a business, mechanical work and the proper use of many tools. I also learned how to deal with people. After using any of his tools, he insisted I cleaned them then, returned them back to where they belonged. I was never to sit in a customer's car when dirty. This was a Cardinal sin. It was my job to keep the shop neat and orderly. He taught me how to drive a car with an old 1941 Plymouth coupe. After giving me one quick lesson on how to drive a stick shift, I practiced driving around the gas station when not pumping gas, changing oil, filters and fixing flat tires. He figured I was good enough when he saw the car rolling around the building in reverse.

One night he gave me the keys to his car and said to drive us home to Lindenhurst, which was about ten miles away. I said "Who me?" "Yeah you, don't be afraid, you can do it." From that time on, he had a chauffeur to drive him to and from work each day. As soon as I became fifteen, we got a learner's permit just to keep me legal while driving the car. When reaching the age of sixteen, I took a road test and failed. The man who gave the test asked "How long have you been driving?" Thinking, I best tell him since receiving a learner's permit, or else it would be admitting that I broke the law for the period of time that I drove without a permit. Therefore, I said to him, "Since obtaining a learners permit." He looked at the date on it and answered, "You've been driving for only two days?" "Ahh, I guess," I told him. This was most likely the reason he failed me.

A few weeks later, I took the test again and passed. I now had a driver's license at the age of sixteen. It was useless, because living in the city one was not eligible to drive until the age of eighteen. However, driving on Long Island was legal.

My Uncle Dan: (Dante) was a professional wood carver. He had a shop with many tools used to fabricate picture frames. He carved different designs into wood, placed a finish on them and shipped them to various picture frame stores. His shop was located in Brooklyn. He lived very close to us, which made it convenient for ma to send us to help him in the shop occasionally. Uncle Dan was one of the greatest people you could ever meet. He had the patients of a saint and the personality to go with it. No one disliked him, or had a bad word to say about him. He belonged to a bunch of different organizations and clubs, such as bowling teams and fishing clubs. He was active in the church and the Knights of Columbus. He was just a regular guy. When they consider someone in Brooklyn a REGULAR GUY, it means that he is a stand up person and very well liked. If someone is called a regular guy, it is considered a complement. Every Sunday friends gathered at his apartment on Glenmore Ave. They came for a drink and a snack after church. Moms Sister, Irene, who was married to Dan, was also a saint. I wondered how my Aunt continuously entertained all the people my uncle invited to their home so often. She never hesitated to put out something to eat while my uncle poured drinks for everyone. In the afternoon, he would light up the Bar B Q in the alley, and began to cook. Friends and neighbors enjoyed an afternoon of fun with eats and music.

When the fishing club gathered for an outing, he always included Billy and me. We never owned a fishing pole but that was no problem. He made sure that we were well equipped. He also included me in his bowling league. When he played shuffleboard at the bar and grill we were there too. He made sure we got something to eat and drink. He also joined us on camping trips in the mountains in the upstate area of N.Y., we would spend a whole weekend pitching tents, hiking, and cooking.

The man could play a guitar and a mandolin. He had a terrific voice and often sung in his apartment or in the alley. Whenever he sang, especially the song MY PRAYER, by the Platters, mom forbids us to speak. "Shut up" she'd say, "My Perry Como is singing."

Dante was the person we all went to whenever we had a problem of any kind. He sat, listened and helped to solve it; he is 'THE GODFATHER' of our family.

Mom's Uncle Tom: Back in the 1950s, a singer by the name of Lou Monte recorded a song called The Sheik of Napoli. It was a takeoff of the song most recently recorded at that time, by Louis Prima called The Sheik of Araby. With the lyrics changed, it now pertained to an Italian dude from Naples Italy. Lou Monte's song became a big hit and it played often on the radio.

Billy and I were hip to all the songs at the time and we knew most of the words. We had a Hi-Fi, which played records, and we often sang along with the music.

Momma had an uncle by the name of Tom who had just passed away. We were getting dressed with suits and ties to attend the wake at the funeral parlor. At the time, the style of the necktie had changed to what they called a Slim Jim. All the fellas were wearing these very skinny ties. It was important for a teenager to be in fashion. As we dressed, mom decided to tell us about her uncle. The man was born in Naples Italy, which made him a Napeleton. She told us that he was a real nice dresser and was very popular with the women. In fact, the women went crazy for him. As she rambled on about her uncle, I went to put Lou Monte's song on the Hi Fi. Both Billy and I began to sing along mimicking the words to the song using Uncle Tom's name. This pissed her off. She told us to stop the crap, go downstairs and wait for her. When she came down, we proceeded to the funeral home to pay our respects to the family.

Upon our entering, the funeral home mom told us to go ahead of her to the casket to kneel, say a prayer, then go and give our condolences to the immediate family. She waited her turn at the rear of the room as we approached the casket. We knelt down, took one look at the gent in the box, then looked at each other and began to laugh like crazy. The friggin dude had on an old out dated suit with a big wide tie that resembled a catchers chest protector. We never had to say a word to each other. The writing was on the wall. What the hell kind of a ladies man could he have been? "This guy aint even got any style." As we tried to hide our faces in our hands, we could hear the old people behind us saying, "Look at Lucia's boys, they cry for Tom what nice boys." This caused us to laugh even harder. We also heard mother's Aunt Lucy begin to cry. The family knew her as the professional crier. She carried on at all the wakes. This made us continue laughing. The more they spoke the harder we laughed. Finally, mom approached the casket. She stood directly behind us and said "I am gonna count to three, both of you better be gone." We heard one two and we both took off in different directions. We ran outside the funeral parlor and waited to face the real music when momma came out. The first words out of her mouth were "Wipe that *Smirk* off your face or I'll wipe it off for you."

Valet Service: I knew the man that owned a parking lot next to our house. I went to school with his daughter. I approached him and asked if he needed any help jockeying the cars when the owners came into the lot to retrieve them. I told him of my junior driving license. I also assured him that I was a competent person. I said to him that I'd be here at the lot every day after school. I will not only pull out the cars for people but, I'd stay in the little shed he had on the lot and keep an eye on things for him. He was convinced enough to give me the job. After school, I took the schoolbooks down to the shed and did my homework next to the little pot belly stove, which burned coal. When the owners of the automobiles arrived, I started their cars and brought it to them. Also receiving tips from them as a gratuity. I had started my own little valet service.

Gang Fights: The street gangs continued to battle with each other for unknown and insignificant reasons. There was a gang called the Crystals, named after Crystal Street, which was five blocks from Crescent Street. The gang consisted of fellas older than me. A friend Richie, who lived across the street from us managed to become involved with this crew. Some of the fellas were the older brothers of the younger gang members of the Crescents. The gang members often talked about the fights that took place at various locations. Richie often shared with me some of the details. I was never impressed. It was good to know these people and stay friends with them; however, I never became involved with them.

The churches always held dances in their gymnasiums or social areas for the teenagers. On one particular evening, there was a very large crowd that attended a local church dance. The music was playing and everyone was having a swell time. A friend who was a gang member of the Crescents warned me about what was developing. He said that there was a rival gang at the dance and the Crescents were going to battle with them right here on the dance floor. He explained the game plan: Each member of the Crescents will stand next to a member of the rival gang. Once everyone is in place while the music was playing, there will be a signal given by a certain person. At that moment, each Crescent was to cold cock the person he was standing next to, and then he will continue to beat on him. After the warning, I went to a neutral corner. They gave the signal, and all hell broke loose. There was blood splattered all over the place. The music stopped and many of the rival gang members lay on the ground with injuries.

The Crescents were very proud of themselves. They had come and they had conquered. However, what did all this mean? The ambulances came to attend to the wounded teenagers. Several of the non-participants were also hurt. The place was a mess and everyone had to go home. The people that ran the dance were pissed off. They thought twice about holding another dance on the church premises.

There was now plenty to talk about on the street corner. I could not imagine standing next to someone who you do not know from Adam. He does not know you either. Then something like this goes down. Guess it is the same thing when a country goes to war. The individuals doing the fighting do not know each other either, but the idea is to kill each other. The whole idea is INSANE!

The Peeping Tom: We had a friend named Paul. He was a nice, clean cut kid. He was also a musician. He played a musical instrument in the school band. I think it was a clarinet. Paul was also one of the boy scouts in the old troop 229. We were in the Beaver patrol together. The fellow had a great sense of humor too. Every time we met, he had a smile on his face.

One afternoon Paul came down to the street corner where all the guys hung out. He had a grin on his face from ear to ear.

"Hey Paulie what's up?" one of the fellas asked.

"Well I got something good to share with you guys."

"What is it?"

"Do ya know that sharp looking chick in school named Gina?"

"Of course," we all answered,

"Who the hell don't know her, she's that real knock out broad."

"What about her?"

"Well one night I was crossing through an empty lot on my way home when I saw a bright light on in a bathroom window. So I walked a little closer and looked inside."

"Yeah, so what the hell did you see?"

"I saw Gina naked taking a shower."

"No shit, how did she look?"

"She looked great. Not only great, but she also played with herself in the shower. She finished her shower then shut off the light, and den I went home, I couldn't get her off of my mind."

"Did you ever go back?"

"Sure I did. I went back several times and watched the same friggin ding each time. She has certain days dat she takes a shower. Do you dink any of you guys wanna go wit me next time?"

"YES!" Everyone answered.

"Thursday night at 9:30 P.M. Dat's when she will take her next shower. If you wanna go with me, meet me here at 9:15 ok?"

"Sure, we will be here."

So, came Thursday night and about five of us showed up for the show. Paulie took us down to the empty lot and told us to lie down and watch. Like a bunch of Numb Nuts, we all lay down on our stomachs and stared at the bathroom window.

"So when the hell does she begin to shower?"

"Shush don't make any noise."

We laid there for about a half hour and the bathroom light never came on. My friend Red said.

"Hey Paulie, I dink your full of shit."

"No I'm not, I swear to God I saw her, I'm not lying."

"Well maybe anutter time," we told him.

Now it is time to go home. Therefore, we all picked up and went back to the street corner.

Paul insisted that we go with him again on Saturday night. "She will be sure to do it then." "OK Paulie, we will try it on Saturday." Saturday night was like deja vu all over again. After another half hour of lying on our stomachs one of the fellas stood up, smacked Paulie in the head, and said, "Let's get the hell outta here. If she wasn't such a hot looking broad I wooda never came here the first time." We all left while listening to Paulie swear once more about all the times he saw hot Gina play with herself in the shower. I did not really doubt him, after all, it is hard to pin point the time someone will take a shower. Nevertheless, we told him to keep blowing all that hot air into his horn and not in our ears.

A few years later when Paulie became of driving age, his grandmother bought him a brand new 1957 Chevrolet Bel Air. It was a beautiful machine and he took good care of it. A year later, he traded it in for a 1958 Bel Air, another gorgeous automobile black in color. He added teardrop skirts and a continental kit. Paulie sported around town always looking good and wearing a smile.

A Local newspaper presented an article along with a photo of a fellow lying in his underwear in a small shanty. The story read something like this: Young man and female companion found dead in a shack located down the Old Mill. The couple, died due to inhaling fumes from an improper ventilated gas burner.

Good old Paulie, he shacked up with some chick and partied with her in the heated shanty. Too bad he forgot to crack open a window, he probably would still be alive today. Everyone missed him however, we were all happy that he enjoyed driving around with the new cars before his shocking death.

Minsky's Burlesque: It was somewhere in the mid-1950s when my friend Red came up with a suggestion that we both go to the Minsk's Burlesque in Newark New Jersey.

"Sounds like a plan. Do ya know howda get dare?"

"Yeah, It's somewhere across the George Washington bridge."

"When do ya wanna go?"

"This Saturday, we'll brown bag a lunch and hitch hike there."

"OK sounds like a plan."

Saturday morning I was set to go. A peanut butter and jelly sandwich, a piece of fruit and a candy bar. "Let's go watch the show." We got to the bridge then decided to walk across the view was fantastic. It was a holiday weekend and a gigantic American flag hung from the top of the bridge. As we began our hike, the flag came loose and began to fall. There were many people including police and Port Authority workers to direct traffic and pick up the flag. It was quite an experience, our timing was just right.

  We had one of those free maps with us, which we took from a gas station, circled out Newark and figured we'd ask where Minsky's was located once we got there.

  Our next step was to board a bus, which would take us to the show place. I recall the two of us numb nuts sitting in the back of the bus while singing:

Hi HO Hi Ho To the burlesque show we go. We paid two bits to see two tits Hi Ho Hi Ho Hi Ho.

    Everything was going great we spoke of all the things we imagined we would see. By the time we arrived, it was noon.

  "Hey dares Minsky's lets buy a ticket."
Upon advancing to the ticket booth and telling the clerk we wanted two seats, he began laughing.

  "Hey what's so friggin funny?"

  "What the hell do you two kids want here?"

  "We wanna see the show dats what we're doin here, now give us two tickets."

The fellow continued to laugh while telling us to get lost.

  "You are too young, still wet behind the ears; now get the hell adda here."

We looked at each other and then decided to go to the Palisades amusement park. As the day progressed, we found our way to the park. We did not allow the creep in the booth to spoil the day. I ate my peanut butter and jelly sandwich along the way and saved the fruit and candy for last. When we get a little older, we will try once again to get into Minsky's Burlesque.

The Negros & Puerto Ricans:

More and more Negros moved into the neighborhood while more of the whites moved away. Most of the white people moved out to Long Island. The blockbusters continued to do their wheeling and dealing, scaring people into selling their homes at a lower and lower price. The Puerto Ricans also began moving into the area. Many of them were fine people. However, some were nasty individuals. Rivals became common between the two ethnic groups. All of them knew how to collect money from the government. Groups of Spanish speaking people greeted the new comers as they disembarked from the planes or ships. The first thing they did was to inform them of all of the available entitlements. They handed out Printed forms along with assistance on how to fill them out properly. It was amazing to interact with these people only to learn how cunning they were and the scams they would pull on various people to defraud them of their money.

As the population grew, so did the ghettos. Different groups of people began to band together. Some formed street gangs with Latin names and wore specific colors to indicate as to which gang they belonged. The blacks also formed their own gangs. It did not take long before the two groups were battling each other in the streets. They were stabbing, clubbing and hurting each other for no reason. This did not happen overnight. The change took place gradually.

The white gangs began to fight with the new comers over turf or any other stupid reason they could invent. The boys in school formed their own little groups consisting mostly of the Italians and the Irish. I recall them trying to lure me in with the Italians but I would never commit to being one of them. They asked me to hang out with them because I was half-Italian, but I always respond, I am not an Italian, I am a full-blooded American. I wanted no part of their foreign groups. I eventually got the nickname *The All American*. I was OK with that. I always stayed good friends with all of them and they respected how I felt. Therefore, no one ever bothered me about it, especially after I told them; I belong to the biggest gang of all. Do you have any doubts?

Franklin K. Lane High School: After I graduated from Junior High School P.S. 214, another new adventure was about to begin. Since I began school, I managed to have every schoolteacher invite my mother up for a special visit. This was not because I was good and they wanted to praise me. Most of the time, it was because of a *smirk* when being scolded. I was now batting a thousand in this category. There are only four more years to go. Can I maintain this average? I have no doubts that I can.

I had made many friends in Junior High School, but now many of us were going into different directions. The students that lived in Queens will most likely attend John Adams High School while the students who lived in Brooklyn will go to Lane. Many others will attend Brooklyn Automotive or East New York Vocational High, where they will learn a trade while others attended academic schools like Saint Johns or similar parochial schools, providing, they had the smarts to pass the entry test along with all the academic credits.

Lane is located on the borderline of both Brooklyn and Queens. It is set on Jamaica Ave. and Elderts Lane. Just across the street stood the old baseball field called Bushwick Stadium. My father took me there to watch semi-pro games when I was a kid. It later turned into a track where they raced stock cars. An elevated train runs along Jamaica Ave. with a train stop right in front of the school.

The walk to this new school is much farther than to the Junior High school. For a nickel, we were able to take a city bus to school each morning. We entered the bus at the last stop. By the time the bus arrived, it was jammed packed with students. In order to enter, everyone pushed altogether while screaming, "make room." Eventually the other passengers moved a little further to the rear, allowing us to squeeze in. What a hassle each morning. Sometimes school buses were available to give us a ride home, if not, we took the city bus again.

The Jamaica Ave. train brought many Negro students to the school. In our Junior High, there were very few Negros. Because of the Blockbusters undertaking, bringing so many low-grade minorities into our neighborhood, it was only natural to develop a bad taste for this race of people. Nonetheless, not all of the Negros that came to our new high school was of the same caliber as those on the next block from where I lived. I tried to rationalize before making any judgments about any of my new schoolmates. I found many of them were fine people. Amongst them were also good athletes. Yet, as in any group of people, there are good and bad alike. I became friends with most of them nevertheless; I kept alert and sustained a good distance between the troublemakers and myself. Not everyone thought the same way as I did. Maybe it was because of their upbringing. Both the black and white students alike had a sort of distrust for each other. It did not take much of an incident to sway one's opinion of the other.

This new school played host to many ethnic groups and their gang members. It also added to the members of many different gangs from both Brooklyn and Queens. The students consisted of gang affiliates from the Crescents and the Crystals from our neighborhood, the boys from Rockaway Ave. and Fulton Street, in Queens, which included John Gotti (Who later became the Mafia boss of the Gambino crime family in N.Y.) and his associates. The Blacks had their groups who stuck together as well as the minority Latin people. Some from the New Lots area of Brooklyn became friends and banded with all of the other Caucasian students. Many of these new schoolmates became notorious gangsters with numerous stories written about them in newspapers, along with several movies, countless documentaries and many books published.

When you put such a mixture of people together, just about anything could happen in a split second, and it did many times. Gangs as well as individuals fought each other on the school buses, the trains and in the streets as well. Fistfights also occurred in the stairwells and hallways of the school. I tried to keep my nose clean and stay out of trouble as best as I could.

Kay Bee Foods: Shortly after starting High School, I landed a job working for a food supplier as a warehouse worker. The warehouse was located on Pine Street one block from the Euclid Taxi stand. My brother and I ran across its rooftop when Red Furman hired the big boys to catch us after we tormented him for such a long time. It also stood adjacent to the old haunted house, which we had entered and found a lot of good stuff.

Five brothers by the name of Kaplan owned the food company. The name Kay Bee actually stood for Kaplan Brothers. The company sold and delivered many different food products to various restaurants. Tractor-trailer trucks delivered pallets of food products, which needed to be unloaded and stacked in the warehouse. We also loaded the various orders onto the Kay Bee trucks, which the drivers delivered to the various restaurants.

By no means was this an easy job. When an eighteen-wheeler backed into the warehouse with pallets loaded with one hundred pound and sixty pound sacks of sugar, flower, beans or other goods I worked along with another fella by the name of Sammy (Fat Sammy) to unload everything. Sammy also attended the same school as I did but he was a senior. He was a big heavy fella and strong too. Sam ran the forklift, which he handled well. I received a pay of seventy-five cents an hour. It does not sound like much compared to the wages of today. Nevertheless, it was a steady job and I always had a few bucks in my pocket and therefore, became less of a burden to my parents.

The Kaplan's are a Jewish family and they made sure to squeeze every ounce of work out of us, earning every cent that they paid us. The mother hung out at the warehouse and became a big pain in my ass. If I had to take a piss, she timed me. If I took longer that she thought it should take, she ran into the office to tell one of her sons. Shortly afterwards I received a lecture from one of them. I put up with their crap because I knew how the Jews functioned. It was part of their upbringing. Therefore, I never let it bother me. Just to piss them off, I gave them a *smirk*. I knew they would never fire me, after all who the hell would work as hard as I did for .75 cents an hour. The old lady hung out around the pickle barrels. To keep herself occupied, she filled one-gallon glass jars with Jewish kosher pickles from the large barrels made of wood. I walked past her one day and gave her a nice smile along with a greeting, "Good afternoon Mrs. Kaplan." Just as I greeted her, the old witch ran into the office. A moment later, she and her oldest son Harry entered the warehouse. "Louie, Hey Sonny get over here right this minute!" As I approached the dynamic duo, Harry started to yell aloud at me with a threatening voice.

"Why are you eating my Maraschino cherries?"

"Who me?"

"Yeah you."

"I didn't eat any cherries,"

"My mother told me that ya did eat the cherries."

"What the hell inspired her to say dat?"

Harry then told me to go into the toilet, look in the mirror and smile. I did what he told me to do. When I exited the toilet, my face was as red from embarrassment as my mouth was from eating a bunch of red Maraschino cherries along with fat Sammy. We ate them from a glass jar that we opened in the back of the warehouse. I never smiled nor did I ever greet the old lady again after that incident.

To make the job even more difficult, Sammy broke my balls every chance he could. He was a nice person but, a ballbreaker. One afternoon while unloading a truck filled with 25 lb. sacks of lentils and one hundred lb. bags of white flower, Sammy decided to have some fun at my expense. He stood on the rear of the truck while I stood on the ground below. He tossed the bags of lentils to me. I caught them then stacked them on a pallet. As I turned to place a bag on the pallet, he tossed another one, hitting me in the head with it. This went on for a while; Sammy was enjoying himself seeing me hit with the 25 lb. bags. I kept telling him to quit the bullshit but he was having too much fun. After the pallet was full, he came down from the truck to drive the forklift, putting the pallet in its proper place in the warehouse. I took the opportunity to jump up on the truck before he returned. I took my pocketknife and cut a large slit in a 100 lb. bag of pure white flower. Upon his return, he told me to start unloading the flower. "OK here it goes Sammy." I lifted the first bag to shoulder height then threw it at him. The friggin thing busted wide open as it struck him in the head. The white powdery flower came out of the bag and completely covered him. He began to scream with rage while running towards the big opened garage door. He ran past the old lady, she thought she had seen a ghost. She ran into the office and came out with Harry. He took one look at Sammy and asked, "What the hell happened to you?" Meanwhile I stood on the tailboard of the truck laughing. Sammy told him what I did. Harry ran to the rear of the truck to question me. I told him it was an accident; the bag had a little hole in it causing it to break as I passed it down to Sam. Harry had to accept my explanation, it seemed logical enough. However, Sammy thought twice before ever breaking my balls again.

The job at the warehouse lasted for more than a year, until one evening as I passed the place while walking down Glenmore Ave. towards my dad's bar. I noticed smoke coming from the large garage door on Pine Street. A moment later flames shot out. I immediately pulled the fire alarm. The firefighters arrived within a few minutes. However, the place was in a blaze. By the time, the firefighters extinguished the fire; most everything inside the warehouse burned or became smoke damaged. I never told the Kaplan brothers that I alerted the firefighters. I knew better than to do that because I am aware of the behaviors of Jewish people, along with how they conducted their business. I assumed that the fire was set in order to collect insurance money. Everyone knew that scam; its nickname is (Jewish Lightning).

I kept in contact with one of the brothers by the name of Bernie. On Saturdays, I worked at his home doing many odd jobs. Which included, scrubbing and polishing the floors for his darling princess wife. She was a JAP (Jewish American Princess.) The Jewish women took pride with the tittle JAP. The husbands were bossy at work. However, when they returned home they could not voice their opinion. The woman of the house ruled.

As a young boy, I watched and listened to many of the Jewish women in the neighborhood, as they sat on the concrete stoops soaking up the warm sunshine. They talked to each other for hours about common gossip. The Jewish term used for these type women is (A Yenta.) When their husbands returned home from a full day of work, the whining began.

"Oh Morty I'm so glad you're home I had such a hard day."

The husband felt sorry and began to pamper her.

"Darling I'm so sorry do you feel OK?"

"What can I do for you?"

"Yeah I'm OK but I am so tired. Go get some takeout Chinese food?"

"OK sweetheart would you like anything else?"

"Yeah before you go, bring me something to drink."

They had their men wrapped around their little finger. The Jewish husbands often sent their wives on a vacation during the summer months. Most of them stayed at nice hotels in the Monticello area of the Catskill Mountains known as the Jewish Alps. The hotels had lots of entertainment. The husbands often visited them on the weekends and paid the bills they had incurred during the week. The fellas on the corner mimicked the husbands by saying things like:

Alvin: So Irving, are you sending your wife to the mountains this summer?

Irving: Na I will bang her myself.

On the other hand, most of the Italian men were just the opposite. When they returned home after work, their wife has had a nice dinner on the table. The women washed and dried all the dishes and put everything away without whining, while the men relaxed after a hard day of work.

Came Friday night they met with their friends at a Poolroom, Bowling alley, a card game or at the bar for a few drinks. Some of them even had a (Gomadda) "a girlfriend on the side." Saturday nights, usually spent with their wives. It was all so typical.

High School Tryouts: It was springtime once more and baseball tryouts at the high school were near. Pop was well aware of this and he wanted to make sure that his son was ready. The tryouts always took place at the ball field in front of the school. Many students tried to make the team. After a couple of days, the tryouts were over. They picked the players they felt would be best for the team and I was not included. When I went home, dad was waiting to hear good news but instead he was very disappointed.

"How could that be?" he asked.

"My arm pop, it's just not there. You gotta be able to pick off the runners stealing second base."

"Well, wait till next year you will do much better." Pop was beginning to sound like a Brooklyn Dodger fan whenever they lost to the N.Y. Yankees. "Wait until next year."

I continued to play baseball with other teams in the parks, and in the schoolyards with friends. A constant pain existed in the right arm. It was my throwing arm. There was no doubt in my mind that the cause of the pain developed from throwing snowballs in the winter. I slowly reframed from playing the game because of the pain. When the following spring arrived, they announced that the tryouts for the baseball team would begin in a week. The week passed and I never went to the ball field to try out for the team. Pop was tending bar one afternoon as the school bus stopped in front of the tavern. Upon my entering he asked, "Hey when are they gonna hold baseball tryouts at the high school?" "They had tryouts last week." "How come you never told me?" He asked. I stood there bewildered. I began looking around the bar not knowing what to say, when he asked again. I took a deep breath, "Because I never bothered to tryout." "What?" "Yeah dad I never bothered to go because of my arm." Pop's jaw almost hit the bar. I never saw him with such a disappointed look on his face. He stood there staring at me as though a crime had been committed. Unexpectedly he said, "Go home; I don't even want to look at you. I cannot believe that you never tried, Go home." While walking down Glenmore Ave. tears ran down my face. Thinking about how pop worked so hard all these years hoping his son would someday become a major league baseball player. He had it all played out in his mind how it was supposed to happen and now he was so very disappointed in me.

When he came home, we sat and had a good talk. Dad finally realized that things do not always happen, as we would like them to happen. It took quite a while until he was back on track and things went back to normal.

During that year, something happened that changed all of our lives. Our parents still owned the Bar and Grill, Billy at the age of 12 attended Junior high school, while I just turned 17, and a student at Franklin K. Lane High, working after school at the grocery store for the Jewish people on Pitkin Ave.

Pop became ill again. We believed it was another stroke. They took him in an ambulance to Kings County hospital in Brooklyn. This time it was bad, very bad. He had a blood clot in his neck. Mom was stuck with the business and had to wait for the bartender named Howie to relieve her before she could go and visit him each day. He was there for several days. The best transportation for me was by bus. It was August 10 1957 when I traveled alone to visit him. Upon arriving, dad was lying in a bed inside of a plastic tent. While walking towards the bed, he motioned me to come into the tent so that he could speak. Leaning into the tent, he began to speak very low. "Listen carefully to what I tell you. You are my oldest son and I love you very much. You have always made me very proud of you. Now, I have one last thing that I want you to promise me." "What is it daddy?" "Promise me that you will always take care of your mother and your brother. Give to him, everything that I would, and watch him closely. Make sure that he continues to be a good boy. Set a good example." "I Promise you, I will do it dad." "Good now give me one last big kiss because this is the last time you will ever see me. I know that I am going to die." After giving him a big hug and a kiss, I sat on the floor in the hallway and cried. Gathering composure, walking back to the bust stop thinking of what just happen I became exhausted. When returning home, instead of going to our empty apartment, I went into Aunt Irene's apartment. After telling her what just took place, I lie down in her bed and fell asleep. Suddenly the phone rang. I became frightened. Aunt Irene entered the bedroom, sat alongside me and said, "Your father just died."

Pop's wake took place at the old Stephen Oddo funeral parlor on Pitkin Ave. under the El. There were many people that came to pay their respects, including all the boys from the baseball team. Representatives from the U.S. Army came and draped a flag over his coffin, which made us all proud of him once again. We later buried him in St. Charles cemetery out on Long Island. Dad left us when he was only 46 years old.

Now! What? Here we are in this decaying neighborhood, getting worse by the day. All of the decent people including our relatives are moving out. We are still living in the same old apartment, which we rented from the stingy Jewish property owner who never gives us enough heat in the winter. Mom continued banging the steel pipe on the radiators while screaming, "Send up some steam." She still owned the Bar and Grill which was open for business seven days a week, while both her sons are too young to help her run the joint.

There was nothing else for mom to do but sell the place. Some time passed before she found a buyer. She worked her butt off trying to keep the place open and to make ends meet. It was not clear to us boys at the time, how she handled all of the legal matters. Momma told us later that some lawyer advised her but then charged her a rather large fee for his work. When she finally exited the place, she had no money left. Between taking a loss on the sale, paying help to keep it open and the lawyer's fee we were broke. Our folks used all of our savings to buy the business after dad's accident. Mom said, one day she would pay us back every cent she borrowed from us. However, that was the last thing we had on our minds. I told her not to worry we will start all over again.

Momma never let grass grow under her feet. She picked up where she left off with her old business. She began making trips to Manhattan to buy clothing wholesale and sell it retail to various people she knew. I tried to earn as much money as possible while keeping an eye on Billy and trying to set a good example.

Our Uncles taught us well, now was the time to use what knowledge we had. I managed to get an additional part time job after school at a gas station on Pitkin Ave. The job lasted for several months. While never giving up the job at the grocery store, working weekends I always seemed to have money. I tried to console Billy long after pop died. Billy took his passing quite hard. Many times, he sat on the floor in our house crying. I tried my best to be his big brother and sort of acted a little like a father to him. I sat next to him and promised him that things would get better. "We have each other and mommy too and no one will ever separate us." Momma often told us the same thing. "We must always stick together." She would also say, "Promise me that you boys will always love each other and never let anything come between you." "We promise mom." She never asked for help from anyone. Nor did she apply for any assistance from the government, not even unemployment. Momma was a very proud woman.

Billy spent a lot of time with our cousins Nick and Celia out at the chicken farm. He watched the kid's ice skate on the twin lakes along Montauk Hwy. After seeing how much he would gaze at them skating, I brought him to a sporting goods store and bought him a pair of ice skates. The little fella became a very good ice skater. He was able to do tricks and a nice figure eight on the ice. Things like this helped take his mind off pop. It took a few years until he stopped sitting by himself crying. I tried to look after him without letting mom know how much he still hurt. She probably knew we could never put anything over on her.

Momma never wanted to become a burden to her two sons, so she enrolled in classes and obtained her high school diploma. Everyone in the family was very proud of her. We held a graduation party for her at one of my cousin's house on Long Island. She later went on to find a job with a municipality. The job gave her all of the necessary medical benefits, which took a load off her mind.

Things went on as usual. I continued my studies at Lane high school, while I became more personal with many of the gang members and the future storybook characters. How can one not become involved with these people, we were always together, we attended classes, played sports, went to church, school dances and hung out on the same street corner. I shared their stories, became friends with their sisters and other relatives. I even spent many hours in their homes playing cards.

Billy also became involved with many neighborhood kids. He developed a good friendship with a Negro boy named Bernard, who spent a lot of time at our house. Mom feed him and treated him just as she did with our other friends. Although we were getting older, she continued to monitor all of our friends. Our house was the place where everyone assembled. That was because she wanted it that way.

As time marched on, mom knew I was spending more time away from our home than usual. Therefore, she had to have trust in me that I would not become involved with the wrong people. She was always a very smart woman. Momma never kept a short leash on either one of us. Instead, she continued her talks at dinnertime. She trusted me one hundred percent of the time. When we were, alone she frequently reminded me that I must set a good example for my younger brother. Also reminding me that whatever I did he will probably follow my example. Please! She'd say, "Don't ever make me ashamed of you. I am trying to be not only your mother but your father too. I love you both so very much."

Mom was much like the German women from the Ridgewood area of Brooklyn. She often swept down the front stoop and the concrete sidewalk in front of the house.

One morning as I was getting ready for school when she entered the small bathroom in our apartment, pushed me aside and began washing the hands and face of a little Negro boy. "Who the hell is that Ma?" "Shut up" she said, "I saw him going to school and he looked so dirty, so I thought I'd clean him up a bit." "Oh" So, I shut up. After washing the little boy, she put a nice clean shirt and one of our ties around his neck. Soon after that, he sat down to breakfast with us. We grew to know the kid and he became one of my mother's inaudible little friends.

Billy also befriended another kid from Doscher Street. The boy named Roger had about four siblings. Roger's mom died and his dad tried to keep the family together the best he could. Our mother knew this and therefore gave Roger a lot of attention. He ate dinner at our home quite often. Whenever we went to Long Island to visit relatives, Roger came with us. Our whole family knew the kid and everyone treated him as one of the family. Our Uncle Danny and Aunt Irene offered to adopt him and give him a good home. He refused. This was the biggest mistake of his life. I will tell more about Roger later. These are a few instances of how things were at our home.

Years later, I asked my mother why she always invited so many of our friends into our home and was always so generous. I told her that none of the other parents did this. She answered; it was the best way I could think of to meet every one of them and make sure that you boys never became involved with the wrong people.

NEIGHBORHOOD STINGS

As the Puerto Ricans slowly moved into the neighborhood, we saw a lot more action in the streets, especially on Glenmore Ave. explicitly on our block. When most people used the expression, (Do you want to go to the show?) It meant do you want to go to the movies. Whenever we used the term, we meant, do you want to go outside and watch a gang fight, which took place frequently.

Any curb space along the street quickly filled with an automobile belonging to someone that took the subway train to Manhattan. They got to the subway station extra early in order to avoid paying for parking in one of the lots. This was a good idea if it were any place else besides our section of Brooklyn. We witnessed some of the scams pulled off by the Puerto Ricans many times. This is how some of the stings went off.

A while after the owner of an automobile boarded the train; a thief would break open the trunk of his car and take everything that is inside. This included the spare tire, tools, clothing and whatever else was in there. When the owner of the car returned from work, a small kid standing behind the car with the trunk wide opened would ask the man if he was missing anything. The poor man answered yes everything that was in my trunk. Well, the little fella said. For twenty bucks, I could tell you where you can find everything. The man paid him and the kid lead him to the hidden stuff then ran like hell.
.

The same type of con took place by jacking up an automobile, placing cement blocks under the axels to hold it up from the ground. Then, all the tires and wheels removed and brought to a garage. Once again, a little kid approaches the man-asking if was interested in buying his wheels back. This gig brought in more than twenty dollars.

A woman does a load of wash then hangs the clothing out on a clothesline to dry. When the garments are almost dry, a kid removes all them and hides them somewhere. He hangs out near her window, when the woman goes to pull in her clothes and finds that there is nothing to pull in, the kid makes a deal. He tells her that he can get all of her clothes returned for some cash.

The Puerto Ricans would steal a car, then drive it to the neighborhood and park it under a tree. A chain block hoist is set in place. The chain then thrown over a heavy branch of the tree. The motor is unbolted from the chassis then hoisted out from the car and brought to a garage, either for a pre ordered sale or for a future sale. Other parts stripped and stored away. The car then lowered to the ground, set on fire and left to sit until the city sanitation removes it. There were many stripped and burned automobiles lying around the streets. Between the burnt out houses and the automobiles, our neighborhood began to look like a war zone.

The Negros were famous for removing copper, brass and lead pipes, from the walls of an apartment, then selling it at the junk yard for mungo. House fires occurred several times a month within a few blocks from where we lived.

On one occasion, while a house was burning on the block next to ours, firefighters came to put out the fire. Suddenly garbage cans and various pieces of furniture began to fly off the roof of the burning building. The firefighters and their trucks were the target of this flying debris.

As they tried to put out the fire while dodging flying debris, a couple of Negro boys began pouring gasoline around the fire truck. A moment later, they threw a lighted match into the gasoline, engulfing the firefighters in flames. Both Billy and I came to the aid of our friends the firefighters. We tore into the Negros with baseball bats. The firefighters eventually put out the fire and thanked us for our help. After that incident, they never began to extinguish a home fire in our neighborhood until the police were on the scene first to protect them.

The fire chief gave both Billy and I keys to a lock, and permission to park our cars behind a fenced parking lot next to the firehouse. He also told us to ring the fire alarm if we ever needed help fighting the bad guys. They will come over to help us. Did you ever hear of such a thing?

In order to operate a taxicab, one must have the proper licenses, insurance and a medallion on the cab. The medallion is quite expensive and they are not handed out to just anybody.

The largest cab company in N.Y. City is the Yellow cab Co. They primarily work in Manhattan, also Brooklyn, Queens, Bronx, Manhattan and Staten Island. If for any reason you needed a ride to the East N.Y. section of Brooklyn, do not try holding your breath until you found a person to take you there. They will tell you that it is too dangerous and then drive away.

Gypsy cab is the name of the game. Anyone with balls, places a magnetic sign on the side of his car reading TAXI. Bada Boom, he is in business. Some of them go a little further and place a sign reading (We aint yellow we go anywhere.)

While constructing a five story Day Care Center in East New York, The contractors were having a problem with pilferage, especially the plumber. Each time he delivered copper pipes to the job site, someone stole them. The Owner of the project provided a German Shepard guard dog for the evening hours. A load of copper materials were deliver during the daytime, the gates were lock for the night. The next morning we found the dog hanging from a steel bar joist dead as a doornail, and all the copper was gone.

Shorty Shoes: My mother sold the bar to a fellow named Frank. His nickname was Shorty. The name matched his height. They also called him Shoes. We never knew how he got that name. Maybe he owned numerous pairs of shoes.

Shoes did not run the bar in the same manner as our folks or the previous owners, Bennie and Abbie did. They catered to the locals in a mom and pop fashion. Whereas, sports, shuffle board and food were the focal points of their business. Shoes, was a different type person. He encouraged Wise guys and hot looking women to patronize the joint. My friends and I were still too young to indulge into alcohol. Therefore, we never entered the place. The law stated that one must be eighteen years of age to drink. We did not have to go hang out inside to recognize what was going on. We already had obtained the skill of being street savvy.

The Gyms: As a teenager, I continued to be very active in sports. Now that mom sold the bar I had to find another place to continue my workout routine. The little space I set up in the basement is now history. My friends Sal and Vinnie teamed up with me and joined a health club in Jamaica Queens just across the street from the extremely large movie theater called Valencia. The Valencia seats close to 3,500 people. It opened in the year 1929. The architect based his designed on Spanish architecture motifs which consisted of wrought iron railings, ornate tile work, sculptures and murals, inspired by Spanish and Mexican architecture. The place was gorgeous. I often took my girlfriend there to catch a flick.

The gym is a bit far from our neighborhood but we took the El that ran along Jamaica Ave. We always clowned around with each other along the train ride and up at the club too. While working out hard we had lots of fun. I never asked my mother for any money to do these things. I would never even think of doing so. I earned all of my own money and took care of myself. The gym changed names more than once while we frequented it. As most gyms do, they sold memberships up until the day they were about to either sell the place or temporarily go out of business. Therefore, we never laid out too much money in advance but always kept our membership.

Throughout the years, I belonged to many health clubs. Yours truly never became a Charles Atlas, but always kept myself in good shape in both body and mind. While always employed, I made time to exercise even if there was no one to go to the gym with. I never used being alone as an excuse. Later, I began to run several times a week. It did not matter what the temperature was, I dressed accordingly and went for a nice long run. On Sunday mornings, I ran around the reservoir up at Highland Park, even in the snow, ran along the sandy beaches in the summer, in the parks, golf courses, gym tracks, school tracks and city streets. I did this all my life. Today I still belong to a gym with my wife Francyn. We work out several times a week. It becomes a part of what you are.

Graduation: Several months prior to the prom, mom reminded me that the whole event was going to cost quite a few bucks, for that reason, she said, "I have a proposition for you." "What is it?" "Many people owe me money for the garments I sold to them and I am having a hard time collecting it from them. I will give you a list of names, addresses and the amount of monies they owe me. Everything you collect, you can use it for the prom and all the other graduation expenses." "OK give me the list. Before she knew it, I collected every penny. Afterwards, she told me that an old neighbor borrowed a few bucks. He promised to pay her back within a month. It was close to a year now, and he never gave her a cent. I called him on the phone and asked him for the money. He gave me a sob story. I reminded him that I was not a kid anymore and did not want to hear any of his bullshit. I told him that if he did not pay her in full by the end of the week, upon my visit him to him he'd have a headache that he would never forget. He paid my mother the entire amount he owed her within two days.

Graduation from High school was approaching rapidly. I had been dating an Italian girl one year younger than me. After school, we watched Dick Clark on Teen Bandstand out of Philadelphia. We knew how to dance just about every dance out there. Part of our school training in the gymnasium was to learn and practice the steps and tempo of all the dances. We attended many high school and church functions. We were good. Everyone was good. How could you not be good unless you had two left feet? John Travolta once said in the movie Saturday Night Fever, "Of course I know how to dance. I'm from Brooklyn."

The big day was near. I could not believe that we were almost finishing with school. The photos were taken, school rings, caps and gowns were on order, and the teachers and students were deciding who was to be selected as the most popular, most likely to succeed, best looking and so on. One of the Gym teachers asked me to come to his classroom because he wanted to speak to me. Upon entering the room he said, "Sit down Louis. I want you to know that the Gym teachers, all but one have agreed to elect you the schools Best Athlete. But, because he did not agree, we had to pick someone else." Just then, the teacher who did not agree with the others entered the room. He told me why he did not agree with the others. "You always had that little grin on your face. I believe that you never took anything seriously, for that reason, I picked another student for the award." "Well that's OK," I told him. "No hard feelings. I never had it so, I'll never miss it." While telling him this, I gave him the good old *smirk*. I knew dam well what he was talking about.

During graduation rehearsals, there was a lot of bamboozling going on amongst the students. The teachers tried like hell to keep everyone in order so that we could all participate in a successful event. The teacher in charge picked out couple of students to set as an example, in order to maintain an obedient assembly. The two students he pulled out of the group were my friend Red and me. He announced to everyone, that we would not participate in the graduation exercises on graduation day. He now had the attention of all the students.

Wow, this is going to be a shocker for my mother. She anticipated this day since I entered kindergarten. How can I break the news to her? When I got home, I began by telling her,

"Mom, I have some good news and some bad news."
"Oh-Oh, give me the good news first."
"I am going to graduate high school."
"So, I already know that. Now give me the bad news."
"Well I will not be participating in the class exercises at graduation."
"And why won't you participate?"

After telling her the reason, she became very annoyed. It was just what I expected. Both our mothers went up to the school and negotiated with the teacher in charge of the commencement. They explained how much this meant to them and that he should not punish the mothers because of this incident. He finally agreed to let us participate in the graduation exercise however; he said, "Both of them shall receive an empty diploma envelope on graduation day. When the new term begins, both of them are to write a letter of apology to the school principle. That is when they will receive their diplomas." This was fine with me.

When we returned home, my mother said to me. "Louis you have managed to have every teacher invite me to a special session since you began school. This event is the cherry on the cake." I knew the day I entered high school that I would continue batting a thousand in that category. I had no doubts about it. It was predictable. I gave mom a *smirk* she gave me a smack and it was the end of another day.

Although I was mischievous in school, mom always trusted me. Awhile after my dad passed away, she decided to trade in the car. Mom allowed me to shop and pick one out of a used car lot. She knew I was coming of age to drive in the city. I believe she felt this would help take my mind off pop. My uncle Charley went to check out the 1956 Mercury Montclair, which I found at a car lot. He said it looked good so mom traded in the old car.

While not quite eighteen years of age, mom allowed me to drive the car into the city on prom night. Wow. Speaking of the RITZ, who was better than I was?

Prior to graduation day, we all went to the class prom. My girlfriend, decked out in a prom dress while I sported a rented tuxedo. The prom took place in a hotel hall in Manhattan. We later attended a show at the Copa Cabana starring Johnny Mathis. Everyone had a great time without any problems.

One year later, my girlfriend graduated. The senior class selected her best-looking girl. This made me feel quite pleased. Here I am going steady with the best-looking Chick in the senior class. I must be doing something right. The whole prom scene took place once more. It is like deja vu all over again.

Draftsman: Jobs were hard to find after graduation. However, I landed a job not too far from our house. I was a Draftsman at the Richmond Screw Anchor Co. They manufactured engineered tying devices for concrete form construction. I started out at $55.00 dollars a week. My job was to produce drawings and details pertaining to the use of the devices. I contributed a portion of my weekly salary to mom to help with the household. I also paid for the auto insurance and continued buying all of my own clothes. Things were going very well. All the people I hung out with also had jobs and a car.

I enrolled myself into the N.Y.C. Community college which was located downtown Brooklyn. In addition, began a major study in Construction Technology. I also indulged in the basic math, English and other elective courses. I attended night school several times a week.

I walked to and from work each day. Mom used the car during the daytime and I used it just about anytime I wanted it. My friends and I began to cover a much larger radius since we had wheels.

Occasionally on Saturday afternoons a few of us stopped at a butcher shop, picked up some hero sandwiches, a can of soda and headed for an afternoon at

Aqueduct race track to bet on the horses. This was one of the many types of gambling which we indulged in.

We scheduled Saturday mornings for a basketball or stick ball game at another schoolyard further from our neighborhood. Red and I played the Jewish boys for money. We won most of the times, then double dated that night and blew whatever cash we won on the girls. We also attended many card games, not only in our neighborhood; we also traveled to play with new acquaintances a distance from where we lived.

We hooked up with a bunch of wise guys on the other side of Brooklyn. These people were from the Red Hook section, near the Brooklyn Navy yard. They were members of one of the five organized mafia families other than the cliques from our neighborhood, which are the Gambino and Lucchese mobs.

I suggested to Red that we get a hedge on these fellas.

"What do you have in mind?"

"Signals I told him, signals."

"Ya gotta be kiddin me? Dat sounds dangerous. If they catch us, they'll whack us right there at the card table."

"Ehh bull shit. Don't be such a candy ass, they gotta catch us first and if they do, we can talk our way out of it."

"Do ya think so?"

"Yeah, where's your balls."

"OK sounds good, let's work on it."

Tell a guy that he has no balls and he suddenly grows a pair. Both of us began reading several books on Poker. We studied odds and techniques of the game. We then developed a system of letting each other know just what cards we held in our hand. We practiced until we were sure of ourselves.

The swindle worked like this: The dealer hands out the cards. If neither of us has a strong hand we both fold our cards. As soon as one of us holds a strong poker hand, he signals what hand he holds. The other man raises the bet while the fella with the strong hand just calls the bet. This continues until the last cards dealt. At the end, the man with the strong hand raises the pot big time while the other fella drops out of the game. By this time, there is a lot of money in the pot. This worked in our favor most of the time. It was extremely important to pay attention to each card player, making sure that he did not suspect any shenanigans. These fellas were not stupid, besides they were all street wise. By the end of the night, we accumulated a stack of cash because these fellows gambled for big bucks.

The card games took place on weekends. After losing a bundle of cash, we offered them a chance to win it back at the bowling alley. Some of them were decent bowlers, and so, we had to hedge this game too. There was a young kid in our neighborhood that starred on a bowling team. He had a friend that bowled with him who was also a very good. This fellow looked like a farmer so; we bought him a pair of coveralls to wear when he came to bowl with us. The wise guys looked at him as some sort of a jerk. That is just what we wanted. They both had a bowling average of over two hundred. We instructed them not to show off, but to allow our opponents to win a game or two. When the hoods thought they had us beat, they raised the stakes. That's when the farmer and the kid turned it on, beating them by only a few points to take their money once again while keeping their interest alive for another shot at us in the future. We rewarded the two skillful bowlers handsomely, which made them available whenever we called on them.

This was risky business. We were not playing with the boys from the schoolyard. One slip up and we both wind up somewhere in the river with cement shoes or bowling balls tied to our feet. However, I explained to Red, that these thugs take from people every day of the week through extortion, prostitution, loansharking or some other way. They probably whack guys too. Therefore, we should not feel guilty to take from them. Just think of yourself as Robin Hood. Besides, it was a lot of fun and a continuous adrenalin flow.

Payback Is A Bitch: One morning the Daily News came out with a tragic story of a shooting that took place outside of Aqueduct Race track. The story went something like this: Young adult male shot to death while trying to assault a N.Y.C. undercover cop. The news article described how the young male tried to bully the cop somewhere near the entrance to the track. The cop warned him to back off while identifying himself as a police officer. The oversized male continued his attack on the police officer. During a physical altercation, the police officer drew his revolver and shot the attacker in the chest in self-defense. A physician pronounced the aggressor dead at the scene.

The newspaper identified the aggressor as Angelo, (Godzilla himself.) Wow! What a story. After reading it over a couple of times I thought to myself, Could this be true? Is the bully dead? The animal finally picked on the wrong fellow. I must admit, I breathe a sigh of relief. There will be no more beatings for me. Yes! Payback is a bitch.

Euclid Taxi Stand: It was a sunny summer afternoon. I was 18 years old. A few of my friends just finished playing basketball in the schoolyard on Crescent Street. I asked if anyone wanted to walk to the Drug store a block away on the corner of Pitkin Ave. and Pine Street. My pals Joey and Sal agreed to walk with me. As we approached the store, one of the Euclid taxicabs sped down the street, never slowing down at the stop sign. We jumped back to the curb to avoid the cab hitting us. Sal yelled out at the driver who then stopped the car, opened the door, walked over to my friend and asked, "What are you a F----- smart ass?" He threw a punch at him. Sal was no slouch; he hauled off and punched the driver knocking him to the ground. The fella got up and a fistfight begun in the middle of the street. Sal gave the older driver a good beating. There was blood all over the street. Sal bounced him off a parked bus several times. The cab driver was no match for my friend. He lay helpless in the street dripping in blood.

Within minutes, several of the older gangsters ran to the scene to assist their friend. These people were dressed in fancy clothes. One with a pin stripped suit, a black shirt and a tie lunged at Sal. I grabbed the dude who resembled Al Capone, dragged him away from Sal, shoved him against a telephone pole then smashed his head into the solid wood structure. Sal and Joey fought off the other thugs while the fella in pin stripes lay on the ground with a headache.

When it was all over, the crew from the cabstand got up and walked away. They had been roughed up. They shouted at us. "We will remember all your faces you are all as good as dead." We gave them the finger and a couple of other rude gestures and told them to tell their story walking. I picked up what I needed at the drug store and headed home. Mom had given me the car for the day but she needed a ride home from the liquor store where she worked few miles from the house in the Bushwick section of Brooklyn.

Sal must have went home too because about an hour later several Cadillac automobiles pulled into the neighborhood filled with gangsters. They were looking for us. The only one they found was Joey. They grabbed him off the street, dragged him into an alley across the street from Henry and Joey Hill's house, put a pistol in his mouth while demanding that he tell them where Sal and I went. Just then, a man named Joe who lived in one of the houses at the alley came out and pleaded with them not to whack Joey. Old man Joe knew most of the hoods from the cabstand because he lived on the same block and often chatted with them. He told them that Joey was a good friend of his son and a nice kid. As a result, they just smacked Joey around a little then let him go. Sal and I got away without any trouble.

It did not take long before the story spread around the neighborhood of what took place in the street that day. Nevertheless, no one ever spoke about it after that. Everyone knew that "lose lips sinks ships."

I knew damn well, what we just done could cost us our lives. These fellas play hardball. Stories about the people they whack are always appearing in the newspaper. Besides, some poor slob suddenly disappears from the neighborhood, never seen or heard from again.

I hung out on the street corner only a block away from the cabstand ate pizza at their store and walked down Pine Street past the cab joint quite often; it was only a block from my house. I used my own street savvy and kept a low profile for a long time, knowing that in no time at all they will be involved in something else therefore, putting this incident on the back burners. I never stopped going to the schoolyard nor did I stop hanging out on the corner, but I constantly kept an eye out for those individuals. After all, a fella has to take care of himself; no one is going to do it for him.

Several years later, a friend of mine who made detective in the N.Y.P.D. sat with me in a neighborhood diner. Unexpectedly, he says to me.

"Ohh-Ohh, don't look around now but someone you don't want to come in contact with just walked in the diner."

Who do you think walks in but the old dude who I smashed his head against the telephone pole. He walked up to our table and said.

"Hey Mateo, how you doin?"

Matty stood up and greeted him with respect.

"I'm doin good. How you doin?"

They hugged one another. This is very common amongst these guys.

"How's ya mother?"

"Fine, she's doin good."

Just then, he turned to me and said.

"Hey; I know you!"

Quickly I responded.

"Sure you do my father owns the bar on Crescent Street."

"Ok yeah your Frankie's boy, Dat's right."

He gave me a hug and told me to say hello to my dad for him.

"OK I'll do dat."

Evidently, he did not know that my father had died. He then told the waiter to give us whatever we wanted to eat and then give him the check. These fells never seize to amaze me.

Military Draft: After reaching the age of eighteen, it was compulsory that every male register with the U.S. Government. There are two classifications. 4-F or A-1. I qualified A-1, which means that I am eligible for draft into the Army at any time and serve a minimum of two years active duty. This was not an option particularly at this time considering my present situation at home. Consequently, after looking at all other ways to serve my country and not be away from home for too long, I decided to join the United States Marine Corps Reserve. What the hell. If I have to serve,

I may just as well be one of the best. Thus, I became one of "The few, the proud, the Marines."

I laid out the whole plan with mom and Billy. I told them this is something that I had to do. I promised to do my best and return home soon. After taking the necessary tests, I told my friends about my plans. My friend Sal threw a going away party at his house. Many people attended and wished me well.

My job at Richmond Screw Anchor will be there when I return. Another fellow named Hugh McHugh who worked with me enlisted at the same time.

I told my mother not to send me any goodies while I was at Paris Island Marine boot camp. She and my aunts sent many packages to my cousin Anthony who was in the Army. Mom never heeded what I requested. She decided to send a box of homemade cookies. Just after my leaving the chow hall, mail call was in order. The drill Instructor called my name.

"Borek."

"Yes Sir.

I stepped forward as he threw a box at me, wrapped in brown paper.

"What's in it?"

"I don't know Sir"

"Open it."

"Yes Sir."

"Its homemade cookies Sir, would ya like some?"

"Pogybait!"

"What?"

"Pogybait!" (Marine lingo means candy and other sweets)

"You piece of shit, don't we feed you enough?"

"Yes Sir."

He then turned to one of the privates standing at attention and instructed him to get my canteen and fill it with hot water.

"Now private Borek start eating your mamma's cookies and wash them down with the hot water."

"Yes Sir."

After I could eat no more, I asked permission to share them with the platoon. The friggin guy went crazy screaming at me.

"No one needs that shit. You are the only candy ass that seems to need mamma's cookies. Throw the rest of then in the G.I. can then write to your momma and tell her not to send any more of that shit to the Island."

"Yes Sir."

That evening I wrote my mother a very nasty letter explaining how she made me look like a fool in front of the platoon. This was an example of how the three months of basic training went.

There were many, both funny and memorable stories during my stay at boot camp. I will sum it up by telling what the senior Drill Instructor confided in me.

"Private Borek, come to my hut I want to speak to you in private."

"Yes Sir."

"Do you get enough to eat?"

"Yes Sir."

"Enough sleep."

"Yes Sir. I get the same as everyone else Sir."

"Do you receive mail regularly?"

"Yes Sir."

"I want you to relax, talk to me as though I am one

of your friends OK?"

"OK"

He began.

"We Instructors walk past all the huts every evening. Each of us have noticed that while all the other recruits are asleep, there is a lot of chatter and laughter going on in your hut, and the reason is you are telling jokes. We have selected to name your hut the late-late hut

"Is there a reason behind this joke telling?"

"Well as I see it, the Drill Instructors are trying to teach us discipline and camaraderie amongst the troops. I noticed many of the privates in my platoon are very nervous and sometimes frightened when the Drill Instructors begin screaming at them. I feel that a little humor in the evening will help them relax and make it through boot camp."

"And what about you, aren't you scared?"

"No I am not."

"We all noticed that when the other privates are getting their asses chewed out, you always seem to have a little grin on your face."

"A *Smirk* sir, it's called a *Smirk*."

"Do me a favor Louie, try to eliminate the F----- *smirk*, it's making our job a little harder."

"I will try sir."

He went on to tell me that I had the makings of an outstanding Marine and that I can walk off this Island at graduation time with every honor available to a recruit. Many of the original recruits that formed our platoon in the third Battalion were set back into other platoons only to extend their stay on the Island a little longer. In spite of this, I managed to fly through boot camp without any hitches. I continued to piss each of the Drill Instructors off with the *smirk*. I literally received a couple of beatings from the Drill Instructors including a punch in the face along with several punishments for my efforts. I graduated with the rest of the class on schedule. I neither received anything special pertaining to a reward nor was I honored in any special way. Nevertheless, I had many new friends that I knew I could trust with my life. I was just one of the guys and that satisfied me.

I served three more months at NATC Naval Air Training Center in Jacksonville, Florida. Afterwards, I returned home to serve one weekend each month at Floyd Bennett Field in Brooklyn and two weeks every summer at various naval air bases as a member of VMF 131, a fixed wing fighter squadron. After six years, I received an Honorable discharge.

Allow me to back up a moment and add a little story about my stay at NATC in Florida. The class, which I was part of, consisted of mostly Marines from the big cities. Our clique was from Brooklyn others from Philadelphia, Washington D.C, New Jersey, Chicago and Detroit, quite a bunch of men, all with the same type of mentality.

All of us had just been out of boot camp at Paris Island only a few weeks ago. Everyone was spit and polish and squared away. A Sgt. Striker assigned to lead our class, which dwelled in a two-story barrack, acted as if he was General George Patton. Whenever he marched us down the street and noticed an officer, he called out flanking, oblique and other fancy commands. He knew we were sharp and wanted to show off to the passing officers as though he trained us. Well between all the crap, he pulled on us in the living quarters and on the Street, we had our fill of him. One morning I gathered all of my classmates and suggested that the next time he tries to show off we can make him look like a jerk. Everyone was eager to participate. "OK, when he starts calling out different drills, all of us execute each command, when he calls out, "To the rear march." Only half of us turn to the rear while the rest of us keep on going forward. He will call it out again to try to get us back as a unit, everyone turn, march towards each other, crash and fall on the ground. "Wow how the hell do ya dink of this shit? Let's do it."

The next morning the class pulled off the little stunt. The officer had a good sense of humor and laughed like hell while Sgt. Striker's face turned the color of the Marine Corps flag. The next morning, still pissed off from what we pulled on him, he began giving everyone orders in a harsh way, which included a lot of petty shit. I walked behind him, wrapped a towel around his eyes, pushed him into a broom closet and locked the door. Our crew went to class that morning without him and did quite well.

The officers granted us liberty while on the new base. That weekend a dance planned at a large hall, with a band, food and alcoholic beverages. People from each branch of the military attended the function. We Marines put on our new uniforms, spit shined our shoes and were ready to party.

The hall was huge; tables were set up similar to the hotel dances back home. I do not know where all of these people came from, both men and women alike. Nevertheless, the place was rocking and everyone was having a ball. Out of nowhere, a Sailor and a Soldier began fist fighting. A few seconds later more guys were slugging it out. I thought to myself, this is just like home, when one of my friends flew past me with a bloody nose from a punch he got from an Army boy. The soldier, still in pursuit of him so, I grabbed him, punched him in the face causing him to land with his back flat on one of the tables. The table collapsed. Damn, I thought this is just like the movies and I felt like John Wayne. After the dance, none of the Marines went on liberty again.

Upon my return from Florida, I went back to work at my old job. I enrolled in classes again at the Brooklyn Community college while serving the remainder of my military commitment. I was glad to be home again with my family. Mom continued to work and Billy became a little older. Everything was back to normal.

After completing my tour of active duty, I made friends with numerous Marines from my duty station at Floyd Bennett field. One fella in particular hung out with me, a Jewish dude named Gene Estner. He was a character with a great sense of humor and was always ready to engage in fun.

Gene often spent time at our house. He could not believe that my mom knew how to make Blintzes. (They are A Jewish type calzone with various fillings.) Mom asked him which kind he liked best, and then pounded them out from scratch. He ate them as fast as she made them. He and mom got along very well.

The two of us decided to take a trip to Fire Island for the weekend. A ferry took us across Great South Bay to Cherry Grove. After disembarking, we encountered a group of men dressed in bright colored costumes adorned with feathers.

"Hey what the hell is dat?" says Gene.

"I don't know they look like a bunch of fags."

As we turned around, the ferry was on its way back to Long Is.

"Well, dares a bar lets go get a drink and scope out the joint?"

"Yeah, sounds good to me."

Inside the bar was no different, there were many more men dressed the same way and they also had balloons, all of them were dancing in line to the Hully Gully.

"Hey Gene there's two broads, lets go talk with dem"

As we approached the girls, one of them caressed the other and sputtered out,

"She belongs to me."

"Wow! These two are freaken lesbians."

"We gotta get the hell outta here."

Unfortunately, the only means is a beach taxi that really had no schedule. After hanging ou for a while, a taxi drove us to Ocean Beach, another town, with straight people.

"This is our kind of place," said Gene.

"Yeah let's check out that bar, looks like lots of action."

The evening went well, lots of laughs and good-looking women. Nonetheless, the evening was ending and we had no place to crash. The locals told us that it is against the law to sleep on the beach, the police would arrest us, besides it was not summer yet and the nights get cold and damp on the Island.

After speaking to some folks in pursuit of a place to sleep, a fellow revealed to us that for a couple of bucks each, a space in his living room is available. "Great take us there." The house was full of people, all the bedrooms occupied; therefore, the floor in the living room will be fine.

The living room had a fireplace that was burning wood and it was cozy. During the night, the temperature dropped considerably and the fire was burning out. It was getting very cold and we did not have any blankets.

"Hey Gene, it's pretty friggin cold aint it?"
"Yeah, Watta ya dink we autta do?"
"I don't see any firewood do you?"
"No."
"How about that rocking chair, it's made of wood?"
Gene busted it apart and placed it into the fireplace. A while later it got cold again.
"Hey, I'm gonna throw one of these draws from that chest in, Watta ya dink?"
"Go for it."

It seemed like a very long night, but before it was over, we had burnt the rocking chair, every draw in the chest, the chest and another wooden chair. As the good Marines that we were, we adapted to the situation in hand. We awoke before anyone else in the house and vacated the joint before the owner woke up. We had successfully burnt more than $4.00 worth of wood, our cost to sleep there. Semper Fidelis (Always Faithfull.)

The Custom Jewelry Gig: The desire to make extra money never left me. With my eyes and ears always opened, I looked for the next opportunity to pick up extra cash. My cousin Rosalie introduced me to a new idea. She and her husband Paul began selling custom jewelry at home shows. She invited me to come to a demonstration just to see how the idea worked. After watching I thought, "I could do dat."

The following week Rosalie and I went to the jewelry center in Manhattan. She asked that I act serious and not joke around in front of her new business associates. "OK let's make it happen." Shortly after an introduction to the merchants, while inspecting the various pieces of jewelry in the glass cases, I swore that I saw a friend of mine walk past the front of the shop. Like a bat out of hell, I ran to get a better look out the large glass storefront. Not realizing that there was an additional glass partition in front of the exterior window display, my head smashed squarely into the glass partition almost breaking it. Everyone in the store stopped what he or she was doing. All of their attentions focused on the loud noise while watching me hold my head with pain. The man whom was helping my cousin was bewildered. He asked her if I was crazy. "What kind of a person runs into a glass window like that?" Rosalie and I made our purchases then ventured back home. We had a good laugh about the incident while my forehead swelled up.

I gave home demonstrations in my spare time and sold some stuff at my construction job site. I also used another technique, which I figured would work. I placed a display of shinny jewelry in the trunk of the car, pulled up to a construction site during lunch hour, opened the trunk in front of a bunch of the workers and told them that the stuff was hot and that I was looking to unload it fast. This idea paid off better that the home shows especially on paydays.

This gig lasted for quite a while. I made restitution with the people at the jewelry store while spreading out to other places to purchase other ornamental bracelets, rings, earrings and trinkets. Jingle-jingle, I hear coins in my pocket.

The Breakup: After dating my beautiful Italian girlfriend for several years, she began to bust my balls about getting married. Her mother always pumped her to encourage me to commit to setting a date. Nevertheless, this was the furthest thing on my mind. My cousins all married at a young age, as did many of the other people in our neighborhood. I was not ready to take the big step. Consequently, I continued to go out with her but never made a commitment to get married. The pressure became unbearable. At that specific time, I should have broken off our relationship but I did not. I gave in and set a date.

I put up a lot of money "Deposits" pertaining to all the crap that goes towards a wedding and house furnishings too. She was happier than a pig in shit and her mother glowed each time she saw me. Her old man always liked me so he was also glowing. Just prior to the main event, Miss gorgeous met another dude at work. She told me to come to her house. While her entire immediate family sat in a circle watching us in their living room, she removed the ring I gave to her and told me in so many words that she did not want to marry me. "Otz" I sat there like numb nuts not knowing what to say while the clan stared at me. "OK If that is what you want." I then said to her younger brother. "Johnny boy, go down to the basement and get me my punching bag. I'm out of here."

My heart was broken and my bankbook was empty. I continued to do my job with the construction company, trying to hide my inner feelings. It took me awhile to return to being my normal self. I figured what the hell, I started over from scratch before, I can do it again and so, I did. I never once saw or spoke to her again. Move on young man. Move on.

Time for A Change: I worked as a Draftsman for three and a half years at the same place. I was now 21 and began to feel closed in. Similar to how I felt on a rainy day in the house when I was a kid. While working at my desk one day I picked up one of the sample iron nuts that was lying on the windowsill and pitched it out of the second story window. The thing bounced off the brick wall about one inch above a large plate glass window of the grocery store located across the street from our office. Wow! What would have happened if it went through the window? I could have hurt many shoppers with the broken glass and the flying nut. I thought to myself, it is time for a change.

One of the salesperson from our company set up an interview for me at a construction site in the Williamsburg section of Brooklyn. The company was looking for a rodman for a layout crew. A layout crew consists of three people, a rodman, a transit man and a chief of party. At the time, I had no idea what a rodman was. After the interview, they offered me the job. The party chief liked the idea that I was a Marine. He was a Navy Seabee and he evidently saw a rival and a chance to harass me. I started work soon after giving my old boss ample notice. I kept in contact with my old coworkers for many years.

Prior to starting my first day of work, my new boss instructed me to buy him hot coffee and have it at the construction shanty by 7:00 A.M. "OK boss" That morning I arrived at 6:30 A.M and stood outside the shanty with the lid off the coffee container. When he arrived at 7:00 A.M, I handed him the coffee container filled with cold coffee with the lid on it. He took one sip and complained that it was cold. I told him that the coffee was not cold when I arrived at work but because he came late, he would have to drink it cold. I then asked if all of his Navy friends were like him. This got the ball rolling. I did whatever he told me to do and jumped on it very quick. He broke my balls every day, but I made sure never to show that it bothered me. This pissed him off. The harder he tried to break me, the faster I did whatever he directed me to do then I gave him a good old *smirk.*

We developed a great relationship. He got me into the International Union of Operating Engineers the following week. I worked with the same group of people for many years. I made more money as a rodman than working at my old job. Before we finished constructing two reinforced concrete buildings at 21 stories and five buildings at eight stories, they promoted me to a transit man along with a hefty raise.

The construction jobs became more interesting, coinciding with all of the classes, I was studying at school and I kept getting raises. Only one problem, each new job was a further distance from my home. We now started a job in New Jersey, near the George Washington Bridge. Work started before 7:00 A.M. Our engineering crew was the first people to begin work and the last people to leave the job every evening. The task of night school was becoming intolerant. There just were not enough hours in the day, besides doing homework. Vacation time each year consisted of traveling with the Marine Corps to an air base to train. I had no choice but to drop out of school. Making a living took precedence.

Most of the time, I traveled to and from work by train. Located on a large platform at the Broadway Junction station in Brooklyn was a fellow who sold cut flowers. I made it a point to stop and buy mom a bouquet every payday. She continued to make a fuss and I ate it up.

Spaceman: Billy never knew that I kept a close watch over him. He continued to hang out close to the neighborhood and I always knew who his friends were. He began smoking cigarettes at the age of fifteen. He thought he was shrewd and that he was putting something over on me but I always knew what he was doing. I also knew he would not stop smoking so; I never pushed the issue at his young age. He asked me only one time to help him in a fight. I gave to him the same medicine that pop gave me. Billy never asked again. He learned quicker than I did that he had to protect himself or learn to avoid getting into a confrontation. He probably heard pop talk to me more than one time.

There was a kid in the neighborhood Billy's age, whose nickname was (Spaceman.) He was a bright kid and was very interested in the space age. He seemed to know a lot about rockets and that sort of thing. Spaceman had a brother a couple of years older than me. We occasionally hung out together. Their dad had either died or divorced the mother. Like many other people in the neighborhood, Spaceman began to experiment with drugs. He literally became a Spaceman. The reason being, the drugs spaced him out.

The kid wandered around the neighborhood doing stupid things, like standing at a street corner with a length of rope waiting for the bus to come to a halt. He quickly tied a large mailbox to the back of the bumper of the bus, then stood on the corner all by himself and laughed like a hyena as the mailbox bounced down the street behind the bus. The kid had a red rash around his mouth, which indicated that something was not normal. I once asked his brother if he was aware of his kid brother's condition. He did not seem to care very much. For that reason, I never mentioned it again. It was not too long afterwards that Spaceman died from an overdose of drugs. They launched him into orbit.

Bla-Bla Blackie: Blackie was a father to one of the Italian families that lived on the next block from us. He lived in the same building as the Godzilla family. He had two good-looking daughters and a son Frankie.

Whenever Blackie was out in the street you could not help hearing him, he was very boisterous. He left for work at the same time as me in the morning. I'd sometimes walk with him to the subway or meet him downstairs on the train platform. Blackie gave me the same old greeting each morning, a big slap on the back and a "Hey boy how ya doin?" It was customary to read the daily news on the way to work. When we boarded the train at Euclid Ave., plenty of seats are available. As the train moved on, it became crowded with standing room only, which created a bunch of what they call strap hangers. During our travel, Blackie talked continuously, burning a hole in my ear. As the train passed through the Bedford Stuyvesant section of Brooklyn, many Negros boarded the train causing it to look like a packed can of sardines. All of a sudden, comes out of Blackie's mouth in a loud voice, "Hey boy, these F----- niggers stink don't ya dink so?" I instantly buried my face in the newspaper and tried to act as if I did not know him. I felt many dark eyes staring at me and could not wait to exit the train. After that morning, I tried my best to avoid him. When I saw him, I ran to the last car.

Blackie's son who they all called Frankie-boy committed a crime and sat in the slammer for a year or two. Frankie did the crime and paid the time, and was ready to go home. He did not want everyone to know that he was in jail and so, his plan was to quietly enter the neighborhood and slowly work his way back into society. On the other hand, his father had different ideas. Blackie made a large colorful banner and nailed it over the front of the building. It read, WELCOME HOME

FRANKIE-BOY. As he walked towards his house, music began to play and there was a big crowd to greet him. Freaken Blackie he did it again!

Sundays: On Sundays, we tended a mass at St. Fortunata church. Mom often took her mother along with us. She always dressed with bright colored suits and dresses looking very attractive. Billy and I were never too fond of the idea because my grandmother often fell asleep then begin to snore very loud, which attracted everyone's attention including the priest and the altar boys.

It was a summer morning when we all packed into our red Mercury automobile. I was now of legal age to drive in the city. My grandmother was sporting a canary yellow dress with a matching hat. She was riding shotgun next to me. I drove the car to the parking lot next to the church that had burnt coal ashes as its foundation. Before I had the car properly parked, Grandma jumped out, then bent over to pull up her garters while leaving the door wide opened. I turned to my left to look out the back window because I wanted to straighten out the car. Without noticing her bending over, I put the car in reverse and backed up. Bada-Bing the friggin door hit her in the ass and sent her sprawling into the black ashes. Mom let out a scream as Grandma rolled around trying to get back on her feet while cursing at me in Italian. Her stockings? Yo, Furgetaboutit! They ripped to shreds and her canary yellow dress now looked like a black crow. Mom who sat in the back of the car smacked me in the back of my head and messed up my hair. My girlfriend began yelling at me while Billy was hysterical laughing. We took grandma home that morning. Mom and my girlfriend got her cleaned up while Billy and I chuckled about the incident. "At least she did not fall asleep in church that morning."

The Good The Bad & The Ugly:
Sometimes things are going good, then they turn bad, then they can turn very ugly.

I was 21 while at home alone with mom one afternoon. Everything was going **GOOD.** Suddenly, there was a knock on the apartment door. When she opened it, standing there was a plain-clothes detective who identified himself. Standing beside him was my brother. "Mrs. Borek, I am doing you a favor by bringing your son home to you." "What is the problem sir?" said mom. "There was a gang fight and he is one of the people that we caught. Many of the other boys are in the police station. However, I felt that Billy is a clean cut kid, very respectful and deserves another chance. I advise you to keep a closer watch over him. Next time he will not be so lucky." "Thank you sir, we will." **Then they begin to turn bad.**

Soon after the detective left, mom asked Billy "what the hell is going on with you? Whatever possessed you to get involved in a gang fight?" He answered; "My friends asked me to help them." Mom almost hit the roof. She told him to get inside, and then instructed me to go talk with him and do whatever it takes to teach him a lesson.

Billy stood there staring at me. Calmly, I asked him what happened today. He explained where and how the incident took place.

"What I do not understand is how did ya get involved in it?"
"Well, my friends asked me to help dem"
"Help dem do what, risk yourself getting hurt to go and fight with someone that ya don't even know?"
"Yeah they needed help."
"Billy! This makes no sense at all. How can ya beat up on someone that ya never seen before?"
"All of my friends went."
"And so, ya felt that that was a good enough reason for ya to go hurt some people that never did anything to harm you?"
"Well, I guess?"
"Ya guess?" He shrugged his shoulders in a manner as if to say yeah that is a good enough reason. I began to get pissed off.
"Let me ask ya something, if you are in trouble and needed help, would your friends come to help ya?"
"I guess they would."
"OK, start making phone calls."
"What do ya mean"
"What I mean is that as of now, you are in trouble and ya definitely need help."

At that moment, I hauled off and punched him in the face. He fell to the ground, looking up at me. I said to him. "Get up" As he got onto his feet I cracked him again and once more he fell to the ground. Mom was inside taking it all in but never said a word. "Do you want to make that call now, because as I see it you damn well need some help?" He got up and stared at me. "Well defend yourself." He would not hit me. This pissed me off even more. I grabbed him by the throat, threw him to the ground, jumped on him and began banging his head on the floor. "Now get up" He got up and the friggin guy never lifted a hand to defend himself. I became angrier; I then threw another punch, smashing him in the face this time knocking him across mom's bed into the dresser. At that point, my mother came in and told me to stop. "That's enough." "Christ I only hope it is. Let this be a lesson for you."

I felt terrible for a long time after hitting my younger brother as I did. However, sometimes "Ya gotta do what ya gotta do."

Sometime later:

Billy was helping mom vacuum the carpet when a few of his friends knocked on the door. After speaking with them for a moment, they left. I approached my brother and asked him,
"What did they want?"
"They asked if I would go to Queens to help them fight a gang of guys."
"What did ya tell them?"
"I told them No! I can't go."
"Why did ya tell them No?"
"You know why."
I felt that he did learn a good lesson.

The next morning there was a picture in the newspaper of a bunch of Billy's friends including the ones that had called on him last evening. The story read something like this: Teenager stabbed to death in Queens by a gang from Brooklyn. All the boys are in jail, awaiting a hearing.

Of course, mom was sad because of what happened, on the other hand, she was also glad that she had made the decision to allow her older son to handle matters a short time ago. She felt like she had nipped trouble in the bud with my younger brother.

A couple of days later:

Billy accumulated a pile of money in his drawer. When I noticed it, I asked, him where he got it from. He told me that he got it selling fireworks.

"Where do ya get them? Do ya go to Chinatown?"

"No some guy in a truck comes around and he sells them to me cheap, then I sell them in school for a profit."

I began to think. If my kid brother can turn such a profit by selling fireworks in school, imagine what me and my friend Red could make if we sold them from our cars in various neighborhoods.

"Could ya get more?"

"Sure do ya want me to get ya some?"

"Yeah, I'll let ya know how much a little later."

I got on the phone with Red; we had accumulated a stack of cash from playing cards and bowling with the mobsters. I told him that we could score big-time with the fireworks then take a nice trip to Mexico for a vacation. Red was easy to persuade. "Get a bunch he said." "OK. I will."

A few days later, we had the car loaded with all sorts of explosives, Roman candles, Cherry Bombs, Ash cans, Nigger chasers, Firecrackers and other bangers. We set out to Queens to make our first sale. Upon pulling up to, a schoolyard Red yells out "Hey do you guys wanna buy some fireworks?" About a dozen kids ran to the car. At the sight of the commotion, a police squad car pulled up alongside of us and asked, "What's going on?" All the kids scattered like a bunch of frightened monkeys. "OK get outta the car and put your hands on the roof," The two police officers searched the car and unloaded all of the fireworks. At that point, we sold for a grand total of fifty cents. The cops took our car, and put us into the police car. They drove us to the police station. There we stood in front of a big desk with a police Sargent sitting behind it with a mean look on his face. "What have we got here?" He asks. The arresting officer says, "We caught these two selling fireworks down near the schoolyard," He then dumped a load of explosives on the Sargent's desk. They began to roll off the desk onto the floor and into his lap. When I saw that, I began to laugh.

"What the hell are you laughing at?" I answered,
"Ehh a lot of fireworks hah?" with a big *smirk* on my face.
"So, ya dink its funny do ya?" I shrugged my shoulders and said
"Ehh."
NOW, THEY BEGAN TO TURN UGLY.
"Take off their belts and shoelaces and lock them up" "Are you kidding me?"
"Shut your friggin mouth and go with the officer."

Red made a comment,

"Damn it Louie that friggin *smirk,* when the hell are ya gonna learn?"

The police officer marched us to the jail cells in the Queens Police precinct. As we walked past the filled cells, each of the occupants greeted both of us by name. Why not, they were all Billy's friends. The police officer gave a double take and asked,

"All these guys know you by name?"

"Ehh"

In the morning, the arresting officer brought us a hot breakfast. He said that he did not sleep at all during the night, claiming he felt he made a mistake by bringing us into the police station. He realized we were good people and did not deserve to be behind bars. He also commented about my laughing at the Sargent. "That's what got him pissed off, and it is what landed you guys in here."

Before the whole thing was over, it cost us about a thousand dollars in fines and court costs. I could not look my brother in the face. He never let me live this one down. I told Red not to let it bother him. We will make it back at the card games. Not long afterwards, we did just that.

The House Next Door: My Grandmother who lived next door from us suddenly

passed away. She was half owner of the four families building that she lived in. My Aunt Viola owned the other half. Our mother thought it would be a change for us if she were to purchase the building. She did not need much cash as a down payment, which made it a sweet deal. Grandmother's half, split six ways divided amongst her children while each of them would accept one hundred dollars every six months from mom as payment for their share of the inheritance. Aunt Viola also collected a monthly payment for her share of the building.

We moved into the building next door in the winter season. The first morning was like something we have never experienced. "Hey ma, it's warm in the house, is there something wrong?" "I know, nothing is wrong, we own it, I turned up the heat." From that day on, she never banged on the steel radiators with the metal pipe. Nor did she warm up our underwear in the gas oven for us to put on before we got out of bed.

Mom made a study on legal ways to raise rents according to the government's rent control rules. She had Billy add electrical outlets in the walls, which he spread apart to the minimum distance allowed in order to add twenty-five cents a month for each outlet. She kept her two boys busy performing various tasks that she laid out. All that we had learned from other people when mamma sent us to work with them was now paying off. There was no profit but we had use of the cellar and plenty of heat. Speaking of the RITZ, who had it better than us?

The Hang Out: Things continued in the neighborhood as usual. The racketeers made their heists on trucks to and from Kennedy airport. Whenever they did, the word was out on the street. It was not long afterwards that we received a phone call to go to a certain address if we were in the market for a couple of cases of scotch whiskey, shrimp or some other freshly obtained commodity.

Henry Hill and his wife Karen had an apartment nearby. We occasionally stopped there to see what they had for sale. It was common to find clothing racks with various kinds of garments taken from a truck hold up. Henry liked selling food products from a heist. He said, after everything is eaten there is no evidence.

A Brinks truck heist, for a very large amount of money took place in our neighborhood. They claimed the amount to be in excess of a million dollars. Shortly afterwards there were plain-clothes man combing the neighborhood seeking information. They questioned most of us about the robbery. Nonetheless, the crime went unsolved.

Less than a year after mom sold the Bar and Grill to Shorty Shoes, there was a murder committed inside the joint. Someone dragged the body outside and left it across the street on the sidewalk. The story in the Daily paper read something like this: Male body found lying on sidewalk on Glenmore Ave. in Brooklyn. The man, shot to death. Evidence indicates that the crime took place in in a local tavern. The victim's scraped shoes and a trail of blood leading back to the bar signify that someone dragged the body along the concrete sidewalk. I do not know the outcome of that incident. There were too many other things going on at the time.

I became of permissible drinking age; now permitted to frequent any establishment that served alcohol. It was no big deal for me because I was not much of a drinker. However, it was nice to be able to gather with all the fellas in an establishment instead of the street corner. The place where everyone met was my parents' old bar. Still owned and operated by Shorty Shoes.

I began to meet many new characters besides the people I already knew. Friday nights being the most popular time, most of the fellas came there to have a few drinks, congregate and decide who was going with who, and where we were gonna go. Everyone rather hung out with his or her own crew. Most of the times, we ventured off into different directions. Some of us went to a dance in Manhattan, a place in Queens with a band, or a Latin joint somewhere in Brooklyn. At the end of the night, whoever did not hook up with a chick went back to the bar and hung out with the guys or tried to make it with one of the local barmaids. After the bars closed, many people congregated in a local dinner for breakfast.

One weekend night a band was playing at Short's bar. He brought in some entertainment, trying to keep everyone from going somewhere else. Red and I had a couple of drinks at Shorty's place then began bouncing around to the local pubs. A couple of hours later we went back to our regular watering hole. "Shorty Shoes place." At this time, we both began feeling a little woozy from our consumption of alcohol. The place, filled with people and loud music. I noticed many different people in the bar including some good-looking women. The band lured in a nice crowed. Red and I continued to drink. At this point, I was feeling drunk. This was something I had never felt before. Red looked worse than I did. We started to walk into the rear of the place where people were dancing when I saw a neighborhood friend of ours named Jimmy catch a surprise punch square in the face from some guy I had never seen before. Jimmy fell backwards his head hit the wall. He then dropped on his ass to the floor knocked out cold from the blow. Red went after the fella that punched him and at that point, all hell broke loose. As it turned out the new people in the place were from Rockaway Ave. in Queens it was the friggin John Gotti bunch.

Instantly, they grabbed Red, threw him down on the shuffleboard table and continued pounding on him, these fellas were giving him a beating while I stood there disorientated. Suddenly I made the decision to rush in and help my pal. I put my head down while grabbing him around the neck with my arm, dragging him off the table. I began to receive blows to my head and body. Nevertheless, I managed to keep my balance, pointing Red towards the door while pushing him from behind yelling in his ear "Run you son of a bitch. Run for your life." We both made it out of the place with a couple of the assholes chasing us. We caught a few more punches but managed to run across the Sunrise highway avoiding any further injury. Looking back, we got off cheap. If one of those characters decided to use a gun or a knife on us, I would not be writing this story.

This experience was the greatest lesson I ever learned. I promised myself from that day on, that I would never drink alcohol again to the point where I am not 100% in control of my mind and body. Realizing that the neighborhood I lived in is very dangerous, I must always be capable of defending myself. Up to this day, I have never become drunk again. Red was another story.

Some of the people who assembled at the bar were real characters. A dude called Cheech frequented the joint. He regularly belted down scotch and soda. He was a very nice fella. I could not enter the place without Cheech buying me a drink. By the way, Cheech was another name the Italians called someone with the name Frank. After a few drinks, he became very loquacious. Cheech had plenty of wild stories to tell. After we developed a relationship with these people, they trusted us and shared things that they never talked about with many other people. Another nickname he had amongst his peers is "The Falcon." While sipping on a mixed drink one evening he told me how he acquired that nickname. He said, "A few of my friends and me were stalking these guys from a rival gang in Manhattan one night. Something happened between us, and this night was showdown night. I stood on a balcony with two loaded pistols. As they entered the hotel, one of my gang members began shooting at them. They drew their pistols and fired back at us. I jumped off the balcony into the lobby while shooting both guns at them. When the gunfight was over, we all took off leaving them in a bloody mess. After that night, my friends began calling me the Falcon because of the way I flew off the balcony."

Now this sounded like a farfetched story, somewhat hard to believe until that one day another strange fella that began hanging out with us. He also knew Cheech as the Falcon. I asked him one night when Cheech was not present, "How did Cheech acquire the name Falcon?" He told me the same story as I heard from the Falcon himself.

Whenever entering any of the bars where my friends hung out, it was almost impossible to walk in and not have at least a couple of drinks bought for me. The first thing someone said was "Give Louie a drink and take it out of here as he pointed to a pile of cash on the bar. No body ran a tab; it was customary for everyone to drop money on the bar in front of himself as the bartenders picked from each pile during the evening. No one ever kept count on whose turn it was to buy the next drink.

During the many years that I associated with these characters, they shared many stories of what they did or what they were about to do. As usual, I listened and never spoke about anything. Some of the fellas from Henry's movie (Goodfellas) also hung out here or occasionally stopped in for a drink. I could write more about the corrupt and ruthless things that happened along with their stories about some poor slobs being wacked and buried. However, that would be against my nature, besides this book is not about them.

Everything went well for me at work as a Field Engineer. I continued to show up very early each morning to layout work for the construction crews while getting raises and a promotion to the position of Party Chief. I am now in charge of running my own crew of Field Engineers.

My company completed a twenty-one story residential building in Fort Lee, New Jersey close to the George Washington Bridge, and then began laying out foundations at the edge of the Palisades along the Hudson River. These foundations supported the superstructure for several buildings, which also contained residential suites.

I considered the trip to and from work each day part of my job. Many people would not do the traveling that I did on a daily basis. However, I did not find it as cumbersome as they may have imagined it to be. Besides, I worked with a great bunch of fellows who felt the same way as I did.

I very rarely worked on weekends; for that reason, I had time to spend with my friends and the girls, often traveling somewhere to have a good time, in addition to hanging out at the bar or going to nightclubs. Eventually, it all became a bit expensive. As a result, I came up with another great idea; Mr. Ricardi who rented one of his garages to park my car on Euclid Ave. worked in a place that rented work clothes to various companies. His firm picked them up, washed and returned them to the shops. When the garments became a little worn, they replaced them with new ones. Mr. Ricardi had access to the worn shirts and trousers. I told him to store them in his in his garage while I arranged to pedal them to the construction workers at my job site. He brought home many bundles tied with string. The bundles, categorized according to size and color. Meanwhile, I had one of the carpenter foreman cut the door to our construction shanty in half, and then attached a counter to it while also installing shelving around the entire room. Once completed, I brought enough of each size to fill the shelves. Each piece of clothing I purchased for .25 cents then sold for .75 cents, tripling my money on every sale. Each morning the various workers bought a set of matching top and bottom shirt and trouser. The whole idea was fantastic. Anytime it rained, they bought dry clothes. I managed to continue the same set up at each job site. Mr. Ricardi never seemed to run out of supply and he was as happy as a pig in shit.

The Swindle: It was a Saturday afternoon, a few friends and I gathered at the Lucky Strike Lanes on the corner of Atlantic Ave. and Crescent Street. While we bowled, a character by the name of Gabe came over to our lanes and asked if any of us were interested in purchasing some clothes. My good friend "Fat Joey" who was also at the lanes knew the fella. Gabe proceeded to show us what he had for sale. Everything he showed us had a good quality. One of the nicest things was a man's suit in several different colors to choose. Everyone was interested in what he had to offer along with the great prices. Consequently, Gabe took a list of orders from all of us while requiring a small deposit in order to clinch the deal. Fat Joey said it was OK to give him the money, for that reason we did. Before leaving, he guaranteed to deliver the goods next Saturday.

The following week I attended a Marine Corps drill. I gave my pal Red the balance of the money to give to Gabe and collect the suit I ordered. When trying on the suit, I could not fit into the extremely small jacket and the pants were about six sizes too big.

"What the hell is this?" I asked Red.

"Didn't you look at the friggin dings before you paid him?"

"No; but don't feel bad most of the socks the utter guys bought had no toes, and a sweat shirt was missing an arm."

"No kiddin."

"Yeah; No kiddin."

"Well, what do ya dink we autta do about it?"

"I'm not sure; ask Joey, he knows Gabby."

"OK I'll do dat."

Joey was a television technician and owned his own business. No one used the nickname Fat Joey when he was nearby. He was a great person, no one wanted to hurt his feelings. Occasionally he managed to piss off one of the guys and they called him a fat bastard to his face. Otherwise, everyone knew him as T.V. Joe.

After trying on the horrendous suit, I called T.V. to tell him about the scam Gabe pulled on us. He told me to come to his shop and he will figure something out to get all of our money back from the con man. When I got there, Joey had a plan already in play. He told me to come with him to Gabe's apartment. He had already called Gabe's wife who he knew personally and told her that Gabe called him asking that he check out their television. Joey already knew that Gabe was not at home. When we got there, the wife claimed that she has no problem with the television. Joey was clever; he convinced her that there was a problem and that he must bring it to his shop for the repair. The television was a console with a large screen and so, it took two of us to carry it down to the truck. When Gabe returned home, he realized that he was not as shrewd as he thought he was. He called Joey and later returned everyone's money, and then Joe gave him his T.V. It is nice to have good friends.

T.V. Joe: My good friend T.V Joe did not have set hours in his business. When the opportunity knocked Joe jumped. He knew how to make money. I occasionally went on calls with him when I had nothing to do. One afternoon while at a customer's house, he removed the broken channel selector from the television then asked the woman which channels she preferred to watch? The woman said,

"Why do you ask?"

"Because the parts that are damaged cost ten dollars each to replace and I want to know which ones ya would like fixed."

"Well I watch all the channels."

"OK I will fix them all for ya."

"Fine." she replied.

The woman paid him to repair all the channels and we then left the house. I later asked.

"What was that all about?"

"Ehh, The tuner has all the channels built into one. I always give them a choice so that I can charge more for the part."

"What if she did not pick all of the channels to be fixed?"

"I would den have no choice but to include all of the

channels and tell her that it was a gift from me. In appreciation, I usually get a nice tip. They most always choose to fix them all. It's a win-win situation."

"Oh. I see."

One Friday evening Joey and I stopped at a bar in Brooklyn for a drink while on our way to a dance at the Taft hotel in Manhattan. The place had a band, which drew a nice crowed. The only space available was at the end of the bar in the rear of the place. Shortly after ordering our drinks, a bar brawl broke out. Beer bottles and glasses were flying all over the joint. I told Joey,

 "Hey T.V. this aint no place for us to be in, let's get the hell outta here."

"OK"

"Hey Joey, wait a second."

"Wait for what?"

"Listen to me; start running along the bar as though you are a fullback with a football, stay close to the bar and I will be right behind ya."

"OK let's do it."

Fat Joey took off running, pushing everyone out of the way. When we exited the place, he asked me why I wanted him to run close to the bar. I showed him a hand full of paper money, which I scooped up from the bar as we ran out. "Hey you missed the coins." "Get into the car you bastard, we have a free night ahead of us at the hotel."

Joe always bought a brand new automobile for himself. When it comes to cars, he never deprived himself from having the best. He drove a brand new Cadillac or a Buick convertible. He knew how to earn a buck and was always generous with his friends. All the fellows appreciated Joe and as a result, never took advantage of him.

Occasionally, we all visited a local pizza joint. Everyone sat at the table drinking a beer, waiting for the pizza to come out of the oven. As soon as the waiter placed it on the table, Fat Joey was the first one to grab a slice. The pizza was very hot, but Joey ate half the friggin pie before anyone of us would dare put it in our mouth. As he ate the pizza everyone cursed at him, in spite of this, it never bothered him. He just ordered another pie and shot the shit while we all finished eating. Afterwards Joe insisted on paying the bill.

The Boat: Our crew was always interested in boats. Everyone enjoyed spending time around the water. Along Cross-bay Blvd. in the Howard Beach section of Queens, was a canal with many boats tied to the docks. At the end of the canal was an old fifty-foot Air rescue boat. It had a registered name GALE painted on it. The boats motors had a conversion consisting of two straight eight-cylinder Packard marine engines. We decided to chip in and buy it. We towed the rig to a marina; hauled it out of the water then began to work on it making necessary repairs.

The hull consisted of heavy solid wood planks, built to take rough seas. When the work was complete, we docked it at a rented space in the Canarsie section of Brooklyn. The question now was, who the hell is gonna drive it? One evening after work I drove to the dock by myself, started the engines and steered the boat very slowly down the canal until I got it into open waters. I found a buoy and practiced maneuvering around it. About an hour later, I drove the boat back to its slip and went home. When we reunited, I told the other partners that I would drive the boat. "What the hell do you know about driving a boat?" "Trust me, I'll drive the boat." We all assembled on the fifty-footer with the new paint job and fancy curtains in the windows. I cranked up the engines and headed down the canal, through the inlet into the Atlantic Ocean.

"Hey you're damn good at this where did ya learn to handle a big boat like this?"

"Yo, it's a piece of cake, did you forget, I'm a Marine?"

"Oh. Yeah"

I had them all wondering. It did not take long before card games and crap games began at sea. We invited people from the bar on board to participate in gambling. Since we were running the games and provided a place to play, we took a cut out of each pot just like the mob guys do. This helped to pay for fuel and drinks.

On Friday nights everyone packed gear for a couple of days of travel. The normal congregation at the bar took place. After a few drinks, everyone took off into different directions with the intentions of arriving at the dock before sunrise. As soon as the sun came up the engines cranked up too. Whoever was late missed the boat. Whoever brought a new girlfriend from the night before brought them aboard too? Off we went to Fire Island or the Jersey shore for a fun weekend.

After knocking around with the GALE for a while, T.V. Joe purchased a 40-foot boat. This rig also needed work. All the fellas helped work to put it into a nice condition. Before we knew it, we were ready for action again, only this time we had a little more class.

Upon our returning home from a joyous weekend at Fire Is. one summer afternoon, I noticed water spraying up from the engine compartment as Joey drove the boat. I opened the hatch to inspect.

"Hey Joe, look at the water coming in through the hull."
"Holy shit it's almost up to the engine."
"Yeah shut the damn ding off."
"Where do ya dink its comin from?"
"It's comin from underneath the hull some place."
"Well dat makes sense, Watta ya dink we autta do?"
"I'm not sure."
"I dink I'll dive under the boat with a mask, snorkel and fins to take a look."
"Ya better hurry the friggin boat is fillin with water."
"OK."

The water had large swells making it difficult to inspect the hull. After a struggle, I managed to detect a missing bolt that held the shaft to the hull.

"Hey Joey, do ya got a pencil?"
"Yeah I do."
"Give it to me."

I pushed the pencil into the hole and provided a temporary fix to the problem. Fortunately, a Coast Guard station was close by. After taking the boat there, we tied it to the dock with heavy ropes to prevent it from sinking until a marine service was able to come and repair it. Our whole crew then took the Long Is. railroad home. During the ride home, one of the fellas removed the captain's hat from Joey's head and flung it out of the window of the moving train.

It was time to sell the old boat, "Gale." After placing an ad in the newspaper, a couple of dudes came down to look at the boat. I was alone when I met them at the dock. They asked if the rig was sea worthy. I told them that it was. They asked if I could take them out for a ride. I replied "sure jump aboard." I knew there had been storm warnings from the weather report nonetheless, this would be a great opportunity to show just how sea worthy the boat actually is. Upon entering the inlet, I saw very large waves on the horizon. I told the two dudes to sit tight because we were in for a nice ride. By climbing through a hatch on the roof of the boat, I was able to sit with my feet on the steering wheel. The waves began to hit the bow of the boat. As we plunged forward through the inlet, the waves became extremely large, they were now breaking over the bow and hitting on top of the roof. There is no turning back. The only thing to do was push forward until we entered the ocean. As the waves broke on board the water rushed off the deck through the escape holes on the port and starboard sides as well as the stern. The bow of the boat dove into the water with every wave. The propellers exited the water with a roaring sound. Man, this was exciting. We looked like the Navy ship on the television show "Victory at sea." When I steered past the heavy waves, I looked down in the cabin to check on the two potential buyers. Both of them were crying.

"Hey, what's the matter?" I asked.

"You are crazy; bring us back to the dock."

"OK but I cannot turn around just now, the waves are still too big, we will be hit broad side and turn over, we have to go out a little further before turning back."

Did you ever see two grown men cry?

I went out a little further, turned the boat around and headed back through the inlet. Only this time I had the waves behind me pushing us. I had done this many times before and knew that if I throttled the motors at the right RPMs we could ride on top of the wave. I did just that, only this time both propellers were out of the water for a longer amount of time giving off a frightening roaring sound. I began to feel sorry for the two dudes in the cabin.

When we returned to the dock a couple of my friends were there waiting for my return. As soon as we got close to the dock, the two crybabies jumped off the boat and began to curse at me. Naturally, I began to laugh while asking if they were satisfied with the sea worthiness of the boat. My friend Richie nicknamed "The Colonel" (because he never made it past the rank of Private in the Army reserves.) Started to yell at me,

"You son of a bitch, you crazy bastard, you took them through the inlet didn't you?"

"Yeah they wanted to see if the rig was sea worthy." Eventually we sold the boat. Unfortunately, we did not sell it to the two whining pussies.

That same year T.V. Joe sold the 40-foot boat and bought a 50-footer, which also needed work. Again, we all pitched in to fix up the new rig.

Joey rented a dock space at a country club in the Sheepshead Bay section of Brooklyn. The boat, now docked alongside of a swimming pool and a large clubhouse. Along with the dock space, Joey received membership for two at the club. He asked me to sign in as a member with him. "Wow! Thanks Joe." The new boat was very nice. It had a kitchen, several sleeping quarters, a head, shower and a large living room area. The friggin thing was a floating hotel.

We never had to go any place with the boat because there were loads of beautiful girls that belonged to the club, and they all used the swimming pool. Besides that, there was entertainment at the club on weekends, which attracted more women. Most of my other friends spend time there too. This whole setup was like something out of the movies.

Although everything was convenient, we still occasionally made trips to Fire Island. There were beautiful women always hanging around with us. It was not because we were classy people, but we all knew how to have fun. Everyone felt welcomed aboard the boat. There was always plenty of booze, music and dancing. The girls lay out on the deck with their bikinis enhanced in suntan oil soaking up the summer sun. There was never a problem taking off on a weekend with a boatload of party people.

Judo: One of us got the bright idea to study judo. There was a dojo (Judo school) downtown Brooklyn. Both my brother and I enrolled in classes. The instructors were of Japanese origin. The three sensei's (Judo teachers) took a liking to us. We played the sport extremely hard and they sensed it. Towards the end of each lesson, was a period when the students paired off to practice the various judo throws and wrestling holds on each other. Billy and I was always a match up. The instructors stood on the side and observed us. They appreciated how hard we fought against each other, making us a couple of their favorite pupils, and we sensed that.

After sessions at the dojo, we practiced at home, performing the maneuvers of numerous holds and throws. Occasionally one of us slipped and pounded the other person to the floor that did not have a mat. This caused a loud noise, which infuriated mom. I am sure it also pissed off the folks who lived below us.

The three Japanese instructors became rather sociable with us. Consequently, we invited them to our home for an Italian dinner. Mom was pleased to have them come over and prepared a great meal. She also learned a little about Japan and Japanese culture, as so did they about our American hospitality.

After a lesson one evening, our instructor (Shina) took me aside; he told me that my brother was the strongest person he had ever played with in judo. I must have had a grin from ear to ear when I heard that coming from a seasoned athlete who held a 5th degree black belt in Judo, a 4th degree black belt in Karate, was named player of the year in the university of Tokyo and gave exhibitions at the world's fair. I was once again very proud of my kid brother. After I told Billy what Shina said, he would flex his biceps and say "Brother strong like bull." In return, I told him "Brother smells like bull."

Neither one of us ever tried to hurt anyone with the new skills that we acquired. WE considered it a sport. Nonetheless, whenever confronted with a hostile confrontation the sport came in extremely handy.

Johnny Esposito: I became friends with a fellow Marine who lived in the Bensonhurst part of Brooklyn. His name is Johnny Esposito. He got along good with all of my friends and became part of the clan. I met this character while driving my car on the base at Floyd Bennett Field where we did our duty as Marines. While driving from the flight line to the chow hall one afternoon, John was walking along the road. As I approached him, he put out his thumb as if to hitch a ride. I had a bunch of fellow Marines in my car and for that reason, decided to drive on past him. While sitting in the chow hall eating, Johnny came up to me and said,

> "What the F--- is wrong with you; couldn't you pick me up and give me a ride to the chow hall?"

I looked at him, gave him a *smirk* and answered,
> "What the hell do I look like to you a base taxi?"

He looked surprised then sat down at another table to eat. I left the chow hall and returned to the flight line.

The next day a bunch of Marines gathered at a baseball field for a game. The big mouth was also there. I kept my distance from him but could not help but notice how agile he was on the ball field. By the time the game was over, we were talking to each other and tossing the ball around as if nothing ever happened the day before. In later years, Johnny moved to California married and raised a family. He has two sons who are officers in the Marine Corps. To this day, we remain best of friends.

Johnny rode a motorcycle when he was not driving his parent's Oldsmobile auto. He could be wild at times, which is one of the things our group enjoyed about him. Sporadically, while hanging out at the bar during a summer night with a bunch of fellas, the large screen door at the entrance flew open, in came Johnny on his motorcycle. He revved up the engine a few times making lots of noise, dismounted then ordered a drink. Many of the occupants thought he was crazy. However, we considered him as our pal Johnny.

Driving a motorcycle seemed like fun. Johnny persuaded me to look into buying a bike. As a result, one evening we rode out to a motorcycle retailer in Port Washington, on Long Is. I looked at many bikes before making my choice. The bike that caught my eye was a 750cc Matchless, made by Norton. I bought it on the spot. I asked the salesperson to drive it around the block one time with me sitting on the back while instructing me on how to drive it.

"What?"

"You heard me, just one time."

The friggin moron began yelling in the store,

"Hey look at this guy; he just bought the biggest bike in the store and he doesn't even know how to drive a motorcycle."

"Shut your mouth asshole and get on the friggin bike."

We rode around the block once; he stopped in front of the store and said,

"OK Now! What?"

"Get the hell off my bike. Jackoff."

I started it up and drove it all the way home on the highway.

That was the beginning of many years of motorcycling. Johnny and I spent numerous weekends traveling to various places while camping out under the stars. Occasionally we took a couple of girls with us to add a little zest to our trip.

In 1969 just the two of us took a long ride upstate N.Y. Not sure as to exactly where we were at the time, we ran into an enormous crowd of Hippies. The streets, packed with people. Police directed traffic while trying to control the crowd on foot. After managing to get thru the mess we found out that, we were in the town of Bethel alongside of Max Yasgur's farm. We did not know it at the time however; we became part of the 500,000 that attended the Woodstock Musical Festival.

Driving home along Woodhaven Blvd. very early one morning, I stopped for a red light. I could not help but notice a vagrant sleeping on a park bench along the Blvd. with newspaper covering his head. As I waited for the light to change, I thought I'd have a little fun at the poor chap's expense, and so, I rolled my motorcycle very close to the sleeping dude, backing the exhaust pipes close to his head. Then placing it in natural, I blasted the accelerator. Upon releasing the throttle, the machine created a very loud popping sound. The dude must have shit in his pants as he went flying off the bench. The newspapers flew down the block as I started to laugh. Instantly a police officer jumped from a hallway, apprehended me and wrote a summons for disturbing the peace. "Ehh, what the hell I did not hurt anyone."

The Hunters: Johnny, his cousin Freddie and I, along with a few other Marines went on several hunting trips in the mountains of N.Y. and Pennsylvania. It was always a blast going away with these guys. None of us ever shot a deer but we had a lot of fun trying. Pheasant hunting was another sport we engaged in. It was not too far of a trip to the opened fields for us to hunt. This involved a shotgun instead of a Hi-powered rifle. Johnny and I always brought home a few birds and his dad Mario who was very handy in the kitchen always prepared a nice dinner.

One of the Marines found a place to go wild boar hunting in Pennsylvania. Johnny suggested that we drive up with my van so that we had room to transport any pigs that we might shoot. The place was a reserve run by some local yokel farmer. He had a large property stacked with the pigs. After checking into his lodge and listening to all of his stories about how dangerous it is to hunt wild boar, we settled down, had a few drinks, mimicked the farmer and shot the shit about what tomorrow will bring. Hanging out with all these dudes involved continuous joking and laughing. As the wee hours approached, it was time to turn in for the night. Freddie, Johnny and I bunked in the same bedroom. Johnny fell asleep right away. Freddie and I continued to joke around until we both fell asleep. I woke up around 2

A.M. to take a piss. Heck, I was up, might as well have some fun.

"Hey Freddie, wake up."

"What?"

"Are ya ready for some laughs?"

"Yeah, what do ya have in mind?"

"Let us set the clock ahead to 6 A.M. and wake up Johnny. We'll tell him it's time to shave, shower and get ready to go hunting, then we will go back to sleep."

"How the hell do ya dink of these things? Sounds good let's do it."

Johnny could not believe it was already 6 A.M. He jumped into the shower, shaved and got dressed. We told him to wake up the other guys and we will meet him downstairs. When he found out it was only a little after 2 A.M. he came running up stairs pissed off. We did not pay any attention to him and went back to sleep.

The farmer prepared a nice breakfast for us, Johnny cooled down from the prank and we went hunting. Since it was a preserve, everyone was sure to shoot a wild boar. By the end of the day all the great hunters had shot a pig, we gutted them and loaded them into the van, thanked the farmer for a nice time and headed back to N.Y.

This trip took place in the mid-1960s. It was the time of drugs, Hippies, Wallflower children, protests and free love. Everything opposite of what a Marine believes in. Our crew was truckin down the Turnpike when on the side of the road was a hitch hiking Hippie. The dude had the long hair and a ragged looking beard to go with it, all decked out in the typical Hippie attire.

"Hey look," yells out one of the guys. A freaken Hippie let's give him a ride."

"Where the hell are we gonna put him?" I said.

"Just pull the friggin truck over will ya?"

The Hippie ran up to the van delighted that we stopped to pick him up.

"Jump in." says a Marine.

"Where can I sit there is no room?"

"There is room in the back,"

One of the guys jumped out of the van, opened the rear doors and tells the dude,

"Jump inside."

"Ehh pigs!" He screams,

"Dead pigs."

Just at that moment, another Marine pointed an unloaded rifle at him and said,

"Jump in with them you're a pig just like them."

After looking at the rifle pointing at his chest, he decided to jump into the van.

"Now lie down and shut your friggin mouth."

I started the motor and began driving down the Pike. The poor fellow started to cry while pleading for his freedom.

"Shut up Pig."

We drove a few miles then let the dude out. He ran away from the van like a gazelle.

The rest of the ride home was full of everyone imitating the Hippie. It made the ride seem much faster. I know that it was not a nice thing to do to the poor slob but what the hell, that's what guys do. "Sempra Fi."

POW: Johnny and I attended a dance one Friday night in the Sheepshead Bay area of Brooklyn. It was a nice facility and we were having a pleasant time dancing and meeting some new chicks. It was summer time, the dance hall became a little warm and so, we decided to step outside for some fresh air. While the two of us stood next to each other talking, someone coldcocked me just above the eye. I never saw the person. He caught me totally off guard. Blood began pouring from the deep cut and entered both my eyes. It ran down my face and all over my clothing.

"Wow! What the hell just happened? Johnny, point me towards the men's restroom."

It was very hard to see with my both eyes filled with blood. After throwing cold water on my face, I was able to see again.

"Hey Johnny what happened, did you see who hit me?"

"Yeah I did."

"Who did it and why did he hit me?"

"I don't know but I'd better get ya to a hospital, the guy had to have a ring on his hand to make such a deep cut."

"Never mind the hospital, show me the guy."

"He's gone, come on I'm taking you to the emergency room you need stiches."

"Ya dink so?"

"I know so."

"OK let's go."

At the emergency room, a doctor sewed up the cut with several stiches and placed a white bandage around my head to hold it together. Time was flying by, it was already early in the morning and we both had to play weekend warriors with the Marines in a few hours.

"OK John, go home and get your uniform on, I'll meet you at Floyd Bennett field later."

"You're gonna go to the meeting after all this?"

"Of course I am, I have never missed a drill in all the years we've been in the core, I'm gonna finish up with a 100% drill attendance record."

"OK, see ya later."

When I arrived home my mother was just getting up from bed, she took one look at me and asked,

"Louie, what the hell happened now?"

After telling her what happened she began to laugh.

"Hey ma, what's so funny."

"You; you're what's funny, between you and your brother and all the judo lessons you took, you both manage to come home looking like something the cat dragged in. Hurry up and get dressed, you're gonna be late for the Marines." "No mercy."

The City's Finest: My brother was washing windows for someone on Glenmore Ave. He had an extension ladder against the building, which he stood on to, do his work on the second floor. Suddenly, one of his friends came running through the alleyway and hopped over a wooden fence. Chasing behind him was a black kid with a large knife. Billy watched the incident from the top of the ladder, then yelled out to the black dude "Hey what the hell are ya doin?" The kid turned, began climbing the ladder wielding his knife. Billy jumped through the opened window to avoid a stab in the leg. He ran to the kitchen, picked up a larger knife and ran down the stairway exiting the building. Just then, the black kid ran past him on the way to his own house. Billy chased after him right up to the front door. The kid's mother ran out to stop him from entering the house while pleading with him not to stab her son. The mother who was a very large woman finally calmed Billy's temper, and managed to save her son.

A gang fight between the Negros and the Puerto Ricans were about to take place, Billy and I went into the street with long iron pipes to prevent a war from taking place on our block. I stood at one end of the block while he stood at the other end holding off the rival gangs. The neighbors thought that we were both nuts as they peeked through the blinds. No one ever came out to help us.

On one occasion, just prior to a street battle, I saw two cops sitting in a squad car under the El. along the dirt road. I approached them to inform them as to what was about to take place. I suggested they put on the colored blinking lights on the roof of their police car while blowing the siren to break up the gangs. At that instant, the two of them drove off. A fight broke out and several people were injured. In addition, automobiles had broken windows.

Sometime later, I was standing outside my house holding one of the iron pipes. A police car pulled up to the curb, the cop said to me "Hey you, what do you have in your hand?" These were the same two people that took off when I tried to tell them about the battle that was about to take place.

"Come over here." I walked over to the police car and asked,

"What's your problem?"

"What are ya gonna do with dat pipe?"

"Why do ya want to know?"

"We are here to prevent any trouble from starting."

I laughed in his face and said.

"You want to prevent trouble? Why you two little fagots, you're the two candy asses that ran away when I advised ya of a street battle that was about to take place a few weeks ago."

At that moment, I smashed the iron pipe across the roof of the police car putting a dent in it.

"My brother and I are the only ones that confront these gangs. You and everyone else around here are afraid of them, and they are afraid of us. So, I advise both of you to get off my block because the next time I swing this pipe I will be putting a dent in your friggin head."

The two police officers drove away, they never approached me again. What an awful way to speak to the "City's finest."

My Brother Billy: My brother did well in his final year of high school, also graduating from Franklin K. Lane. He joined the swimming team just as I did but; he was a diver and became the captain of the team, a lifeguard at Rockaway beach in Brooklyn, scored the most points of anyone on a physical test given to high school students by the U.S. Marine Corps. He had a talent for art and was selected the best-looking boy in his graduating class. I was very proud of all his accomplishments. He was a natural in so many ways. For that reason, I pushed him to excel even further. Consequently, my brother had a mind of his own. He would do only the things he wanted to do, and when he wanted to do them. Sometimes I felt I was pissing in the wind.

Shortly after graduation, Billy decided to marry his high school girlfriend Phyllis. Although mom and I had hoped, he would cultivate one of his aptitudes but he had other things in mind. The two of them set up house in one of mom's apartments. About a year later, they became the parents of a bouncing baby boy. They named him William Jr. He was our pride and joy.

The construction company I worked for started another city housing project in Harlem N.Y. I introduced Billy to a carpentry contractor who built wood protection rails around each stairwell and elevator opening at every freshly poured concrete slab. I told him to work with this contractor until there was an opportunity for me to hire him as a Field Engineer with my company. That time came; we hired him as a Rodman and got him enrolled into the union. He now worked with me.

I told him that there was much for him to learn, and that he was now working for a good outfit and a great bunch of people. The rest is up to you. I conveyed to him at the very beginning that I would not stand behind him if he slacked off. "From now on, I want the company to look at you as William Borek, not Louie's brother."

I pushed him very hard to be the best he could be. At times, he got pissed off at me. He as much as complained to my mother about how I treated him. She told me to loosen up and stop pushing him so hard. I told my mother not to interfere, because when this job is completed, our crew will be broken up and we will probably all go to different jobs, that is if there are more jobs. By that time, he should have established a good reputation for himself so that the company will keep him because he is a good worker, and not because I am his brother.

It took a long while from the time my brother told me "I hate you" until he realized that everything I did was for his benefit. I will never forget the day he told me, "I understand why you pushed me as hard as you did, thank you, I love you." He worked with the company for several years and worked along with other crews. Everyone liked him and liked working with him because he was "William Borek" and not Louie's brother.

Our stint in Harlem transpired during a time when riots took place in the area. The Black folks found just about any meaningless reason to destruct anything around them, just like back home. We now had to put up with the same crap at work, only Harlem had a much larger volume of black people. We had to be on our toes at all times.

When laying out Axis lines to construct a building we placed checkered targets on top of the tallest buildings in the area. We set up our surveyor's transit between these targets on a daily basis. Upon entering the buildings to go to the rooftops there was often a very foul odor in the hallways. Looking over the roof into the courtyard, there was garbage piled as high as the windows of the first floor. The tenants often tossed bags of trash out the window instead of walking it down and placing it into the garbage can. As a result, the place was crawling with rats, mice and insects.

On several occasions, the morons heaved a couch, garbage cans or another type of heavy obstacle off the rooftops at a passing police car. The thieves often approached us trying to sell drugs, stolen articles such as televisions, watches or many other items. We also were very vigilant when traveling on the subways. A person can easily become a victim of a mugging or thrown onto the train tracks. Yes, Harlem is a great place.

Construction Stories:
Construction sites are a dangerous place to work:

Besides knowing and performing your job, you must always think of safety first. I have seen several men die on numerous jobs. I have also lost some friends to accidents. I have almost lost my own life on more than one occasion.

Harlem job: After driving steel piles into the ground, an engineer has tons of solid steel blocks stacked on top of a platform made of steel I-beams to test the rigidity of the piles. Because of the cold weather, a tent is set up to enclose the testing area and the mechanical instruments that took movement readings. I had just stepped out of the tent along with the engineer, when we heard an enormous crash behind us. It was so loud; people opened their windows to see what happened. The platform collapsed causing tons of steel to crash to the ground, smashing everything inside the tent. It was a narrow escape.

At the same job, while setting survey targets on a roof and looking through the transit's telescope, I noticed a black dude sneaking up behind my rodman with a hatchet in his hand. I warned my coworker with the "Walkie-Talkie" handsets that we used to communicate; I told him not to run, "I will be up there in a minute." I ran up to the top of the roof and confronted the hatchet man. I kept calm while explaining to him that we are construction workers. He thought we were cops in plain clothes and was going to throw the rodman off the roof.

City housing project in Manhattan: During a concrete pour, a large crane lifting a four cubic yard steel bucket filled with concrete was going onto the deck of a building adjacent to the one I was working on. While lifting, the bucket hit a telephone pole. Somehow, the bucket came unhitched from the crane's cable then fell to the ground. Because the boom of the crane had so much tension on it, it sprang straight up pulling the loose cable into the air. The crane operator quickly swung the large boom away from the city street while winding the treacherous rambling cable, which is capable of cutting a human in half. The boom then began to fall again as it passed over the building I was working on. The massive steel boom was now dropping on top of me. It came so close; I could jump and grab it with my hands. I saw my whole life flash by me in an instant. Suddenly the cable was tight enough to allow the boom to bounce up again. Everyone working on the deck ran for his life. The boom dropped a couple more times. Each time the cable wound tighter around the drum until the operator gained complete control of the rig. There were many men with brown spots on their underwear that afternoon.

Twenty-one story building near the George Washington Bridge: I was laying out lines on the plywood deck; an ironworker by the name of Red Dalton leaned over the building while he gave signals to the crane operator who was lifting materials up to the nineteenth floor. I noticed Red standing very close to a part of the deck, which the carpenters had not secured yet. I walked over and warned him more than once of the possibility of the lumber not supporting him. He continued to signal the operator when suddenly the wood he was standing on gave way. I watched him fly down nineteen stories to his death. The other ironworkers stopped for the day and went home.

Rutgers University Newark, N.J: Three buildings were under construction in the heart of Newark. We were working on the third floor of the science building. The masons erected a concrete block wall approximately twenty feet high. The lunch whistle blew and everyone began to leave the site. Unexpectedly, a strong gust of wind came blowing across the construction site abruptly blowing the wall down. The heavy blocks tumbled on two of the construction workers, injuring one of them and crushing the other one to death instantly. The poor fellow never knew what hit him. Ironically, the superintendent told the timekeeper to pay him only up to 12:00 P.M.

On this same job, while laying out lines on a concrete slab with a friend of mine nicknamed "The Rooster" I was holding the dead end of the tape measure while calling out numbers to him off my blueprint. He then marked the concrete with a pencil according to the number I called out to him. As we ran along the concrete slab, I paid attention to reading the blueprint. I called out a number and suddenly felt a heavy tug on the tape, I looked up and the Rooster was gone. I dropped the tape, ran and looked over the edge of the building; there he was laying in the dirt three stories below me with steel rods sticking up out of the concrete beside him.

"Holy shit; are you OK?"
He struggled to get back on his feet and said,
"I think so."
"What the hell happened?"
"I think I read the tape wrong and fell off the building."
"You friggin dummy."
He was extremely lucky because when he fell, his head hit a plank that was set up as a scaffold; this broke his fall, he then bounced off the plank and landed in the dirt just missing the sharp steel rods. I took him to a local hospital for a checkup. Nothing was broken, However, He had a terrible headache and he now knew that roosters could not fly.

Housing Project Staten Island: One of our crews were working on a concrete
Job when the crane toppled down on them. Several workers died when the heavy steel boom crushed them. A friend of mine by the name of Tommy, another Field Engineer, was very lucky. There was a stack of wood pallets lying in the field. The crane landed on top of it, squashing them into the dirt. Tommy's back took a massive blow from the steel boom prior to the smashing of the pallets. The boom landed on top of him. As he lies on the ground, the boom barely pinned him into the dirt. They were able to dig him out from under, and rushed him off to a hospital. Upon visiting him, his body was black and blue. A day later, we spent time at the funeral parlor paying respects to the families of a few other friends.

N.Y.C., Housing project: It happened atop the seventeenth floor of a newly framed wood deck. I was laying out marks in a spandrel beam. (Exterior beam) The carpentry crew began using brand new waxed plywood that day. This type of plywood can be re-used many times. However, when sawdust lay on top, it becomes exceptionally slippery. An older Haitian fellow named Gerry was working with me at the time. I held the dead-end of the measuring tape while adding numbers in my head. As I called out a dimension, Gerry marked the location. He had one foot in the beam and one foot on the deck as he hobbled along. Suddenly I felt a pull on the tape, looked up at Gerry. He had slipped, lost his balance and was falling backwards off the building. I dropped the tape and lunged myself into the air grabbing him and using my weight to pull him back onto the building. Gerry began to cry for joy while hugging me and yelling, "Louie you saved my life" He said the same thing repeatedly, then began to kiss me. Finally, I had to push him off me. For the duration of the job, the fella never wanted to leave my side.

The company I worked for constructed the skeleton of the buildings, which included the concrete footings, columns, beams and slabs. As we worked above, other trades began to do their work, such as the electricians, air condition and amongst others, the bricklayers.
Scaffolds were set up outside the buildings and the bricklayers worked their way up setting bricks.
Suddenly, appearing out of nowhere was Henry Hill. (Goodfellas) He had a pad and pencil and began taking lunch orders from the construction workers. The title of his job is Water-boy. I walked over to him and asked,
"Hey, what the hell are ya doin up here?"
"Hey Louie I didn't know ya were working on this job."
"Yeah I've been here since the beginning."
"Oh good, ya know a bunch of the guys are here too working with brick layers."
Shortly after that, I began to recognize some of my friends from the neighborhood.
"Hey Henry what's the gig, besides getting lunches?"
"The numbers Louie, numbers."
"Oh, this is a great place for dat."
"Ya aint kiddin, I'm cleaning up here."
The guys from the Lucchese crime family who operated the Euclid Ave. cab company also controlled some of the unions, for that reason, Henry became a

Water boy while running the numbers gig. Here we were, just like back in the neighborhood, the gangs all here. The last three numbers in the total attendance at aqueduct raceway is the winning numbers. It works similar to the cash 3 lotto.

New Jersey: Our Company came out of New York to do work in New Jersey. For some unknown reason this did not sit well with the union workers in New Jersey. There were many conflicts as the job progressed. According to the union, none of the N.Y. supervisors could give instruction to any of the N.J. carpenters. They had to first instruct a N.J. supervisor and then; he would relay the instructions to the N.J. carpenter. This was extremely childish and time consuming. It added unnecessary cost to the job, while building animosity amongst the workers.

It was just after lunch when the whistle blew for the men to return to work. The job superintendent stepped out from the construction field office and shouted out some instructions to the workers. The super's name was Tom. He was a very nice fellow with a good sense of humor. His nickname was "Tom Terrific." As Tom was giving instructions, the N.J. workers began to shout and cuss at him. They objected to the fact that he dare speak to them without a N.J. supervisor at hand. Tom shouted back at them, after all he was the big dog of the yard. The workers attacked him right there in the middle of the street and beat him to a pulp. Poor Tom, when they got through with him he laid there all busted up dripping blood onto the street. He no longer looked like "Tom Terrific." This was the simple mentality of the union delegates and the union workers. I continued to do my job while getting along with the people from both sides of the Hudson River. However, I could never comprehend how grown men could act in such a childish manner.

Pennsylvania Station Manhattan: While constructing a thirty-two story building over Pennsylvania station, attached to the Madison Square Garden building, a freak accident occurred however, no one was hurt. This job is a "Goulash job." A goulash job is a manner in which structural steels erected, and then covered with concrete to protect it in case of fire. Each floor also consists of a poured concrete slab.

The main entrance to the building faces Sixth Ave. A marque of structural steel, erected very close to a subway train entrance stood about four stories tall. When completed it display the Madison Square Garden sign. While pouring concrete, a laborer driving a motorized buggy on top of a temporary wooden track, lost control of the vehicle. He fell off the machine and slid to the edge of the building. While holding on for dear life he watched the buggy fly down twenty-two stories and land on the marque. I was standing alongside of a concrete truck when the incident took place. I watched as it landed on top of the structural steel beam wrapping itself around like a pretzel. Laborers cut the machine apart with an acetylene torch. This one buggy could fly.

The method used to bring concrete to the higher floors is a hoist, constructed through a hole at each floor starting from the ground floor up to the roof. A steel cable hoists a large bucket filled with concrete. This type hoist is strictly for the use of lifting materials. Another hoist exists on the opposite end of the building, which acts as an elevator for lifting people. One of my many tasks as a Field Engineer is estimating and ordering concrete. Towards the end of each day, it is important to calculate the amount needed to complete the pour while trying not to run short, or having any concrete leftover without a place to put it. Several calculations are required as the job progressed. Cell phones and hand calculators did not exist at that time. After each calculation, it is essential to call the dispatcher at the concrete plant. All this took a lot of time. If there was not any concrete on the job, numerous workers stood idol costing the company an abundant amount of money. Therefore, I frequently rode up and down on top of the material hoist to save time. Although regulations do not permit personal to ride on top of the material hoist, randomly someone did ride on it. Therefore, the workers above and the hoist operator below have a bell to give signals to each other. One ring of the bell signaled the operator to drop the hoist. He allowed it to free fall until about the fifth floor; he then applied the brake to slow it down prior to stopping. Three rings alerted him that someone is riding on top of the hoist and he should drop it slowly.

Late one afternoon while pouring concrete on the thirtieth floor, I climbed on top of the hoist for a ride down to the ground floor. The laborer who signaled to the operator thought it would be funny if he gave him only one ring of the bell. I stared at him in anticipation of hearing two more rings. He looked at me and smiled. I instantly took a good grip of the cable and a deep breath. I was in free fall for the whole ride down. When I reached the bottom, the operator took one look at me and his face turned white. I took a good look at him and my underwear turned brown.

The Round House, N.J.: My brother went on a new job constructing a round building. The Field Engineers were laying out for the footings as the carpentry crew set up a mill on the site to fabricate concrete forms. The site is inside of an area, cut out of the side of a mountain.

The lunch whistle blew and everyone left to go eat. About five minutes later the side of the mountain gave way and caused a landslide covering the newly set mill and all of the tools. Luck was on their side that day. The men left just in time to avoid being buried alive.

Mob Guys: I signed up with a new gym on Queens Blvd. It was a nice place to work out, a bit far from the house but what the hell; you go where you have to go if you want to work out in a gym.

Very close to the new gym Henry Hill opened, a nightclub called The Suite. He was working his way up the felonious ladder and was not a Water boy any longer. The place was exceptionally nice, including a large bar for everyone to hang out, shoot the shit and drink. It was a convenient spot to go to after a workout. Therefore, I did. I never made it a habit because it would have defeated the purpose of busting my hump lifting weights. It was something like the old T.V. shows Cheers. "It is nice to go somewhere, where everyone knows your name."

The party crowd sporadically shifted to new locations. A nightclub could be doing a bang up business every weekend. Then suddenly, the pack swarms to another location. Wherever the crowd went, you can count on seeing the same people always duking it out in the parking lot with someone else. These individuals became notorious. As they grew older and well known, they became involved with the hoodlums from my neighborhood.

Outside the Suite, a brand new white Cadillac pulls up at the curb, double parks, and out steps a dude in an expensive white suit, tie, cufflinks, the whole enchilada. He walks into the bar. Who do you think he is? You are correct if you said one of the people who busted up everyone's face outside of the nightclubs. He managed to work his way into the crew and was now playing the part of a Goodfella. These type fellas were useful for collecting monies for the mob from innocent people that made loans from them and then charged exorbitant rates in interest. The name of the games is Loansharking and Extortion.

They were also part of the big swindles. For instance, I have witnessed this transaction take place in a nightclub on Long Island. About five hooligans come in sit at the bar and order drinks as they scope out the establishment. After a couple of drinks, they pick a fight with another patron. This disrupts the whole evening and customers begin to leave the place. A week later, the same thing happens. The regular people who frequent the nightclub stop coming in fear of being hurt.

Then one evening, unexpectedly an older gent sits at the bar and asks to speak with the proprietor. The bartender summons the owner. The gent offers to buy the owner a drink then tells him.

"I understand that you are having trouble here lately."

The owner nods in a yes motion.

"Well, I can put a stop to all of this nonsense."

"Oh, how can ya do that?"

"It's gonna cost ya but at the same time I can assure ya that not only will the regulars return but, I will bring in a lot more customers than ya have now. The choice is yours either ya go out of business or prosper."

The poor fella just cannot refuse this offer. He now has a new partner along with a small amount of cash from the gent.

The gent keeps his promise and packs the house with customers. He also allows his friends to open a tab at the place. They spend plenty of money eating and drinking while entertaining lots of fine-looking women. The place is now swarming with the *In Crowd*. Money begins flowing into the joint like water from a hose. However, the tabs of the gent's friends are never paid and the business slowly becomes drained until the original proprietor can no longer pay the bills. The time has come for some "Jewish Lightning." As a result, one evening the place is set on fire leaving nothing but ashes. The insurance pays and both the original owner and the mob split the proceeds. This is not a bad deal for the mob.

What a Coincidence:  Years went by since I saw my old friend Patty Mafia. I once battled outside the church with this guy. His father is the man that gave me a beating on the steps of the church. Pat was now married with a kid of his own when he moved into the apartment below ours on Glenmore Ave. We were now neighbors.

I bought a brand new car and had it parked outside the house. Pat walked over and told me,

"Lock the doors."

"Why?"

"Because I'm gonna show ya how fast I can break into it and start it up."

"OK its locked do your ding."

He took about the same amount of time to enter the new automobile and start it up, as I would have taken with the keys.

"Should I drive off wit it?"

"Wow how the hell did ya do dat?"

He showed me his key ring, a mass of various car keys. He was now in the business of stealing cars. Patty often sat and shared many good stories with me pertaining to his new venture.

Occasionally I would run into Pat's dad when he came to visit them. The man always greeted me and tried to start a conversation. I showed him respect by saying hello but that is as far as I went with the small talk. After failing to exchange too many words with me, he realized that I was avoiding him. Unexpectedly, one afternoon he stopped me and asked,

"Hey, why do ya never talk wit me?" I looked him in square in the eye and said.

"Sit down and I'll tell ya why."

The old man sat on the concrete stoop and gazed at me. I said,

"Let me tell ya a story about a little kid."

"What kid?"

"Shut up and listen."

"Once upon a time, dis little boy was fist-fighting with another boy across the street from a church. It was a fair fight between two boys of the same age. The young father of the boy who was taking a beating appeared and chased the other boy for several blocks until he finally caught him on the steps of the church. The young father gave the little fellow a thrashing in front of all the other kids."

Pause.

"So?"

"So, does dis ring a bell?"

"No."

"Well, the kid that took the beating from the man was me. The man who beat the kid was you."

He sat there staring at me in awe.

"Now that you are an old man and I am a young man in much better physical condition than you. How would you like it if I were to give to you the same beating you gave to me many years ago?"

Sill staring at me, I told him.

"Relax ya don't have to worry because I am not like you. Now ya know why I refuse to carry on a conversation with you. I have no respect for ya."

I then walked away from an old man who was humiliated. I continued to greet him when I saw him but I never went any further than that.

The Good Times: I hung out with a bunch of fellas that lived to party. There was never a dull moment. Besides all the action in and around the neighborhood, it was always nice to get away for a weekend.

In the winter, it was snow skiing at various ski lodges in New York Vermont or somewhere in between. Summertime, meant trips on the boat either to Fire Island or somewhere down the New Jersey shore, trips on cruise ships. Sometimes boarding a ship for just a weekend called (The Cruise to nowhere.) The ship was full of party people that wanted to get out of the city for a while. There was always lots of action on those short trips. Another good get away was a vacation place in the mountains of Pennsylvania or New York. Dude ranches were also lots of fun and quite different. It is always nice to have fun. However, everything costs money. All of us probably partied more than we should have, but we had ways of cutting the cost. For instance, on a Friday night after we all finished work, everyone piled in a car, each fella brought along a bedroll and a change of clothes. Then off to the mountains we went. Just outside of a very large vacation place in the Pocono Mountains in Pennsylvania. We knew of a special area in the woods with a cleared space next to a stream of running water.

This is where we set up camp. None of us had a tent so we all slept under the stars.

In the morning, we awoke jumped into the stream, washed and shaved, put on some clean duds and were now ready to crash the expensive tourist joint. In the rear of the resort, was an entrance for all the commercial vehicles including food deliveries garbage trucks and us? Once we entered the place, we began to fraternize with the guests. They served buffet style breakfast, which we all enjoyed. Everyone then split up while taking part in the various sports and competitions they had to offer. All of us had the knack for mingling in with the crowd. When they served lunch, we all indulged. As the day went by, we each intended to hook up with a chick to spend the night. There was always something going on in the evenings, like a show or a dance, which we also participated. At the end of the day whoever did not hook up, went back to the camp to sleep with the stars. The rest of us snuggled up with our new acquaintance.

The Jewish Alps: Upstate New York had many great places to party. Monticello, in the Catskills Mountains was one of them in the 1940s, 50s and 60s. It is known as, the "Borscht Belt," named after beet soup. This is a favorite dish of Jewish people. There were many vacation spots of choice for New York Jews. So much so, that the Catskills are nicknamed the *Jewish Alps.* Popular kosher resorts included *Brickman's, Grossinger's, the Granit, Brown's, the Concord, the Nevele and Kutshers*

One of my good friends Irwin Levine was a Jewish fella who swam with Red and me on our high school swimming team. One-summer Irwin's dad who had connections with someone at Grossinger's resort set him up with a job as a bus boy in the dining room. Red and I decided to go see him at the resort. Irwin was glad to see us and took the liberty "after a little nudging" to find us a place to sleep free.

Irwin gave us a tour of the place and then got us something to eat. We told him not to worry about us for the evening. "Go do your job we will be fine." Red and I partied all night and had a great time. In the wee hours of the morning, we turned in to get a few hours' sleep. When the sun came up so did all the workers including Irwin. A supervisor entered the sleeping quarters and caught Irwin talking with us. "Who are these guys?" The supervisor became very irate and asked us to leave the premises. He then looked at Irwin and told him to pack his gear and take off with us because he no longer had a job at the resort. We did not allow the rest of the weekend to waste. The three of us continued to party at another hotel.

When Irwin returned home and told his father what happened, it went over like a lead balloon. His pop was pissed off. He was not only mad at his son but also with Red and me. We managed to stay away from the Levine residence for a very long time.

Not every weekend was a freebie. We visited the Concord many times. The place had class. There were great entertainers, music and dance halls. We watched Wayne Newton sing when he first got his start in show business. He just recorded his hit record Danka Shane. I met Buster Crabbe one day and carried on a conversation with him. I told him that we often watched him and Gabby Hayes in the cowboy movies. He told me that Gabby was a great fellow and he always had a lot of fun with him. Buster also played the role of Tarzan and won a gold medal as a swimmer in the 1932 Olympic Games.

One of the nicest things about going to these hotels is meeting good-looking women with a little class, and most of them came from Brooklyn. We never had to travel too far to date them afterwards.

The Best Bartender I Ever Met: It was a Friday night and five of us decided to visit some clubs in Manhattan. There was a popular place somewhere in the mid-town area where a few of the baseball players from the New York Yankees drank.

The very first time we entered the place we found it packed with people. I mean five deep from the bar. The Bartender noticed the five of us when we made our entrance. He called out while he pointed his finger at us "Hey fellas what can I get ya?" We ordered five different drinks. Within a couple of minutes, he reached over the crowd and handed each one of us just what we ordered. He introduced himself as Ray then asked our names. We hung around until we finished our drinks then left to go to a different club. After knocking around the city that never sleeps, we stopped at the place where we began the evening, for a nightcap.

The moment we walked in, Ray started mixing drinks for us without asking any questions. He then served each of us exactly what we had ordered the first time, and as he gave us our drinks he mentioned our name and got everyone right. Now, that is a good bartender.

We made the joint one of our stops each time we went to the city. Ray remembered us and we eventually became friends. I drank with Whitey Ford (Yankee pitcher) there one night. He was with another Yankee player. I do not remember his name.

I in particular, developed a good relationship with bartender Ray. I eventually revealed where I came from. Afterwards, he trusted me. He shared something with me that he did not dole out to just anyone. He had a friend that was doing credit card frauds. He told me that if I ever wanted to travel anywhere with an airline, he could get me tickets for 25% of the original cost. He said,

"You will have to fly under an anonymous name."

"What are the odds of getting caught?"

"Next to nil, no one has been pinched yet."

"Sounds good to me I'll let ya know when I'm ready."

My pal Johnny Esposito and I planned several vacations after I made the contact. Ray got us tickets to Puerto Rico, St. Croix in the Virgin Islands, along with several other places. Hell, at that price we went somewhere every time there was a three or four day holiday.

One year, Johnny and I spent time at the El San Juan, a swanky hotel in Puerto Rico. We met the Supremes, the popular singing group who was appearing there at the time. For a couple of days we sat and talked with Diana Ross Mary Wilson and Florence Ballard at poolside. Johnny and I did our thing off the diving board. We performed, doing somersaults, twists and flips. We had a great time on that vacation.

Several months later, while working in Manhattan, Johnny ran into Diana Ross in a crowded elevator. When he saw her, he said hello and asked her if she remembered him from the El San Juan hotel? In front of the crowed of strangers she said. "Oh yeah you were the big show-off on the diving board." The doors to the elevator opened and she began walking out. Johnny, being himself yelled out, "You bitch." Then the doors closed as his face turned red in front of the crowd on the elevator.

I spent two weeks with the Marine Corps. At a naval air station located at Roosevelt Roads Puerto Rico. On weekends, I went to the hotels in the downtown section of San Juan. At the pool, I recognized a familiar face, the third baseman for the (Philadelphia Phillies,) "Mike Schmidt." I approached him and started a conversation. I did not want to impose, so I told him that I enjoyed watching him play baseball then bought him and his wife a cocktail. Mike was quite pleasant. He thanked me then invited me to have a drink with them. It was one of the highlights of my weekend.

I partied with one particularly nice woman while on a trip to Puerto Rico. She owned a public relations business. We had drinks and danced to Latin music. While on the beach one day, she introduced me to the comedian Buddy Hackett. We spent a couple of hours sitting together on a beach while I exchanged jokes with the popular entertainer.

Before parting company, my new outgoing acquaintance told me, that she had a very pretty sister back in N.Y.

"I would like you to meet her. I have a birthday party planned for her," then invited me to attend.

"I would like to attend the party."

About a week later I arrived at the sister's apartment, my friend greeted me. She introduced me to her sister who turned out to be a real knockout. When the party ended, the sister insisted I stay for the night. How can a fella resist such an offer? I wound up dating her for a reasonable amount of time. She unexpectedly insisted that I meet her parents. Therefore, I did. Soon after, I felt things getting too serious and ended the relationship. "Sorry doll, but I have been down that road before."

Some Encounters

Both Billy and I never looked for trouble. We never had to because it seemed to find us. I always tried to avoid any kind of altercation. I do not like violence. However, whenever my brother or I faced a confrontation we never backed down. Just about every time either of us became involved, was to help a friend or to prevent anyone from taking something that belonged to us.

Billy became involved in a clash with some Puerto Ricans one afternoon because of a friend. Before the squabble was over, he wound up with a large cut across his back from a knife. The scare remains there today.

Another time he entangled with a bad bunch of thugs under the El on Fulton Street. They over powered him, beating him severely. This crew brutalized him, and then thought twice about running his head over with an automobile. They decided to kick his face in instead. When he came home with blood all over him and a disfigured face, I could not recognize him.

Most of my friends never seemed to remember what took place the night before. They always blamed it on alcohol. I reached my limit. Gathering them together, I told them, "From now on, all you numb nuts are gonna have to take care of yourselves. I'm tired of all these brawls and the next day nobody remembers what the hell happened." It never really worked out that way but it made them think twice before getting into any trouble.

Three Wise Guys: The house my brother and his family moved into had a rental apartment on the second floor, which he leased to a young couple. One morning Billy came to our construction office and told me the ceiling in his house has a large water stain and the house smelled like fire. I asked him,
 "Did you go upstairs to check it out?"
 "Yeah but nobody was home."
 "Don't ya have a key to the apartment?"
 "Yeah but I can't just walk into someone's home."
 "Why can't ya?"
 "Ehh?"
 "Come on I will go with you we'll look into it."
 Upon entering, we found a trashed apartment with the remains of the burned bed that they poured water on to extinguish the fire. The stove and oven was a complete mess.
"Lets change the locks; we can't allow these animals to come back here." I said. That evening the couple, who

turned out to be druggies, returned, only to find the place locked. After quarreling with Billy about returning their security deposit, which they did not receive, they left the premises.

A couple of days later three goons walked into our office and asked for Billy. They were dressed in overcoats; one had a large stevedore's hook over his shoulder. The hook is a tool that dockworkers use to move cargo. I instantly advised our secretary to leave the office.

"We are here to collect the money ya took from the tenant for a security deposit."

"Oh Yeah"

"Yeah, make it easy on yourself, give us the money and avoid getting hurt."

Billy turned around winked at me. I knew right then what was coming next?

"Come on outside, I'll give ya the money."

Everyone walked out to the sidewalk along Atlantic Ave. The three of them stood looking at Billy as I positioned myself for his next move. Billy reached into his pocket, the bullies figured they scared him into returning the money and were now relaxed when out of my brothers pocket came nothing but a cocked fist. BAM! The first creep received a knuckle sandwich to the face then Billy smashed his head against a metal light pole. I pounded the dude with the hook he dropped to the ground. I picked him up by his coat and thought, Hey; this coat is just like a judo jacket so I began throwing him all over the street corner like a rag doll while I practiced my judo throws. Billy took care of the other two, bouncing one creep off a moving car. The three of them took quite a beating before running away. We never heard from them or the tenants again. We kept the hook as a souvenir. "It was just another day at the office."

Weddings: Because marriage was the furthest thing from my mind that did not mean everyone else felt the same way. I attended many weddings at exclusive banquet halls. Some of these weddings included the gangsters from the neighborhood. As the guests partied inside, The Federal agents were out in the parking lot taking photos of the license plates on everyone's automobile. This took place whenever the Goodfellas attended a wedding. The photos, kept on file in the event that a crime was committed in the neighborhood. The Feds investigations began with the questioning of the owners of the plates. Their logic being, "Birds of a feather flock together."

The Rooster's Car Flew the Coop: My brother bought a Pontiac Grand Prix from one of our co-workers and a friend "The Rooster" It was not long before the car was stolen from our neighborhood. After reporting the robbery, Billy sat tight waiting to hear something from the police but never heard anything.

One late afternoon while riding home from a job site in New Jersey, I gazed out the window and in the distance; I saw a large lot that contained many automobiles. I told my Bro to get off the next exit and head towards the lot.

"Why?"

"Because I have been observing the cars in dat big lot every day and I dink I saw ya car."

"How the hell can ya see dat far?"

"Just drive da friggin car dare."

"OK."

We pulled up to the large chain linked fence with a sign reading, "Police Auto Pound." They allowed us to enter the lot in order to check out the automobile. Sure enough, it was Billy's car. After showing the right credentials, they turned the car over to my brother. About a week, later mom got a phone call from Billy.

"Ma, I am in the police station and they have me handcuffed to a hot iron radiator. They claim dat I stole a car."

"Are you fooling with me?"

"No Ma, they don't believe dat it's my car because it was never taken off the hot sheet."

"Where the hell are you I'll be right there."

Mom went down and gave them a piece of her mind and they released him. Now why did the police keep the car impounded for several months and never notify the owner that they had the car?

"IS THIS INCOMPETENCE?"

The Rooster was a good friend of ours. He got the nickname due to his hairstyle. It stood up high in the front and resembled a red comb of a rooster. He claimed to be a nephew to the notorious and ruthless gangster "Albert Anastasia." from Brooklyn. Albert made headlines in the newspapers after a rival mob gunned him down as he sat in a barber's chair. It was his last cut.

This killing of Albert took place in 1957. I recall the many killings that took place afterwards. The members of the five crime families went on a rampage. There were news stories every few days of multiple killings in the streets of Brooklyn. All this led to the famous Apalachian Meeting in upstate N.Y. The heads of all the five families were called together to discuss the future of Cosa Nostra.

The Marriage: After knocking around for so long, I met a nice girl. After her constant needling me to get married, I decided to tie the knot; Most of my friends were married while I was still running around. The wife's did not like the idea of their husbands hanging out with me. They thought I was a bad influence. I had some money saved and put it all towards the wedding and furniture. I never had the desire to move out to Long Island as most people from Brooklyn did. I worked in the westerly direction and L.I. was east. I did enough traveling to get to work and I did not need any more besides bucking all the traffic. My mother had previously left the neighborhood and moved to L.I. Therefore, we decided to stay in the apartment on Glenmore for a little while, save up some cash then buy our own house somewhere.

I guess when you are in love with someone you overlook many of their faults. After living together, she became extremely jealous of everything. Upon my returning home from work, I'd pick up my little nephew in the hallway and give him a hug and a kiss before going upstairs. The door slammed with a big bang before I reached our apartment. "Hey what's up?" I asked. "You gotta kiss that little brat downstairs before me?" Her little antics never stopped me from hugging my nephew when I came home.

It was almost impossible to attend a party without her causing a scene if ever; I spoke to some other girl. On the way home from a party, she jumped out of a moving car into the snow. I once had to rush her to the hospital to have her stomach pumped out. She became pissed off at me for some stupid reason then swallows a bottle of aspirins.

I finally had enough of her crap and told her that it is best if we go our separate ways. She agreed then decided to quit her job and asked me to pick up some of her items at her office in Manhattan. I did her the favor, which caused me to get home later that evening. Upon my returning home, the apartment was empty. This woman left me the bedroom set that Billy and I built downstairs in the cellar, a knife a spoon a fork and a bunch of crumbled newspaper on the floor. She also took the brand new Buick automobile I had recently purchased. I eventually got the car back but everything else was gone including my money. She managed to get that too. I figured "What the hell, I will start all over again I did it before and I can do it again. Within about a month thieves stole my Buick. My friend Red drove it home one night, instead of me driving him. He said he'd' return it the next day. Early the next morning he called to tell me that the car is gone. I told him not to worry about it. I will report it stolen. The police found it weeks later, stripped and burned. The insurance company offered me peanuts to replace it. I asked a lawyer to write a letter to the company. He did and I received an amount much closer to what the car was worth. However, the son of a bitch took half of the increase just for writing a letter. Each time I deal with lawyers, they gave me more reasons to dislike them.

My mother insisted that Billy get out of the neighborhood. She did not want my nephew growing up in this environment. Mom sold the building to Puerto Ricans. She lost money in the transaction but wound up with a few bucks. It was a down payment on a house in Howard Beach, Queens for my brother and his family.

I am now the last person of all the friends and relatives who lived here on Glenmore Ave. since I was a baby. I have no choice but to work my way back. I live amongst the blacks and the Latinos by myself in an almost empty apartment. "I shall return again, I know I can do it."

During that same year, the construction company I worked at for many years was going bankrupt. It will not be long now and I will be unemployed. "Oh well, what else can go wrong?" *MURPHY'S LAW?*

Billy and I decided to go into business for ourselves. We started a construction company and did many jobs in our local area. Some of the Puerto Rican blockbuster (Realtors) knew us and asked if we wanted to do work for them. "Yeah why not" We built out a Real Estate office in a space they rented on Pitkin Ave. They paid us well. Afterwards, they hired us to make repairs at various locations all over Brooklyn.

We experienced some strange people during the time we worked for them. For instance, upon entering a home around the Williamsburg section, chickens were running throughout the house. I asked the people,

"What's up with the flock of chickens?"

"Oh, we fatten dem up then eat dem"

"Oh."

Another house had a loaf of bread, some vegetables and a piece of meat hanging from the ceiling attached to a string.

"Yo what's with the hanging stuff?" I asked.

"Oh we keep it there until dinner time so the rats don't eat it before we do.

"Oh, I see"

N.Y.C. came up with a new building code. All fire apparatus, for heating, will have to be enclosed, using concrete block. (Boiler room enclosures) This created a lot of new work. Some of the houses needed a treatment by an exterminator prior to us starting work just to kill the rats.

The Real Estate people were very friendly. Each time they closed on a house they threw a party and invited us. We knew they were screwing the folks out of money whenever they bought or sold a property but we did our own thing, received our pay and went about our business.

On one occasion, this fellow named Phil swindled a fellow out of his home. The man was outrageous. Phil was sitting in a tavern across the street from his office having a cocktail when the fellow walked into the joint. He walked up to the contented realtor and said. "Phil, finish your drink, because this will be the last one you will ever have I am gonna blow your brains out." Phil smiled, and said, "OK" then downed the drink. The fellow pulled out a pistol, put it to the smiling man's head and pulled the trigger. Bada-Boom. Phil was history. "Never corner a rat or a poor man, if he has nowhere to go, he will attack you."

The New Policeman:
My pal Red began toying with the idea of becoming a N.Y.C. Police officer. He asked me,
"What do ya dink of the idea?"
"Who you! Become a cop?"
"Yeah don't ya dink I would be a good cop?"
"Well of course ya would, but do ya dink ya could ever give a guy a traffic ticket?"
"Why couldn't I?"
"Knowing you as I do, you will probably look the other way, and besides you will most likely get yourself in trouble on the job."
"Ya dink so?"
"Yeah I dink so. But what the hell give it a try."
"OK I will."

It did not take long before Red was sporting the blue uniform of N.Y Cities finest. He had a brand new badge and a pistol.

My brother loaned his friend his car. I just bought the new Buick, instead of trading in my old car; I gave it to Billy and traded his in instead. My car was much nicer and I wanted him to have it. He had it for about two weeks when his pal Ajax wrapped it around a tree and totaled the friggin thing.

The insurance refused to pay Billy what the car was actually worth to replace it. Therefore, His friend agreed to pay him the difference. Well, that never happened. Each time Billy asked for the money, Ajax had an excuse why he could not pay him. One night Billy and Red were having drinks at the corner bar, Ajax walked in. Billy asked him for the money. Ajax came up with another sorry ass excuse. Before you knew it, push came to shove and Ajax pulled out a pistol and threatened my brother. At that moment, Red identified himself as a cop. Ajax took off running with Red on his heels. Ajax let off a shot and Red fired back at him. Ajax got away when he ran down into the subway tunnel. I did not think that this was quite a good start in Red's new career.

Red became partners with a real seasoned character on the police force. Often telling me stories about how the dude had a sixth sense for finding trouble. His new companion also had a knack for pulling in some extra dough.

They worked out of a precinct known as one of the asshole sections of Brooklyn. (Brownsville) When the government's entitlement checks are delivered by mail which is twice a month, all hell breaks loose. He shared numerous stories of when the Puerto Ricans and Negros cashed their checks, hit the liquor stores or bought drugs. They then proceeded to commit assaults on each other or their own kind. The police had their hands full trying to keep peace in that district while the emergency rooms at the hospitals overflowed with injured citizens.

The dynamic duo decided to shake down a bar owner for some extra cash. The gig was to protect his establishment from any lawbreakers. This special attention would require a weekly payment. On the day they tried to arrange a deal with the owner, the owner asked, "How many of youze freaken guys do I gotta pay to be protected, I already have you're captain on my payroll?" Meanwhile, sitting at the end of the bar was the captain himself dressed in plain clothes. When they saw him, they ran out of the bar, but the captain spotted them as they made their exit. The bar owner clued the captain in on what they had just tried to do. "This was not a good thing."

The captain now had it in for them. He set up a plan to dispose of Red. Early one morning Red's wife called me to say that two police officers came and took her husband to jail.

"Why?" I asked.

"They accused him of rape."

"Rape? Wow!"

After obtaining some information, I went to the police station to try to help my friend.

"Hey Red what's up?"

"Yo, Louie, remember the story I told ya about the shake down at the bar?"

"Yeah, I do what about it?"

"The captain wants to get rid of me so he is setting me up."

"Tell me how"

"He has a couple of hookers he knows from the street. They are gonna put me in a lineup. According to the law, if two people identify me, they can then convict me of rape."

"When is dis gonna happen?"

"In about one hour."

After thinking about the problem he was facing, I told him that I'd return shortly.

"Where are ya goin?"

"I am gonna go buy ya a different color shirt. They

probably told both hookers to point to the guy in the grey shirt, which you are wearing. After the first one points you out, quickly change shirts and see if the second whore gets it right."

The second tramp picked a different person in the lineup.

My plan worked like a charm. They released Red and I took him home to his wife. This did not please the captain.

Red managed to get away with that incident. However, the captain was still looking for a reason to terminate him. Red had enough sense to keep his nose clean and avoid trouble for a while. All went well for him for quite some time, until our crew decided to go to a N.Y. Mets baseball game at Shea Stadium one evening.

I took a big bullhorn from the job. I thought it would be fun to holler through the thing at the ballpark. The ushers were wise to that idea and confiscated it prior to entering the stadium. They told me to pick it up after the game. We always brought something to drink at the games and this night was no different. We had gallon jug of Ginny red wine that we slipped past the ticket takers. Everyone drank until all the wine was gone. None of us was feeling any pain. The game was over and it was time to leave. I picked up the horn and we all jumped into the two cars. Our next stop, get something to eat at a pizza stand in Queens.

"Hey guys, let's not let the bullhorn go to waste." I said.

"Watta ya got in mind?"

"Before we go eat let's stop at the big parking lot over at forest park. You know, where all the lovers park and do their ding."

"Den what?"

"You'll see."

We drove into the parking lot and waited for a while. Then I clicked on the horn and made an announcement.

"Attention! Everyone please give me your Attention. There is a dangerous violent sex maniac on the prowl and he was last seen driving into this lot. I advise everyone to leave immediately. This is a warning."

Within two minutes, we were the only two cars in the lot.

"Are we ballbusters or what?"

From there we parked both cars outside of the pizza joint. (An outdoor counter, buy it by the slice.) Now here is where it gets ugly. My friend Charley began to sprinkle salt on his slice of pizza when the top came off and the whole bottle poured on his slice. One of the fellas unscrewed the top just to bust his chops. The owner of the place came outside and started making a scene right there on the sidewalk. He should have let the little hoax ride but instead a fistfight broke out. All the pizza workers ran out and fists were flying. Red decides to take out his badge and announce that he is a cop. (Bad move.) The owner ran back into the shop dialed 911 and told them that a cop has gone wild and is shooting at his workers during a brawl in front of his place. "WOW! I'm out of here." I quickly jumped into my car with whoever else managed to get in and took off. Red on the other hand, non-chalantly backed up his car up and before he knew it, there were police cars all around him. This was a dream come true for the police captain. Shortly after that night, Red was on the unemployment line looking for another job.

Let Us Paint The Town: While Red was in a cooling down period, I told him to come and work with Billy and me. My brother and Red know each other very well. They both served in the U.S. Army Reserves and managed to get into trouble together. Therefore, Red fit in well with both of us. We had a small machine that paints neat accurate lines in parking lots. It consisted of a five-gallon tank, a hand pump and a guide. It operates off pressure and a simple tool to handle.

I told Red "This machine will be used as a lead item, after introducing ourselves to an owner of a building, we will seek other work. It will help us to get a foot in the door. In the meantime, we also will pick up a few bucks painting lines." "Sounds good to me let's get goin. We owned a small white Ford van that we used for work every day; we took a good supply of both white and yellow traffic paint and loaded it into the van. Things were going well. After completing two jobs, we signed a third contract to re-paint the lines in a parking lot of a diner on Long Island. The owner chose the color yellow. Red filled the tank then began to pump air into it. After painting the first line, the hose came off the machine, squirting bright traffic yellow paint all over a brand new Buick Electra 225 with expensive fancy wheels. Just then, the owner of the diner walked outside and saw what happened. He placed both his hands on his head and yelled "Holy shit." I told him not to worry we will clean it up. Red ran to the dumpster and pulled out some newspapers while I asked the man if he knows who owns the car. "Yeah a black dude about 6' 3" and built like a brick shit house. "Oh." The owner went back inside the diner while we made more of a mess trying to clean up the paint. It was impossible to clean. The freaken paint went down the windows, thru the grill, the wheels and covered the whole car. The parking lot was also a mess. We stood there looking at each other bewildered. I said,

"Hey Red let's get the hell outta here."

"Louie, the guy has a signed contract with all your information on it."

"Yeah I know but let's take a chance and leave."

"OK good idea."

I cranked up the van and we drove away. We could not help laughing at what just happened. "Keep your fingers crossed Red, maybe we will never hear from the guy." Thank God, we never did.

It did not end there. On the way home we were going a little too fast as I drove over a curved overpass. The Van Wyck Expressway was below us with heavy traffic. Suddenly a large five gallon can of white paint tipped over; the top came off while the heavy can fell against the side doors of the van. Both doors flung wide opened. The can flew out. It bounced and hit the guardrail as paint flew down onto all the cars on the expressway. Red said, "Louie you do not want to see the mess, put the pedal to the metal and keep on truckin." "OK." Some days it does not pay to get out of bed.

The Hot Chick:

In the midst of my travels around Brooklyn, I met up with a girl, which the guys considered a hot chick. Besides her good looks, her body could stop a clock. She liked hanging out with us because she always had a fun time. Her favorite two people to hang with were Red and I. We took her to interesting places including some private after hour clubs.

A bar opened in Queens, with music and entertainment. The establishment also had a new permit, which enabled them to exhibit topless female dancers. It was new at the time and drew a large crowd. Red and I visited the place a couple of times and met the owner. One evening we decided to take our hot chick friend with us. Once again, she was impressed with our choice of place we took her. After watching the girls dance topless for a while, I asked her if she thought she could dance on stage.

"I don't know if I could take my top off in front of so many people."

Suddenly Red chimed in and assured her that she definitely could do it and that she had a better body than any of the dancing girls.

"Do ya really think so?"

We both answered simultaneously,

"Sure ya do." I told her,

"The owner would probably pay ya too."

After a little persuading, she agreed to try it.

"OK wait here I'll go set it up with the boss."
Red bought her another drink and told the bartender to make it a double.

She went behind stage and prepared herself for the new venture. The DJ announced her and she stepped out on stage. The music began to play she hesitated for a moment. Both Red and I began to clap and yell and she started to dance. Everyone in the place thought she looked great and also yelled and whistled. Her confidence began to build. Suddenly her top came off and all the people yelled louder. Before the music stopped, she looked as though she did this all her life. She not only looked, but also felt like a pro.

It was about a half hour later; the three of us were drinking at the bar when Red suggested that she go up and dance again. Taking her top off was no problem. She broke the ice and to her it was like a second nature.

"Hey" I said,

"Lets blow the freaken roof off this joint."

"How?" Red asked.

"Next time she goes up, we get the place all riled up, then we give her a signal and she takes everything off."

"Yeah sounds great let's do it."

We asked her if she is game for the idea and she said,

"Hell yeah! Let's go for it."

Since the idea of topless dancing was relatively new in the area, the people that issued the permit kept an eye on the establishment. Therefore, there were a couple of plain-clothes detectives in house. The DJ introduced her once again and the commotion began. Red and I inspired the crowd while she did her thing on stage. The place was rocking.

Red gave the signal for her to (drop trou.) Without hesitation, she took off her panties and began swinging them in the air over her head. The friggin place went wild. At that moment, the plain-clothes men approached the owner and threatened to shut him down. The music stopped and the crowed began yelling more, we want more.

The chick came off the stage, the owner walked up to us and told us to leave the premises and do not come back. "Ehh, what the hell, it was fun while it lasted.

Hotel Dance: It was a Sunday afternoon, five of us headed to Manhattan to attend a hotel dance. We have all been there several times before and enjoyed ourselves. The hotel has a nice polished wood dance floor, a band and tables that are set up around the dance area.

After ordering a set-up of two bottles, one Scotch and one Rye, the place started to fill up with patrons, which included many fine-looking women. Each of my friends would ask someone to dance then invite her to our table for a drink. Everyone was having a good time when suddenly, I saw one of my pals in a shoving match with another dude on the dance floor. Abruptly a bunch of people came running onto the dance floor and began pounding on my friend. I ran over, pulled a fella off him, gave him a foot sweep while pulling him backwards. The dude smashed his head on the floor and laid still. By this time, all of my friends were also on the dance floor combating.

All the lessons and the many hours of hard work at the Judo school were now coming in handy. The brawl lasted for a couple of minutes. At the end, I managed to knock out three of the hostile rivals. The music stopped and several security guards began swinging nightsticks at the brawlers. I instantly made my exit and waited for my friends down at the corner.

When everyone was accounted for, all in one piece, we headed back to Brooklyn. There was another dance about to begin.

Get to Know the Right People: I was approximately 27 years old when our construction company began to grow. I told Billy that it is time to branch out and try to sign up bigger jobs in Manhattan. He agreed with me. Therefore, I drove into the city, parked my car in the Mid-town section and began to walk through the city streets.

I came across a demolition job in progress located at 14 E. 60th Street. It was the Hotel 14. It also housed the famous Copa Cabana nightclub. I struck up a conversation with a fellow that looked like a supervisor directing his workers. I picked his brain and got all the information I needed to contact the right people that would enable us to get a foot in the door. Before the day was over, I acquired the opportunity to build out an office space in one of the demolished areas. We built a suite according to plan and the owners were satisfied with our work. Shortly afterwards, we sat at a meeting with the owner of the building who was Fred Wilpond and the General Contractor. We submitted a bid with unit prices to build out office spaces for the remaining fourteen stories of the building. In addition, we would finish all the common areas. Two of the biggest drywall companies in the city bid against us but we gave a lower price and convinced them that we are the right people to do the job. My next step was to sign up with the Carpenters union.

We could have walked into the union with no questions asked avoiding the red tape by merely mentioning it to one of the fellas down at the tavern we hung out. After all, these people knew all the big shots in the unions. However, we remembered what mom told us when we were kids. "Never do business with them, and never ask for favors." Instead, I made friends with the demolition contractor, a fellow called "Willy the Coat." He got the nickname because Willy covered everything. This dude knew all the right people. He told me to put $5,000 in cash into a brown paper bag and give it to him and he will put it in the right hands that will open all the necessary doors for us. After that, I went up to the main office of the union hall to meet the right people. I was asked where I came from. I told them. After that, they clued me in on how everything worked. We now had the freedom to go anywhere we pleased in the city and perform work. The union big wigs kept me abreast of everything that went on. They told me in advance, as to when the union was going to audit our record books. They sent one of their cronies to our office to check out our books prior to the union audit, just to make sure everything was in proper order. As he looked over our payroll book, the fellow asked me who a certain person was.

"He is a good friend of mine and he occasionally works for us."

"Is he from the family I think he's from?"

"Yes."

We never had a problem hiring whoever we wanted to work on our job. We never even had a union Shop Steward. They once advised us that there was a cancer amongst our crew of workers. "This guy is a troublemaker, fire him. When he comes to the union hall looking for work, we will send him to work out in the snow on the Williamsburg Bridge." Our union connections worked out well for many years. Our associates were there whenever we needed them. Many things go on behind closed doors. However, when you connect with the right people and you are not afraid to come up with a little cash, many of those doors open for you.

Fred Wilpond: I feel that I must write about this individual. (Fred Wilpond is the major owner of the New York Mets baseball team.) We worked extremely hard at the Hotel 14, stacking it with sheetrock, metal studs, lumber and other materials. The job was going fine. We built out many tenant spaces while also finishing the common areas of the building.

We hired union workers as well as our own men, keeping the job fully equipped with both labor and materials. Gradually, Mr. Wilpond fell behind on paying us. This caused us to cut down on our labor force. Fred demanded that we hire more men. I told him that I must pay all of the workers each week, and for that reason, he must pay us. Conversely, Mr. Wilpond had other ideas. He said that if we did not add more men to our payroll, he would throw us off the job. I told him that if he did that, there would be no one to do the work. He said that he would have a complete new crew on the job early Monday morning. Monday morning came and so did a new crew of workers ready to work. I stood on top of the hotel steps in the lobby in front of the workers and Fred. I explained to them what Fred did to us and that he could do the same thing to them. I may have just as well have spoken to the wall because all they wanted to do was to start working. Nevertheless, I held my ground by telling them that all of the material on the job site belonged to me and if anyone thinks he is brave enough to touch it he would have to go through me first. I am pissed off so do not try it unless you want to brawl with me. The workers all backed off and left the job.

Wilpond gave us a small monthly payment, so we went back to work with the same amount of men. This annoyed him. He returned to the job site and said,

"You guys are young in this business and are still wet behind the ears. Let me tell you how it works. I hold all the marbles and I can out last you. Before I pay you any more money you will have to take me to court. Just before the case is ready for review, I will settle with you. However, by the time you pay for a lawyer, spend an abundant amount of time preparing your case and possible court costs you will both be out of business. Do you understand me?"

I could hardly believe what I just heard. This man must be some sort of a tyrant. Who besides an evil, brutal dictator would speak like this? Why would he want to destroy two young men struggling to succeed in the construction business?

Meanwhile our suppliers were hounding us for payment for the material we stacked on the job site and the union wanted the money we owed them pertaining to the workers benefits. We could not start another job because of lack of cash. While all of this was happening, someone broke into the tool room and stole all of the carpenter's tools. Our company was responsible for replacing them immediately. We were in trouble.

Back at the neighborhood, our mobster pals repeatedly asked us, do you guys need help collecting money from anybody or do you need help obtaining work. Once again, mommas' words came into play. "Never take any favors from them." We told them that everything was going great and if we needed any help, we will let them know.

One afternoon the pressure became overwhelming. Billy happened to call the office to tell me something. I told him how angry I am and was just leaving to go see Wilpond. He asked me,

"What are ya gonna do?" I said,

"I am not sure."

"Wait," he said,

"Don't go anywhere until I call ya back OK? Give me about an hour."

"OK"

An hour later, he called and said.

"Start paying everyone, I have a check in my hand for all the money that Wilpond owes to us."

"What? How'dja get it?"

"I'll tell ya when I return to the office."

"OK, see ya later

Billy returned to Brooklyn and handed me the check with a large number. I could not believe my eyes.

"How the hell did ya get it?"

"Well; after hearing how angry ya were on the phone, I knew ya would do something irrational. So, I daught I'd do something before ya got yourself into big trouble. I walked into his office and told everyone in there except Wilpond to leave."

"Yeah; and den what?"

"I dragged him to the window and I told him that I would give him only one chance to write a check for the full amount he owes us or else I would throw him out without any hesitation and forty stories is a long way down."

"Oh"

I thought to myself, he should have thrown the bastard out.

However, maybe that is why he did not want me to go there.

I deposited the check then paid everyone his or her money and continued working the job. Fred made the rest of the payments on time until we finished the job. "Hang in there Mr. Wilpond." I later found out that Bernie Madoff (Ponzi scheme) swindled the Wilpond family out of an enormous amount of money. "Good for you Bernie." I will bet that Fred Wilpond did the same thing to many other people before he gathered enough bucks to buy the N.Y. Mets. "A leopard does not change his spots."

Roger: Billy stayed friends with his old pal Roger from Doscher Street. The dude, hooked on drugs and so deep into the habit that he had to stay awake about twenty hours a day committing robberies in order to support his habit. They arrested him several times and he spent time in the slammer.

My Bro. always stood loyal to his friends and therefore, tried to help Roger. We decided to bring him to work with us to keep him busy. Both of us kept a close eye on him. Roger became interested in the job and was ready to work every morning. We picked him up and dropped him off at his apartment each day. He kept his nose clean and was doing well. Since he was on probation, he had to report to his parole officer periodically. I received a phone call at our office from his parole officer. He said to me, "I don't know what the hell you and your brother are doing with Roger, but keep it up. The fellow has never been in such good spirits and in good health too."

As time went by Roger became involved with the carpenters on the job. They influenced him to join a union. He approached me and asked me to get him into the union. I explained to him that we do not have a contract with the laborer's union, only with the carpenters and the tapers. Besides, why do you want to belong to a union, we take better care of you than they could ever do. You receive a decent salary besides us bringing you to and from work each day. I may have just as well have been talking to an empty chair. He insisted he become a union member. I then told Billy to speak with him. I figured he might listen to him. A short time later, another friend Nick gave us a note that Roger sent to him. It was a suicide note. He killed himself. What a freaken tragedy. I previously mentioned in this book that I would tell you more about Roger later. I also mentioned that his biggest mistake was not allowing my Aunt and Uncle to adopt him when he was a kid. I am sure that he would have had a wonderful life, a good education and he may still be alive today.

Ironically, my Aunt Irene and Uncle Dan adopted two babies at birth. Named them Joseph and Mary and provided them with a wonderful life.

New Red Car: We were building a great crew of workers. I constantly looked for work to keep them busy. Billy watched over the jobs in the field while I managed the office. We included our mother on the payroll. We could not afford to give her too much. However, we sent her a check each week.
While riding in the car with my mom I asked,
 "Hey Ma, what kind of a car do ya like?"
 "The new Dodge Swinger."
 "If you had your choice, what color would ya prefer?"
 "I like Red. Why are you asking me these questions?"
 "I don't know why, I was just wondering."
"OH, OK"

After extracting the information from mom, Billy and I purchased a brand new red Dodge Swinger. We tied a bow on it and drove it to her home. We told her to come downstairs because we had something we wanted to show her. Mom was so thrilled she began to cry.

"What the hell is wrong with you two, what makes you do something like this?"

"Maybe it's because we love ya mom."

Stolen Cars: Meanwhile, the neighborhood was getting out of hand. Before Billy moved to Howard Beach, we had four cars stolen from us.

My brother had a very close friend who he went through school with. The dude was a close companion to John Gotti. (The Mafia Don.) One of their businesses was dealing with cars. They owned a junkyard in Brooklyn. When his friend heard that another car was stolen he called my brother and told him to come down to the junk yard.

"I just got in a beautiful Cadillac; I want ya to have it for what I paid for it."

After arriving at the yard,

"Wow thanks Johnny it is a nice car."

"Billy, ya take good care of it, you hear me?"

"Yeah, don't worry I will. Thanks."

On the way home from the junk yard he stopped for a red light. A sanitation truck towing a burnt wreck turned the corner. The bumper was sticking out of the wreck and sliced a hole from the front bumper to the rear bumper. His new car looked like someone tried to open it with a can opener.

My sister-in-law became disgusted. She told Billy to pick up a cheap clunker that no one would steel. After buying a clunker, she took it shopping. The car was full with groceries; she stopped at the drycleaners to pick up some items. When she came out, the old car and all the groceries were gone. "Sometimes you just cannot catch a break."

The same friend that sold the Cadillac to my brother took him to his home one day. He told him in front of his wife,

"Look here, you see this box?"

"Yeah, what about it?"

John opened the box. It overflowed with money.

"Any time you need cash, just come here and help yourself, do you understand me? My wife will always let you in. Just do me a favor. Whatever you take, use it, then put it back OK?"

"Yeah sure, danks."

The good friend is doing a prison term of 50 years. We never saw him again. Momma's words rang out once more. Never take any favors. As a result, in spite of all our problems, Billy never helped himself to any money.

Older fellas advised us not to make visits to the penal institutions to call on any of these guys. Nothing good will ever come from it. Therefore, we left well enough alone.

Time to Go: I was in my apartment one evening when I heard gunshots, a gang war started in the street in front of the house. While watching from my window, I saw a fella shooting a flare gun at another dude. The ball of flame bounced along the concrete sidewalk until it reached its target. However, before it struck the fellow he managed to deflect it with a garbage can cover. The fella with the gun then pointed it at my window. I stuck my head out while waving my arms yelling No-No. The fella then took aim at another house on the next block and let off a shot. The ball of flame busted thru a window and set the house on fire. "It was a close call."

The Mayor of New York, John V. Lindsay tolerated everything that the minorities did to the neighborhood. Instead of putting his foot down, he sent out a public notice "Do not agitate them." The minorities knew this and took advantage of his compassion for them. It was like tying the hands of the police officers. They had to follow the new rules or lose their jobs.

I watched a young Negro boy piss on a cop. The cop kept backing up as the little boy ran after him while peeing on his leg. Other people cussed at the cops as they walked by on their beat. The police stood by and only watched the scumbags tear apart the neighborhood. Buildings burned, automobiles that were stripped and burned lined the streets. The garbage piled up in front of their homes. People were too frightened to enter the area. The place looked like the photos shown after a city was bombed during a war.

The Puerto Rican proprietor was giving me a hard time. He wanted my apartment for his family. He and his family treated me like a misfit. I felt so out of place. What a change from only a few of years prior when the building was full of warmth and laughter. I reminisced of the times when all of the old neighbors were still living here. I remembered the parties, boxing in the alley, the kids playing in the streets, the ice cream truck, catching baseball with pop, watching the fights and baseball games on the little television. It was all gone now. Just memories are left. "It is now time to go."

The Condominium: At 28, I managed to save up a few bucks. I drove the little white van for a while. It was all I could afford if I wanted to leave the ghetto. We used it for work and for carting debris to the dump. I recall going on dates with it. Each time I hit a bump in the road, dust flew all over my date and me. "What the hell, things will get better. I will make it happen; no one can ever hold me down."

I purchased a condominium in a six-story building in the Howard Beach area of Queens. I took whatever furniture I had and moved in. My new home is less than a mile away from my brother. This is quite different from Glenmore Ave. Here I am on the top floor looking out over a brand new neighborhood and feeling like king of the mountain.

The new location was a great place. Most of the Wise Guys lived here too. John Gotti and his family also lived less than a mile, along with many other Goodfellas.

Billy and I rented a construction office on Atlantic Ave in Brooklyn. We leased it from a retired boxer by the name of Mario Micelli. Mario ran a body shop in the same building where we often sat with him and drank coffee. Mario and his friends knew my grandfather Louie Fuccillo. When they heard us mention the Fuccillo name, they told us the story of how my grandfather blew up the house while making alcohol with his still in the cellar.

Our business took off due to our hard work. We did jobs in all the five borrows of New York, building out interiors in banks, office buildings, stores and many Day Care Centers. Every Tom Dick and Harry with a few bucks built a Day Care Center. We were knocking them dead while adding more workers to our payroll. At one time, we employed as many as thirty-five people. I bought myself a car and we sent mom a few more bucks every week.

Jack of Spades: In New York, there are many construction contractors. The people building the Day Care Centers, who were mostly Jewish, knew this. Consequently, they tried to beat each contractor out of money. Every builder held a retainer of 10% on each monthly requisition we submitted. At the end of the job, they fabricated an insignificant reason for not paying us in full. They knew that there are so many other contractors available that they did not need us any longer. They pulled this swindle with all the contractors.

I told Billy to come to my apartment one evening. I pulled out a deck of cards and told him to sit and watch as I turned over each card from the deck.

"What am I supposed to be looking for?"

"Just sit and pay attention."

I turned over each card one at a time and laid it on the table. When I turned over the Jack of Spades, I gave him a smack in the face.

"Hey what was dat for?"

Pause,

"Let me do it again, pay attention."

After shuffling the cards I began turning them over again. As soon as he saw the Jack of spades, he leaned backwards. I stopped and asked,

"Why did you back away?"

"Because the last time dat card popped up ya smacked me."

"Exactly, ya got the point."

"Watta ya mean?"

"OK, each of those creeps out dare that we do work for rips off every contractor at the end of the job right?"

"Yeah right"

"And they all allow it to happen because they are afraid of starting trouble."

"I guess." "

"We cannot afford to allow dat to happen to us. For that reason, we must pretend to be the Jack of spades.

Each time they try to rip us off, we whack em good. When it comes time to collect all of our money they will dink twice about not paying us. Let them rip off all those utter poor slobs, not us."

"It sounds good to me."

We worked with many other sub-contractors and watched them lose money to the fraudulent owners. We never lost any money to a swindle in all the years we labored out there in the jungle. I cannot say it was easy, because we had to rough up a few characters to be paid. We took care of ourselves, never once asking for help from the felons we knew.

The Goodfellas did their thing. They always had plenty of money to party. I continued to hang out at the bars with them. Shorty Shoes had sold out his place to a new owner who catered to the same type of crowd. I kept on playing cards with my pal Red at various places that the Goodfellas set up. The games sometimes started on Friday evening and lasted until Sunday while good-looking women served refreshments cigarettes and alcohol.

I began to have second thoughts about all this gambling that I have been involved in since a young boy, especially after spending a whole weekend in some abode with a bunch of friggin losers. Sure, we managed to beat the wise guys at their own game and come out winners most of the time, but whenever we won, we spent it on wine, women and song. We bought new suits, sport jackets and all the rest of the crap to look dapper. However, when we lost, it seemed like a big waste of time. This life style is going nowhere. It is time to quit gambling. I told my friends not to include me in anymore of the games. I quit cold turkey.

Besides doing what Wise guys do to make money, some of them received a salary from big construction jobs. They are "phantom employees." Most of them could not find the job site if they were told to report to work. Guys like Gotti were on contractors payrolls. A plumbing outfit employed him. I bet the friggin dude did not even own a wrench. Others needed to show employment in order to file income taxes proving that they were Legit. For that reason, they asked us to place them on our payroll. They were willing to give back all the money plus an additional kick back for the favor. My answer,

"Hey Are you my friend or not? Why would you want to put me on the spot if anything happened and you wound up in jail? If they checked my books and it showed you worked on that day, what the hell could I tell them?"

"Yeah you're right, Fugeddaboutit, let's have a drink."

"OK"

Moms words rang clear once more, never accept or do any favors, but keep them as friends."

Unions: Working with the unions was never easy. Each job location is under the management of a different local or district. This meant, if a job is starting just a couple of blocks away from an existing job, a different local might manage it, requiring the

contractor to hire different men from the new local. It can make the job much easier if the contractor were able to place his own workers at each job because he knows the people and the type of work they are capable of performing.

The union rules: The union delegates will place a shop Stewart to handle any job grievances between the contractor and the union employees. The Stewart receives overtime pay whenever any union man receives pay for overtime, which is usually time and a half. He also appoints a supervisor to direct all the men, plus the first two people to staff the job. All this can become very expensive to the contractor, especially if the delegate sends inadequate workers. Therefore, it is very important to try to set ground rules prior to starting a job.

On many occasions, I have met with delegates in a coffee shop or a tavern to make my peace with him. The name of the game is always cash. "Cash is king." A contractor must also be a politician. You cannot just walk up to the person and hand him a roll of money. You have to feel him out first. There is always the possibility that you cannot buy the fellow, then you look like a fool and you start the job on the wrong foot.

This is where many contractors get themselves into trouble. It takes a special skill to schmooze a dude. It comes with the turf as being a knock around guy.

Before I ever began negotiating with a delegate, I made a mental list of exactly what I wanted from him. Usually the first thing is to allow me to place the first two men of my own on the job. Second is to appoint my own supervisor. Third is for him to send me men who specialized in the type of work I am about to perform. If a contractor handles the negotiation in the correct manner, things will work out in his favor and as long as he runs his job properly, he should turn a profit.

The Greedy Inspector: After signing a contract to build out the interior of a five story building in the Red Hook section of Brooklyn, I met with the union delegate and set the ground rules. All went well and we were deep into the job.

The owner of the building called me to his office to tell me that he cannot pay me for the last month's work and the materials until I settle with the building inspector.

"What are you talking about?"

"Well he will not sign off on the drywall inspection until you grease his palm."

"Me grease his palm? You are the owner and the general contractor. It is up to you to take care of him, not me. Besides there is nothing wrong with the work we performed."

"I cannot pay you until I hear from him; he wants to meet with you."

This is not my first rodeo; a building inspector in this manner never shook me down. This creep must be pulling this with every sub-contractor. OK, I thought. I had best go meet with the fellow in order to be paid.

"Give me the guy's phone number."

I made an appointment to meet with him the following day. I instructed him to meet me up on the roof of the building at 1.00 P.M. sharp.

This fat dude showed up on the roof with a long smelly cigar hanging out of his ugly face. He introduced himself as the building inspector and gave me a big smile. I walked him to the edge of the building and told him,

"Look over the side."

"It's a long way down, isn't it?"

"Yeah, it is"

At that moment, I pulled out a one-dollar bill from my pocket, showed it to him and then stuffed it into his shirt pocket. I told him,

> "Go buy a cheap cigar just like the one that's sticking out of your fat ugly face, then call the owner of the building and tell him that I took care of you, do ya hear me God Damn it.?"

"Yes I do"

> "If ya do not intend to do what I just told ya to do, let me know now; so that I can throw your fat ass off the F----- building."

The poor bastard must have pissed in his pants.

> "Yes Mr. Borek I will call him right away, calm down, I did not find anything wrong with the drywall work."

"Good then call the G.C., I want to be paid."

Each day that I step out of my house, I walk into the jungle. I have learned as a young boy that "*The strong in the jungle win.*" I have created the phrase of my own after learning about (Survival of the fittest) in elementary school. It is simple logic and pertains to not only animals but also humans. As in the jungle, the big animal eats up the little animal unless the little guy is tough or cunning enough to escape from him. Consequently, I always keep this in mind and so far, I am still able to walk the jungle.

As time marched on, the economy had its difficulties. After living in Howard Beach for several years, we found that finding work was becoming tough. Slowly, our construction crew began to dwindle. The unions demanded pay raises along with additional benefits. Between the higher hourly wages, the increase in the price of materials and the rise in interest rates, people began holding back on construction start-ups.

I recollect speaking with my Uncle Danny over lunch one day. We met on Fridays at a local pub that served shrimp with a hot sauce and Italian bread. He reminded me of the time we sat down many years ago when discussing a family problem. "Louie; he said, life is full of peaks and valleys, you are always going to have your ups and downs, learn to ride the waves." He told me, be prepared to take another ride into a valley. There is nothing to do but change your course to avoid hitting bottom. You have already experienced many disappointments in life and survived, you will do it again.

The Paint Store: As each job came to a completion, we laid off more men, saving our supervisors for last. Finally, it was time to let go of our secretary. The two of us then sat in the office staring at each other contemplating our next move. Although there was no work for us, monies for the jobs completed still needed to be collected. Our company still owed the union a bunch of money along with a few suppliers.

An old friend invited me to spend some time in Florida. Upon my return, Billy and I spoke about making a move. Things were still happening in the South and it seemed like the thing to do. Therefore, I made the first move while he stood behind to tie up loose ends and then follow me down.

Collecting our money will not be an easy task and I anticipated it. Our firm built out the interior of a paint store in a busy section of Manhattan. The General contractor never paid us, claiming that he never received money from the owner. (He is another jack of spades victim.) I sent several bills to the owner over the course of several weeks but received nothing in response. Billy suggested that I return to N.Y. to deal with the person since he did not know too much about the job that I handled.

About a week later, both of us drove to Manhattan to pay a visit to our friend at the paint store. I suggested my bro stay with the truck while I go to the second floor where the office was located. The head honcho sat behind a large glass partition at a large fancy desk. I entered his office and introduced myself.

"What do you want?"

"Sir, I am the sub-contractor that did the interior work in your store. I could not help but notice on my way up here, that your store is up and running and seems busy."

"Yeah, so?"

"Sir, I have not received payment for the labor and materials I invested into your store renovation. I mailed you several invoices, as did the General

Contractor but never received payment for our work, nor have you ever acknowledged any of my invoices. Is there a problem?"

The fellow sat there looking at me as though I had two heads.

"Well, I want you to know that I came here from Florida to collect the monies you owe us; the amount is in excess of several thousand dollars."

The fellow sat back and placed his feet on his desk in an arrogant manner as he looked at me, then said.

"OK I'll write you a check."

I sat there in anticipation of accepting my payment, thanking the fellow and then leaving. He wrote me a check for $500.00 and added a note on the back, which read: Upon the signing of this check, the individual accepts payment in full for the services rendered.

"Sir the check is made out for the wrong amount. Furthermore, what kind of a scam are you trying to pull with the note?"

He stood up and told me that I should accept what he gave me and leave his office.

"Are you kiddin me, who the F--- do ya dink you are Jesse James.?"

"Don't speak to me like that."

"Sit down ya piece of shit and listen to me, I am gonna count to ten, if ya do not write another check for the balance I am gonna get violent wit you."

I placed the check in my attaché case and started counting. He said.

"You do not scare me now get out of here."

"Now you have only five seconds left, don't waste them."

393

After counting to ten, I threw him a left jab hitting him square in his nose, followed by a right to his face. Blood splattered over the freshly painted wall behind him as he began to cry like the friggin candy ass that he is. He screamed for his staff to help him and to call the police. I turned and locked the door to his office. As his employees banged on the window and rattled the door to his office, I said to him,

"What happened all of a sudden, you are not so tough anymore? Don't think this is the end, I am not gonna get involved with the police, but ya can bet your sweet ass on it that I will return."

I opened the door and went back downstairs to tell my brother what just took place.

"Where's the check?" He asked.

"O man; I put it in the attaché case and forgot to bring it down with me."

"You friggin dummy."

"Yeah you're right, I'll wait around the corner, the police will be here shortly."

"OK I'll wait here, see ya later."

When the police arrived, the first cop was a big Irishman. Billy greeted him and told him that he was glad to see him.

"I came to collect payment for the construction work I did here at the paint store and a Jewish guy upstairs took my attaché case."

"Oh yeah, lets go upstairs."

When they approached the boss, he began telling the cop that Billy hit him. The cop asked,

"Did you hit him?"

"No, but there's my brief case, you see it has my name Borek on it."

The cop asked the boss once more,

"Did dis guy hit you?" After taking a good look he said,

"No."

"OK, go pick up ya brief case and get atta here."

Billy said thanks and left.

We met around the corner, waited for the police to leave and chuckled about the event, before I started back upstairs to get the balance of the money. Billy decided to wait downstairs. When the boss saw me, he began screaming once more. I told him to shut his mouth and write another check. He said he would not deal with me or the other fella that picked up the attaché case. Send someone else and I will pay the balance of the money. I picked up the phone and called my sister in-law Phyllis, told her where I was and to come here and pick up the check.

After several hours, we had our payment in full. I told Phyllis to warn him that if the check bounces or if he puts a stop order on the check I will return and bounce his freaken head on his desk.

Was all this nonsense necessary? Of course, it was not. Did he have to try to beat us out of what is rightfully ours? Of course, he did not. Then why do so many people do this type of thing? The answer is GREED. "The strong in the jungle win."

End: Several other encounters took place before we finally collected all of the money that people owed us. However, I will end it here. With all the money now in our account, I went to visit my friends at the union hall, to square up with them. I brought along my Agreement Contract, issued to me when I first met them. I told them, "Since there is not enough work in the city to keep us going, we decided to pack it in and move to Florida." When the fellow opened their books to see how much money we owed them, he noticed that the original agreement did not have any signatures. I told him that I am aware of it. He then said,

"Legally, you do not have to pay us anything."
"I know dat, but I did not come up here to try and beat ya out of anything."

With a bewildered look on his face he said,

"The total you owe us comes to over $13,000.00."
"I know exactly what I owe ya, please accept my check."

I told him how familiar I was with the problems of collecting money from people.

"It is not supposed to work that way. I want to thank all of ya for the help ya gave me for the last few years; it has been a pleasure working with ya."

They in turn told me the same thing and added.

"You are welcome back here anytime; hope things go well for ya in Florida."

I suppose many people think that living in East New York was a rough life; I say this because numerous people have told me so. Nevertheless, just as a kid that is raised in a well to do environment, he knows nothing else. The only time he realizes anything different is when the golden goose is no longer there to supply him with his wants and needs. Just as the well-to-do boy, I did not know anything different other than where I came from and what I had and consequently, never missed. I learned to fend for myself because whining was never an option.

Throughout my life, I learned to ride the wave's peaks and valleys. An old timer once told me, "Be nice to people on your way up, because you are going to meet the same people on your way down." How true.

When things got tough, I set myself into a different mode, asking yours truly. Do I need it or want it? If I did not need something, I chose to do without it. I accepted denial as a part of life and played the cards dealt to me.

Good things seldom came easy. I earned all of my possessions. Therefore, I appreciated everything I had, and I took good care of it. Unlike the affluent, that has everything handed to him and is seldom cherished, because it came too easy.

The most cherish-able thing in life is a loving family. I feel like the luckiest guy in the world to have had such loving and caring parents, a wonderful brother and a beautiful devoted wife. Francyn, I love you. Who could ask for more?

I hope you have enjoyed my stories. If you did, tell your friends to read them. If not, keep it a secret.

Made in the USA
Charleston, SC
11 June 2013